MW01119643

X400 Message Handling

Standards, Interworking, Applications

Data Communications and Networks Series

Consulting Editor: Dr C. Smythe, Surrey University

X400 MESSAGE HANDLING

STANDARDS, INTERWORKING, APPLICATIONS

B. Plattner   C. Lanz
H. Lubich   M. Müller   T. Walter

Swiss Federal Institute of Technology (ETH), Zurich

Translated by Stephen S. Wilson

ADDISON-WESLEY
PUBLISHING
COMPANY

Wokingham, England · Reading, Massachusetts · Menlo Park, California · New York
Don Mills, Ontario · Amsterdam · Bonn · Sydney · Singapore
Tokyo · Madrid · San Juan · Milan · Paris · Mexico City · Seoul · Taipei

© 1991 Addison-Wesley Publishers Ltd.
© 1991 Addison-Wesley Publishing Company Inc.

All rights reserved. No part of this publication may be reproduced, stored in a retrieval system, or transmitted in any form or by any means, electronic, mechanical, photocopying, recording or otherwise, without prior written permission of the publisher.

The programs in this book have been included for their instructional value. They have been tested with care but are not guaranteed for any particular purpose. The publisher does not offer any warranties or representations, nor does it accept any liabilities with respect to the programs.

Many of the designations used by manufacturers and sellers to distinguish their products are claimed as trademarks. Addison-Wesley has made every attempt to supply trademark information about manufacturers and their products mentioned in this book. A list of the trademark designations and their owners appears on p. (viii).

Cover designed by Chris Eley and
printed by The Riverside Printing Co. (Reading) Ltd.
Printed in Great Britain by Mackays of Chatham PLC, Chatham, Kent

First printed 1991. Reprinted 1992.

British Library Cataloguing in Publication Data
X400 message handling : standards, interworking
    applications.
    I. Plattner, B.
    384.34

    ISBN 020156503X

Library of Congress Cataloging-in-Publication Data
X400 message handling : standards, interworking, applications / B.
    Plattner ... [et al.].
        p.   cm.
    Includes bibliographical references and index.
    ISBN 0-201-56503-X
    1. Computer networks.   2. Electronic mail systems.   3. Computer
network protocols.   I. Plattner. B. (Bernhard)
TK5105.5.X15   1991
384.3'4--dc20
                                                                91-19212
                                                                    CIP

Preface

The functioning of our society is based not least on the existence of reliable, convenient and fast methods of exchanging messages. This means that automation of the events in industrial and service companies must rationalize not only data processing but also data communication. One important step towards office automation is the introduction of electronic mail. This has been in use for a long time, largely in and between universities, but also as an internal means of communication within large companies. In addition several companies offer this service to their subscribers in the form of electronic mailboxes.

In the early eighties, it was recognized that a broad introduction of electronic mail could only be achieved by international standardization. In particular, general communication between companies is only possible if standardized protocols define the communication between computers from different manufacturers over a variety of transmission media. Thus services and protocols for electronic mail are standardized within the framework of the international standardization of telecommunications. In 1984, the standard was published as recommendation X.400 in the CCITT Red Book and led to great interest on the part of computer manufacturers and potential service providers such as the PTT. All major computer manufacturers and some software houses set up projects to develop software conforming to the standard; corresponding products have recently become available on the market. In 1988, as part of the four-year cycle of revision of CCITT recommendations X.400 was corrected and new functions added.

The aim of this book is to provide a solid introduction to the concept of X.400 (architecture, services and protocols) and to the embedding into a given environment. This should provide the reader with the necessary knowledge to enable him to evaluate a possible use of systems conforming to the standard, in his environment. Furthermore, it should enable him to penetrate standards documents which are dry and difficult to understand and should provide him with the qualifications to discuss the topic with specialists.

A considerable part of the book is devoted to the ISO reference model for open systems interconnection which underlies the X.400 recommendations. In addition important areas associated with X.400 (for example, security, electronic data exchange (EDI), directory services and the testing of software for its conformance to standards) are discussed.

There is also an important discussion of the problems which arise when X.400 systems are connected with (often existing) systems based on other protocols.

By means of a topical example of the use of X.400, the authors pass on their personal experiences of the design and realization of a distributed electronic mail system which is now in operation.

The book is divided into four parts. Part I describes, so to speak, the pure and undiluted world of the modelling and the standardization of communication systems. Part II takes account of the fact that an operational system must be implemented and embedded in an existing environment, which poses a variety of problems and raises a number of questions. Part III describes previous experiences of X.400 together with new approaches and discusses various aspects which will be of crucial importance to the future of X.400. Part IV, which is in the form of appendices, contains or refers to a number of important sources.

Acknowledgements

The authors would like to thank all those who have contributed to the success of this book for their support. In particular, we are indebted to Albert Kündig, Andreas Zogg, A. Lyman Chapin, and Walter Lange.

Chapter 1 is based on lecture notes written by Albert Kündig; with his consent, we have taken this as the basis for our text.

Andreas Zogg contributed actively to the first drafts of Chapter 11.

Appendix B is reproduced with the kind permission of the author A. Lyman Chapin, from 'Computer Communications Review', a quarterly publication of the ACM SIGCOMM.

Walter Lange very generously made his documentation on EDI available to us.

Advice to the reader

The first three parts of the book are consecutively structured. Thus, a reader for whom the topic of 'electronic mail' is new is best advised to read the book right from the beginning. A reader with a basic knowledge (OSI reference model and X.400) may start with Part II and use Part I for reference. However, we note that Chapter 1 on the OSI reference model contains some new developments which are not generally known and which are crucial to an understanding of the sequel; these relate to the structure of the application layer (Section 1.3) and to the ASN.1 description language (Section 1.4).

Part II should be of interest to the professional who is concerned with the introduction of electronic mail in his working environment. The viewpoint is extended from that of a 'pure OSI view' so that the normal case in practice, namely the necessary inclusion of existing systems, is considered.

Part III turns again to standardization and discusses themes which have only become important since the first experiences of X.400. The practical user should pay attention to this material, since within a short time he will be confronted with corresponding systems and their associated problems.

Finally, Part IV is a reference section which (we hope) will provide the reader with fast access to the information he desires once he has read the book for the first time. Among other things, it contains an Index which refers to explanations of all the important terms, a List of Abbreviations and a current List of OSI Standards (Appendix B) which extends beyond the main theme of the book.

The book contains many references to international standards which often have the same form as bibliographic references (for example, (ISO 8878) in parentheses) and which may occur without particular indication in the flow of the text. In both cases, the reader is advised to consult the List of OSI Standards for further details.

New terms, and possibly associated abbreviations for them, are introduced in italics. As a rule, corresponding entries are given in the Index and in the List of Abbreviations.

> *B. Plattner, C. Lanz, H. Lubich, M. Müller, T. Walter*
> Zurich
> May 1991

For reasons of simplicity, the pronoun 'he' is used to relate to both male and female throughout the book.

Trademark notice

MS-DOS^R is a registered trademark and Windows^{TM} is a trademark of Microsoft Corporation.

Sun Microsystems^R is a registered trademark and NFS^{TM} and Sun^{TM} are trademarks of Sun Microsystems Inc.

UNIX^{TM} is a trademark of AT&T.

DEC^{TM}, PDP^{TM}, VAX^{TM}, VMS^{TM} and DECnet^{TM} are trademarks of Digital Equipment Corporation.

IBM^{TM} and IBM PC^{TM} are trademarks of International Business Machines Corporation.

Contents

Introduction

Forms of communication

By way of introduction, we investigate the *forms of communication* associated with a typical office workplace and point out simplifications, increases in efficiency and other possible forms of communication that may result from the use of computer-supported communication aids. We characterize known forms of communication in terms of geographically distributed objects according to the following criteria or modes of communication:

- According to the temporal properties of the interactions between the objects involved in a communications relationship:
  Many forms of communication require the simultaneous availability of all those involved; we call this a synchronous mode of communication. Clearly, *synchronous communication* has its advantages, since it enables each partner to be continuously sure of the state of the conversation and to react immediately to reactions of the partner. As a disadvantage, we must include the fact that all those involved must be simultaneously available. Thus, synchronous communication between several partners is often only possible after careful planning. This mode of communication is problematic if those involved are in different time zones; every European who has frequent contact with business partners in the USA or the Far East is aware of the problems that the time difference causes as far as telephone calls are concerned.
  Technically, synchronous communication is most often realized using a *connection-oriented service*, where the dialogue between the partners occurs during the period of a connection which is established at the beginning of the communication relationship and released again at the end of it.
  In contrast, participants in *asynchronous communication* are not linked in time in any way. Here, the information belonging to a dialogue is sent by the sender at a certain point in time (which he may specify) and may be read later (again at a suitable time) by the recipient. Clearly, asynchronous communication of this type is only possible if the system used has an intermediate storage capability.

1

Table 1   Forms of communication.

	1:1 association	*1:n association*	*n:1 association*
synchronous communication	dialogue	group meetings, conference, radio, TV	monitoring and collection of information
asynchronous communication	written correspondence	circulars, bulk mail, printed papers	

Asynchronous communication also has a technical equivalent, namely *connectionless service*, in which messages may be independently sent, transmitted and received without prior arrangement or warning. We stress that, as mentioned above, asynchronous communication is associated with the ability of the system to store information (possibly for long periods) in intermediate storage; this exceeds the services normally offered by connectionless transfer networks.

- According to the associations between the set of originators and the set of recipients:
    In addition to a 1:1 association between an originator and a recipient, $1:n$ and $n:1$ associations are also of interest, where n stands for *many*.

- According to the possible directions of the information flow:
    We distinguish between *one-way communication* in which only a monologue is permitted during a communication relationship, and *two-way communication* in which a dialogue is possible.

Table 1 describes common forms of communication in terms of the temporal relationship and the nature of the association.

In a traditional office environment, the following well-known means of realizing the various forms of communication are available:

Dialogue   Face-to-face conversation, telephone conversation.

Written correspondence   Company-internal mail, public postal services, courier, telegrams, telex[1].

---

[1] From the technical point of view, telex is a connection-oriented service. However, most telex terminals are operated in such a way that the service becomes asynchronous as far as the user is concerned.

Group meeting   Meeting of the participants in a suitably equipped meeting room, possibly with presentation aids (projector, flip chart, blackboard).

Conference   Meeting in a suitably equipped conference room (mostly with projection aids). Group meetings and conferences differ in that the former are informal and involve a good deal of interaction between the participants.

Bulk mail   The sending of a communication to several recipients using a distribution list (today, this is well supported by specific functions of word processors, for example, mail merging).

Circulars   'Cheap' form of bulk mail. A single copy of the communication, with the distribution list attached, is sent to one addressee after another.

Bulk mail and circulars are normally realized by written communication (external or internal mail).

Message handling and electronic mail

The term 'electronic mail' is used to describe a computer-supported telecommunications service that transfers machine-processable documents from originators to recipients, and that is able to provide intermediate storage on request. Thus, it is a service which can support the asynchronous forms of communication described above. The documents transferred may in principle contain text, graphics, raster images, speech sequences or data. However, electronic mail also implies that the primary reader of these documents is a person, although it is not to be excluded that electronically transmitted documents may be processed using electronic means.

On closer consideration of such a service, we note that the transmission of documents for the purposes of interpretation by humans is only one of many applications of an asynchronous communications service. For example, a general service for asynchronous transmission of information represented in any form might be used by a software manufacturer for computer-supported distribution of new software packages to his clients. The received data would be automatically archived by the client and (if necessary, after checking with the system administrator) automatically installed. Such a service might also be used to automate business, in that it could elegantly facilitate the reliable transportation of business documents (proposals, orders, delivery notes, customs documents, invoices, advices of payment, etc) to the different recipients.

In the following, a system which supports the computer-supported asynchronous transfer of documents (messages) will be called a *Message Handling System* (MHS); it provides a message handling service. With a suitable implementation, it should be possible to attain transfer times of the order of a few minutes within a country and tens of minutes to a few hours worldwide. Moreover, in addition to 1:1 associations, we also expect a message handling system to support *n*:1 and 1:*n* and thus also *n*:*n* associations. In particular, the sending of a message to several recipients *in a single step* is of great importance, as is clear from the previous examples.

As a consequence, we speak of *electronic mail* as one of many conceivable applications of a message handling service. In order to distinguish between the documents transmitted by these two services, we shall in future refer to documents seen in the framework of electronic mail as *communications*, so as to distinguish them from the *messages* of a message handling system.

Support by electronic means

After introducing the terminology, we now investigate the extent to which electronic means may in the future be used to support the forms of communication in question.

Dialogue

Today, when conversation partners are unable to meet in the same place, making a face-to-face conversation impossible, the telephone is used as a means of communication. However, the telephone may only be used to transmit speech efficiently and as soon as illustrations or text are involved the medium proves inadequate. The introduction of the *Integrated Services Digital Network* (ISDN), and later of the *Integrated Broadband Communication Network* (IBCN), will enable us to transmit speech accompanied by images, text and even moving images.

Written correspondence

While for telephone conversations the quality of speech transmission, versatility and ease-of-use may be considerably improved using modern information technology, the area of written communication will undergo a fundamental change with the widespread use of computer-supported message handling services.

Bulk mail, circulars

Just as today we use letter post for the above forms of communication, we shall in the future be able to use MHSs. Clearly, the electronic medium will offer a better service:

- It is cheap to copy stored messages, removing the main motivation for circulars which can no longer be distinguished from bulk mail. This also removes one of the major disadvantages of circulars, namely the long and often uncontrollable distribution time.

- The short message transmission time makes for greater interaction in the case of written correspondence. This leads to individual discussion forums in which, within a group, themes of common interest are discussed by distributing contributions to the discussion over the MHS. Such a discussion, held over a period of time appropriate to the subject, often acts as preparation for a decision to be taken later at a meeting of the group, or even replaces the meeting. Thus, MHSs may be used for asynchronous conferences where the participants do not need to meet either at the same time or in the same place.

Group discussion, conference

As previously noted, the new medium of an MHS may be used to support a new form of conference, an asynchronous conference.

Modern means of communication are also available for traditional synchronous conferences. *Videoconferencing* is offered as a standard service by many public telecommunications suppliers. IBCN can be expected to considerably extend and improve the services on offer and the connectivity, with its provision of sufficient bandwidth to transmit images.

Moreover, we also expect that new multi-functional terminals (intelligent workstations with facilities for speech and moving images), with suitable communication protocols, will in the long-term supersede the techniques currently used for videoconferences, and will allow subscribers to take part in conferences from their own places of work.

In this section we have shown that new technologies will irrevocably alter communication in the workplace. Here, message handling systems play a special role, since they support previously unautomated forms of communication and thus also facilitate new forms.

Standardization

In view of the importance of message handling systems, various international organizations (*Comité Consultatif International Télégraphique et*

Téléphonique (CCITT); *International Standardization Organization* (ISO); *European Computer Manufacturers Association* (ECMA)) have for some years been involved in standardization work. This cooperation has resulted in a set of recommendations being released by the plenary meeting of the CCITT in 1984 and included in the CCITT Red Book (in the part concerning the X series recommendations) (CCITT, 1985). The relevant recommendations, which have the authority of international standards, are numbered X.400 to X.430 (referred to as X.400 (84) in the sequel). Chapter 2 of this book summarizes almost 300 pages of the standards document in a way that is easy to understand.

The release of these standards also has a particular importance in the general context of the development of the *ISO Reference Model for Open Systems Interconnection* (OSI-RM) and the associated standardization, as this is the first international standard in the application layer. Since a fundamental understanding of the OSI model is essential in order to assimilate the material in the book, in Chapter 1 we give an overview of the way in which the OSI model describes complicated communication systems.

The similarly introduced and originally parallel standardization process in ISO remained behind the work of the CCITT and was only taken up again after the release of X.400 (84) with a view to a revised standard. At this point, it should also be noted that the underlying concept of X.400 was developed in Working Group 6.5 of the *International Federation for Information Processing* (IFIP).

The release of a 'standard to facilitate international message exchange between subscribers to computer-based store-and-forward message services' gave rise to feverish activity in the research and development departments of almost all computer manufacturers and many software houses. Early implementations, such as a software package EAN developed at a Canadian university (Neufeld, 1983), appeared almost simultaneously with this release. In the meantime, a respectable number of commercial products have been announced or are already on the market. By the combined efforts of interested manufacturers, so-called 'multivendor demonstrations' have been organized at several large exhibitions (for example, CeBIT in Hannover) to demonstrate the interworking of independently-developed prototypes or products. Rumour has it that in each case extensive tests and various software modifications were needed before the connections could actually be demonstrated. The systems exhibited at CeBIT in '89 and '90 show that it is today possible to purchase user-friendly implementations which interoperate well with implementations by other manufacturers.

However, initial experiences showed that X.400 (84) had various shortcomings. Thus, projects to improve and extend X.400 were started both in CCITT and in ISO. A new version of X.400, X.400 (88) (CCITT, 1989), which corrected the problems identified, was released in 1988 after the end of the four-year CCITT study period, at the plenary meeting of

Table 2   Notation used to refer to the various versions of standards for message handling systems.

Designation	Meaning
X.400	CCITT series X.400 recommendations, when no distinction between the two versions is needed.
X.400 (84)	CCITT series X.400 recommendations of 1984.
X.400 (88)	CCITT series X.400 recommendations of 1988.
ISO 10021 or MOTIS	ISO standard for a message oriented text interchange system.
MHS	Generic designation for a message handling system which conforms to the standards.
MHS (88)	Both X.400 (88) and ISO 10021.

the CCITT. In parallel with the work of CCITT, the standard 10021 for 'Message Oriented Text Interchange System' (MOTIS) was developed by ISO (ISO, 1988); this is aligned to X.400 (88).

In this book, we shall retain the notation given in Table 2 for referencing the different versions of the standards for message handling systems.

In Chapter 9, we discuss the most important properties of the new recommendations (X.400 (88)). In Chapter 2, however, we refer to the 1984 version of X.400 (84), since we assume that it will be some time before implementations of the 1988 recommendations become widely available.

We do not wish to give the impression here that the computer-supported transfer of messages is something completely new. Nearly all multi-user operating systems have a set of commands which provide the user with just such a service. In addition, various suppliers offer electronic mail in the form of electronic 'mailboxes', to which those interested may subscribe. In fact, corresponding services have been in existence for more than 15 years in the academic world, since the development of the large US research network ARPANET which even in the 1970s contained protocols for the electronic transfer of communications between subscribers. The innovative aspect of X.400 lies in the fact that it is the first international standard for message and communication transfer. Under X.400, the potential connectivity (the number of subscribers that may be attained in the future) is very large and it is possible to implement a global messaging network including public (for example, national PTTs) and private suppliers and millions of subscribers.

PART I

Foundations

1

The OSI reference model

Many systems which support computer-to-computer communication developed in a pragmatic fashion. A requirement for a new distributed application would always be met by the development of a new application-specific recipe for the dialogue between the computers involved, in other words, by a new *protocol*. This led to a large number of different protocols, which were both application- and manufacturer-dependent and mutually incompatible. Although some protocols, such as IBM's *Binary Synchronous Control protocol* (Bisync, BSC) did achieve a certain circulation, a generally-applicable communication architecture was not defined.

In the second half of the sixties and at the beginning of the seventies, several research projects in the area of computer networks led to the development and operation of experimental networks for wide-area communication (ARPANET (McQuillan and Walden, 1977)). One result of these research activities was the recognition of the urgent need for a universally applicable architecture for communication networks and corresponding worldwide standardization. In addition, the research provided the technical know-how needed to convert this recognition into reality.

While the development of the reference model for open communication systems described below took place largely in the grey zone between research and standardization, there was also a second group of beneficiaries of the early experiences mentioned above. In the second half of the seventies a number of the larger computer manufacturers defined their own communication architectures, which were to serve as guidelines for the development of hardware and software products to solve their individual communication problems. In this respect we mention IBM's *Systems Network Architecture* (SNA) and DEC's *Digital Network Architecture* (DNA, DECnet).

Common to all these formulations is the concept of an integrated network of computers of various sizes and capacities (in the case of manufacturer-oriented architectures – all from the same manufacturer) which are able to carry out similar functions. The *Reference Model for Open Systems Interconnection* (OSI), developed by ISO, was designed to be a manufacturer-, application- and transmission-medium-independent model for the standardization of communication systems.

In this context, we also note that the development of the above concepts was also associated with a change in the sense of the term computer network. The latter was no longer viewed as a set of computers and screens, interconnected in a fixed topology with fixed transmission facilities (Figure 1.1), but rather as an integrated computer network of end systems connected to a universal transport network, where the latter virtually but not necessarily physically guarantees full connectivity between all the end systems involved (Figure 1.2).

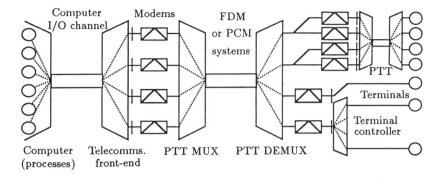

Figure 1.1 Integrated computer network based on conventional transmission facilities.

1.1 The solution and its history

The underlying structure of the OSI reference model is essentially based on fundamental research work on operating systems since Dijkstra's THE system. In what follows we shall give a short overview of these foundations.

The concept of the hierarchy

In addition to his work on programming methods, Dijkstra has also made major contributions in the area of system structuring. In particular, he was

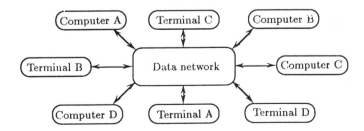

Figure 1.2 Integrated network of heterogeneous end systems based on a universal transport network.

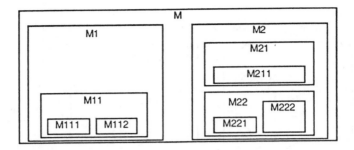

Figure 1.3   Illustration of module hierarchies.

the first to describe a well-structured computer system, namely the often quoted THE system (Dijkstra, 1968). Over the following years this led to frequent misuse of the term *hierarchical system* as an unjustified quality feature, until Parnas clarified this in a very valuable paper (Parnas, 1974). In particular, Parnas put forward two points:

- In a hierarchy, the nature of the relation in question must be defined. Mere association of objects without statements on the nature of the relationship is meaningless. According to the nature of the relation, a system may have various, not-necessarily-coincident partitions into connected networks. Typical examples of such relationships for technical systems include:
  - The offering of a service.
  - Hierarchies in the sense of modules in MODULA-2 or blocks in PASCAL. The layering principles of these languages correspond to a hierarchy, as shown in Figure 1.3.
  - Process hierarchies in the dynamic creation of processes etc.

Figure 1.2 may be interpreted in the sense that the data network offers a service for the participating end systems. Thus, we deduce that the relationship 'offers a service' (and Parnas's converse relationship 'uses a service') takes on a particular importance. A useful system might thus be thought of as a set of objects which cooperate in some way to offer a collective service, as specified by the user.

Illustrations of the concept of the hierarchy

We shall now use two examples to underline that the concept of the hierarchy in the sense of Parnas must be viewed very subtly. At the same

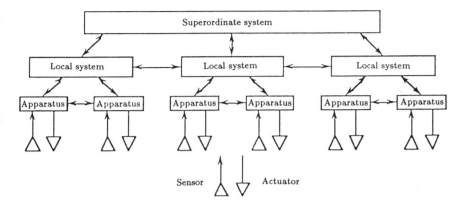

Figure 1.4   Hierarchically organized system in control engineering.

time, the examples are intended to show the principles on which systems may be organized. Figure 1.4 shows a schematized solution for a typical system in control engineering (embedded system). In this system a hierarchical functional division is primarily achieved in accordance with the following points:

- Organization into steps with different reaction-time requirements. Critical tasks are handled in a process-oriented manner.

- Subdivision in such a way that subsystem outages lead to as gradual as possible a deterioration of availability. Should subsystems at low levels fail, only a part of the whole system is affected (for example, in the case of a telephone switchboard only a limited number of subscribers). Should the higher-level system fail, the subsystems may still provide a restricted service.

- Centralization of all those functions that it is impossible or difficult to distribute, for example, the collection and processing of measurement information.

- Organization from the point of view of data flow. Communication out from the local area (if more frequent than communication within the local area) is conducted over a higher hierarchical step. This corresponds to a fixed network hierarchy and in certain circumstances provides better conditions for data exchange.

Although we have already recognized that the reliability requirements on a system may have a considerable effect on its structure,

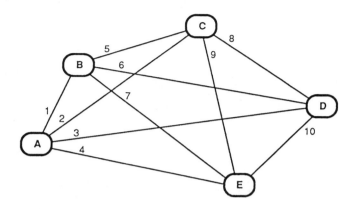

Figure 1.5 Communication in a distributed system with specialized transmission channels.

we would refer the reader to the literature on this subject (Birolini, 1981). Nevertheless, we note that in certain circumstances, a design for a reliable system may be compromised if infrastructure systems such as power and timing facilities do not create additional links between the subsystems (and thus become the weakest links in the chain).

Figures 1.5 and 1.6 are based on another premise. The five spatially distributed objects shown have different communication requirements. The first solution with ten fixed links, shown in Figure 1.5, is a good solution from the point of view of reliability, but has a cost which increases quadratically with the number of objects. A particularly undesirable circumstance occurs if the introduction of new objects requires all the existing objects to be modified.

The solution in Figure 1.6 delegates all tasks relating to the transport of data to a common communication subsystem. The hierarchical structure is then shown by the fact that the communication subsystem provides a service for all connected objects and is hierarchically subordinate.

The advantages of such an organization are obvious:

- On extension, new objects must only be linked to the common subsystem at *one* connection point.
- The development of the communication subsystem may be decoupled from applications development.

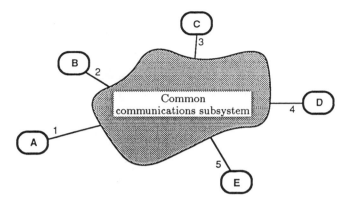

Figure 1.6 Communication in a distributed system over a common communication subsystem.

Note that within the communication subsystem, there may be a second hierarchy in the form of a hierarchical ordering of network nodes (see Figure 1.9).

Service hierarchy in an operating system

The 'hierarchy of services' defined by Parnas is based on the assumption that, beginning with the basic hardware functions at the level of logic elements, increasingly application-oriented machines will be constructed in various steps. Depending on the functionality of these machines (instruction set, programming language) a more-or-less-complicated abstract machine may be used as a model. For example, one simple model would be a finite automaton. Figure 1.7a illustrates a corresponding model and Figure 1.7b fixes the terminology used later.

A service consists of various *service primitives*, together with parameters (data) which may flow in both directions over the *interfaces* between two layers N and $N+1$. We may think of a *procedure call* as one possible implementation of such an interface.

Another example, the construction of a hierarchically structured operating system, is shown in Figure 1.8.

The problem as to the ways in which a system may be decomposed into subsystems has already been discussed on a general level. In an article (Courtois, 1975), Courtois showed that it is advantageous to choose a decomposition into a hierarchically structured system in such a way that the most commonly used functions (or resources) are implemented at the lowest level of the hierarchy. Now the question arises as to which services

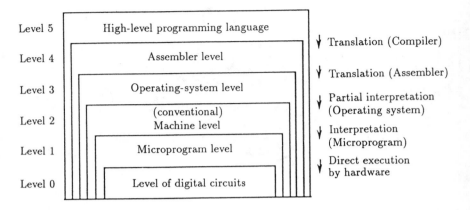

Figure 1.7a   Layer model of a computer system.

in a real-time operating system should be qualified in this way. If, based on Figure 1.8, we assume that, while the number of external processes is large, the number of real processors (to implement them) is comparatively small, then we must require that the *process switching times* in a real-time operating system should be minimized. Thus, the following considerations provide a first criterion for structuring:

- The mapping of the real processor (processors) to individual processes, in other words the provision of different virtual machines, should occur at the lowest possible level.

- For process management and synchronization, we require elementary operations on data structures such as lists and queues, which are consequently assigned to the lowest level above the real machine.

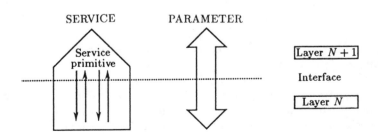

Figure 1.7b   Conventions for services.

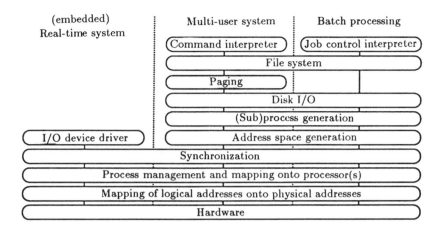

Figure 1.8   Hierarchically structured operating system.

Approaches to an appropriate structuring may be found, for instance, in the studies of the *European Workshop on Industrial Computer Systems* (EWICS, 1982), which were, for example, implemented by Maier (Maier, 1984) on a PDP-11 computer. If the real-time requirements are not dominant, another functional principle may be determined to be optimal, as for example, shown by Parnas for the realization of systems with virtual memory (Parnas *et al.*, 1976).

1.2 The OSI reference model and its description

Elements and structure of the model

The OSI reference model is comprehensively described in the standards documents ISO 7498 from ISO and X.200 from CCITT (see Appendix B). Thus, here we shall only give an overview. For the moment, Figures 1.9 and 1.10 illustrate the basic idea of the model in a very simplified representation.

End systems communicate with one another via a *communication network* consisting of interconnected *intermediate systems (relay open systems)*. The end systems A and B and the intermediate systems 1 and 2 of Figure 1.10 may be identified with the corresponding systems of Figure 1.9. The intermediate systems 3, 4, 5 and 6 of Figure 1.9 are not shown on Figure 1.10. It is possible to conceive other systems between the two

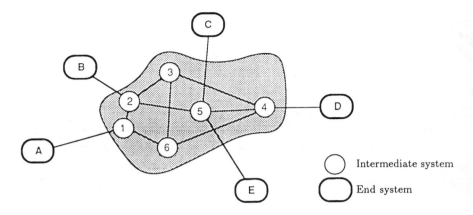

Figure 1.9 Functional model of a connection between open systems.

intermediate systems 1 and 2, communicating between themselves and with systems 1 and 2 via network-internal transmission protocols.

In the ISO terminology, open systems are end or intermediate systems which cooperate with one another according to the rules laid down in the OSI reference model and the other accompanying standards. They are abstractions of *real open systems* (computers, software systems, peripheral devices, etc.) in which only those aspects which are important for communication are considered.

The main idea of Figure 1.10 is to produce a layered system similar to Figures 1.7a and 1.8. As a *supplier of services*, every layer provides certain *services* to the layer above (the *service user*) at the *Service Access Point* (SAP), via the *interface* between the two layers (Figure 1.11a). Two *subsystems* in adjacent layers exchange both control information and data via this interface.

Subsystems contain active elements called *entities*. Entities are intuitively comparable to processes in software systems. Entities in the same layer are said to be *peers* and may communicate with each other according to the rules of a *(peer) protocol*. A protocol is a recipe for a dialogue between peer entities.

Unlike actual physical communication, which only takes place below the lowest layer, the protocols of the higher layers determine a *virtual* or *logical communication*.

Figure 1.11b illustrates the relationship between entities. Both of the $(N+1)$-entities use one or more services of the underlying layer N for their dialogue, in that they are either executed or informed of an event in

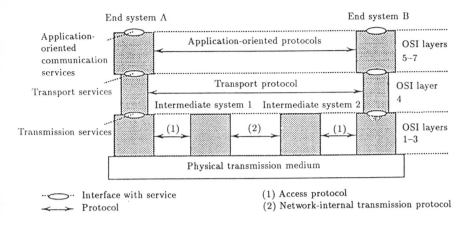

Figure 1.10   Simplified OSI reference model.

the underlying layer by *service primitives*. The service primitives are used to exchange a (possibly large) number of *parameters*.

ISO 7498 defines four different types of service primitives for a service D (Figure 1.11c):

D.request   Service D is requested.

D.indication   Tells an entity which service is required.

D.response   An entity may use this to reply to a D.indication.

D.confirm   The requesting entity receives confirmation of the execution of service D.

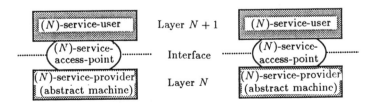

Figure 1.11a   Model of the interaction between the service provider and the service user of two neighbouring layers.

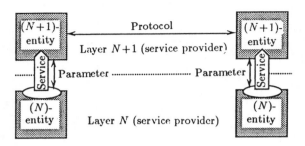

Figure 1.11b   Relationship between entities.

A service may be confirmed (all four primitives are used) or unconfirmed (includes only D.request and D.indication). In addition, a service primitive may be issued by the service provider, for example, termination of a connection in the event of a fault in a network, which is normally signalled by a corresponding 'indication'.

Figure 1.11c shows a *time-sequence diagram*, giving a graphical illustration of typical temporal relationships between service primitives.

Service user	Service provider	Service user	
D.request		D.indication	
	defined sequence	D.response	confirmed service
D.confirm			
D.request	defined sequence		unconfirmed service
		D.indication	
D.indication	undefined sequence	D.indication	e.g. release of a connection by a service provider

Time   Time

Figure 1.11c   Time-sequence diagram for service primitives.

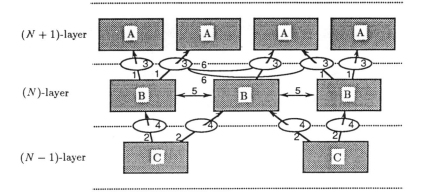

Figure 1.11d   Elements of the OSI reference model.

Figure 1.11d summarizes previous elements and other elements (denoted by letters) of the OSI reference model and their interrelationships (numbers):

- The active components of an (N)-subsystem (the (N)-entities) are denoted by A, B, and C.

- A layer N offers its services (1, 2) at the (N)-SAPs (3, 4).

- Virtual communication between two (N)-entities is defined by an (N)-protocol (5). If this protocol is connection-oriented the corresponding (N)-SAP between the entities involved is an (N)-connection (6).

- An entity may make its services available to several entities in the overlying layer. Conversely, an entity may make use of the services of several entities in an underlying layer. These possibilities are in direct accordance with the definition of a hierarchical system in Section 1.1.

Figure 1.11e illustrates the interplay of layers and entities. The user of layer N in the end system A requests a service, for example, the transmission of a data block, using a 'request'. The service is executed by an (N)-entity which sends a *Protocol Data Unit* (PDU) to the other entity in the same layer in end system B. The PDU contains the data to be transmitted and control information which is added and interpreted by the entities. Successful receipt of the PDU by the entity in end system B gives rise to a corresponding 'indication'.

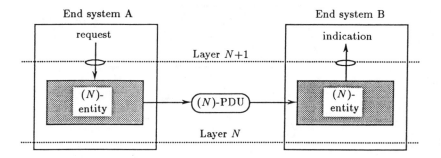

Figure 1.11e Cooperation between entities (schematic).

Only when the considered layer N is layer 1, is the PDU also transmitted over the physical medium as part of this cooperation. Otherwise, transmission of the PDU to the underlying layer $N-1$ leads to a further 'request' and to the transmission of an $(N-1)$-PDU (Figure 1.11f). We note the terminology used:

- The (N)-PDU is delivered by the (N)-entity of the layer $N-1$ to the $(N-1)$-SAP as an $(N-1)$-*Service Data Unit* (SDU). The SDU is a parameter of the service primitive used ('request').
- The $(N-1)$-SDU together with the $(N-1)$-*Protocol Control Information* (PCI) becomes the $(N-1)$-PDU.

The given representation is, however, only appropriate if in fact the whole SDU is packed into a PDU. *Segmentation* may be used by an entity to distribute an SDU across several PDUs, where the receiving entity has the job of *reassembling* the data parts of a PDU belonging to a single SDU, so that the user can receive the complete SDU. Similarly, *splitting* may be used to transmit an SDU over various connections with *recombining* used to piece it together again correctly on the other side.

Repeated use of the process discussed above leads to a nesting of PDUs, so that the information finally transmitted over the medium contains the data delivered to the uppermost layer and control information for each protocol which may only be interpreted by the corresponding entity (Figure 1.11g).

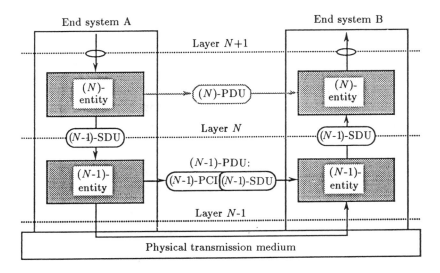

Figure 1.11f   Cooperation between entities.

Now the question is how make a sensible assignment of the necessary communication functions to different layers in a distributed system. From the discussions in Section 1.1 we immediately note that this assignment must be the result of a compromise:

- On the one hand, according to Courtois, a system should be structured so that the most frequently used functions belong to the lowest layers (Courtois, 1975).

- On the other hand, for economic reasons, we would like to offer a certain basic transport service with as few communication networks as possible, on which as many applications as possible could be executed.

The assignment of functions to layers described below is based on additional principles which have been successfully applied for some time in the development of modular software systems. In particular, these include the following fundamental principles:

- We should define as few layers as possible, so that the cost of describing the model and the associated protocols is not unnecessarily high.

- Similar functions should be implemented in the same layer, dissimilar functions in different layers. Related to this principle is the objective of collecting functions and data of the same level of abstraction within the same layer.

- The boundary between two layers should be chosen in such a way that the resulting interface is as narrow as possible (to minimize the interdependency of layers) and easy to describe. In addition, the boundary should be laid where previous experience shows it to be sensible and where future standardization of the corresponding interface could be useful.   .

- Finally, it should be possible to alter a layer, partially or completely (in other words, to modify the corresponding protocols and adapt them to technological advances), without this having any effect on the upper and lower interfaces of this layer.

The resulting model consists of seven layers, which are illustrated in Figure 1.12 (this is a refinement of Figure 1.10).

Application layer (A, layer 7)   The *application layer* has a special role in that it is the only one of the seven layers that provides the end user (the application processes on a computer) with requested services. This layer does not contain the application itself, but communication services that support the application. These may be standardized services or services which are valid for a specific application agreed between the users.

Presentation layer (P, layer 6)   Since computers of different types often also use different representations for information, cooperation requires an agreement over the syntax and the coding of data to be exchanged. The *presentation layer* contains functions to *negotiate* one of various possible so-called *transfer syntaxes* (rules for the representation of information during transmission) together with functions for conversion between local representations of data and the chosen transfer syntax.

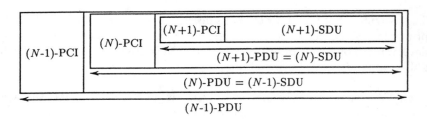

Figure 1.11g   Nesting of PDUs of various layers.

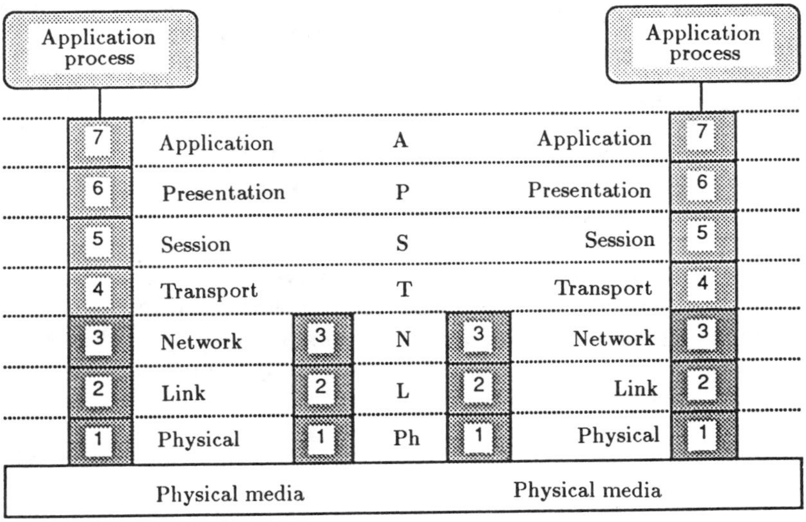
Application process
Application process
7 Application A Application 7
6 Presentation P Presentation 6
5 Session S Session 5
4 Transport T Transport 4
3 Network 3 N 3 Network 3
2 Link 2 L 2 Link 2
1 Physical 1 Ph 1 Physical 1
Physical media
Physical media

Figure 1.12 The seven layers of the OSI reference model.

Session layer (S, layer 5) While layer 7 provides application-specific, computer-system-independent services, and layer 6 ensures that the information exchanged is syntactically correct and coded in a representation known to both entities, the *session layer* provides a service whereby data (in the sense of bit sequences) may be exchanged between cooperating entities. It contains functions which can be used by two communication partners to control and structure their dialogue. In particular, it is possible to transmit important data (so-called priority data) with a higher priority than normal data and to define synchronization points for the structuring of the dialogue. This particularly facilitates orderly restart after a planned or unforseen interruption of a communications link. In addition, duplex or half-duplex connections are optionally available. Most services of the session layer are made available to the application layer through layer 6 without major alteration.

Transport layer (T, layer 4) The *transport layer* uses an end-to-end protocol to provide a data-transport infrastructure the quality of which is independent of that of the underlying transmission service. This means that, if necessary, data-protection measures must be taken, over and above those of the link layer. The transport layer may use *segmentation* to divide a long transport SDU into a sequence of small PDUs which are adjusted to a given maximum size of network SDU. It may also *multiplex* several transport connections onto a single network connection, or *split* a single transport connection into several network connections (for improved performance).

Network layer (N, layer 3)   The *network layer* provides communication paths for the transparent transmission of data between any end systems, over various intermediate systems the subsystems of which are designated as *network relays* in layer 3. The network service screens the higher-level subsystems from the task of *routing*.

Link layer (L, layer 2)   The *link layer* serves to transmit data blocks over the channels between the intermediate systems and over the lines that connect the end systems. In addition to the formation of these blocks and the implementation of error detection and correction measures, the functions of the link layer include the following:

- Control of access to the transmission medium if this is used by more than one user. This includes the avoidance of 'call collision' in circuit-switched systems or the coordination of simultaneous access of several stations to a common transmission medium in local area networks.

- Data flow control, since the buffer memory space and processing capacity of real systems is often limited.

Physical layer (Ph, layer 1)   The *physical layer* defines a procedure for transmitting digital data over a given transmission medium (for example, a cable or a band in the radio frequency spectrum). Thus, the service of layer 1 provides a path for the transmission of a bit stream; however, this service is normally responsible not only for the transmission of individual bits, but also for the provision of synchronization signals.

In Sections 1.3 and 1.4 we give more details of the application and presentation layers, since these two layers are particularly important for an understanding of standard applications such as message transfer.

Comparison: a model of the shipment of goods

Comparison with systems for transporting people and goods provides a simple illustration of the somewhat abstract OSI reference model. First we note that these systems are also hierarchically organized. Figure 1.13 illustrates this ordering.

A	Transportation of goods/people on the road network
P	Goods declarations, handling rules
S	Rules for delivery and receipt
T	Transportation rules
N	Road maps, signposts/diversion signs
L	Lorries, cars; prohibitions and requirements
Ph	Roads, streets, tracks
Medium	Ground surface

Figure 1.13   Hierarchical ordering of the functions in systems for transporting goods.

At the lowest step of this hierarchy are the individual transport bearers, in the form of roads, canals, railways, air lanes, etc. These bearers form coherent networks; their fundamentally different properties necessitate the use of correspondingly different means of transport (road vehicles, ships, trains, aircraft, etc.). In turn, these means of transport support various grades of transport services, which are already to some extent independent of the underlying bearers: transport of people, of material goods of various classes of weight and volume, etc. A dependence on the transport bearer only arises because not all types of transport services are possible on every transport bearer (for example, bulk goods in units of 10 000 tonnes are not usually transported by air). From the user's point of view, a specific transport service may actually involve the consecutive use of both different types of transport bearers and different means of transport (for example, the international parcel service involving air, rail and road transport).

Where two different types of transport bearers meet, special facilities (for example, equipment for reloading, conveyor belts, cranes, escalators) must be provided to enable the transport services to use both bearers with the changeover being as transparent as possible. Many transport bearers also have the interesting property that they permit the use of various means of transport (for example, the carriageway in a street may be simultaneously used by various types of cars, bicycles and horse-drawn vehicles).

Certain standards also exist for material communication systems at the higher levels of the transport system. For example, application-specific packaging facilitates the use of goods from the user's point of view, while a wholesaler's distribution system is determined by the requirements of the retailer.

In summary we may identify the following features of the system to transport goods:

- The system is hierarchically ordered. Application-specific functions are based on multi-purpose, universal transport services such as rail and road transport, and the latter are in turn supported by different types of transport bearers.

- Construction, operation and maintenance of the different transport hierarchies are entirely in the hands of different types of entities, and at the higher levels there may even be a plurality of service bearers. For example, the road network is in the hands of the state, the individual transport services on the other hand are provided by a large number of public and private concerns and by individual and private users. The same holds for the material communication functions at application-oriented levels, from the state-run monopoly of letter post to the private transport of goods.

- Even public and very liberal material transport systems are subject to a number of laws and rules. Specification of the latter ensures open access to whole systems: standards for road construction enable us to build vehicles for an international market; standardized road signals and traffic regulations facilitate cross-border traffic and ensure the compatibility of different means of transport.

1.3 The application layer

This section describes the structure of the application layer as defined by the OSI standards (ISO 9545). The underlying concepts are described in ISO 7498. As the hierarchically highest layer of the OSI reference model, the application layer allows the *Application Processes* (APs) access to the *OSI environment.* In a real system, application processes are found outside the abstract OSI environment. They represent those parts of a computer-based implementation of an application that rely on communication services in order to fulfil their task. The communication requirements of application processes are only handled in the application layer. Statements such as 'our application uses the services of the transport layer directly' thus stand in contradiction to the OSI reference model.

The aspects of an AP that are relevant to communications are modelled by an *Application Entity* (AE). This consists of a number of *Application Service Elements* (ASEs), which jointly describe the

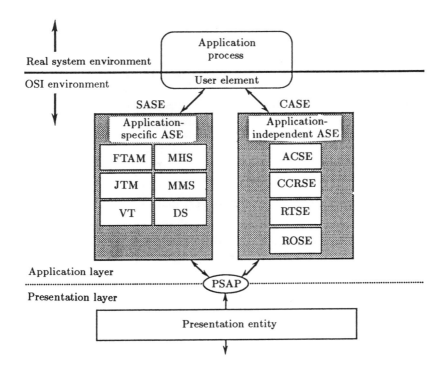

Figure 1.14   Application layer and application process.

communication functions of the application entity, together with a *user element* which models those parts of the application process that use the application service elements. A concrete expression of the user element is often found in application software in the form of application-specific libraries which provide programmer interfaces to implement application processes.

We distinguish between *Common Application Service Elements* (CASEs) and *Specific Application Service Elements* (SASEs) (Figure 1.14).

CASEs are general service elements which may serve many applications. They include the following service elements:

Association Control Service Element (ACSE)

ACSE provides services to establish and clear associations between application entities (it deals with connections at the level of the application layer). The establishment of an association involves a statement of the set of language elements to be used for the subsequent dialogue. This set is called an *abstract syntax*. The language elements of an abstract syntax are described for transmission purposes in the *transfer syntax* which provides for consistency between the presentation entities. In the context of OSI standardization a data description language has been developed for use in the formal description of abstract syntaxes (*Abstract Syntax Notation One*, ASN.1) (ISO 8824), and the corresponding *encoding rules* have been specified (ISO 8825) (this is the only standardized transfer syntax to date).

Associations between application entities can only be established via the ACSE, so that this ASE is needed for all applications.

ACSE is specified in CCITT recommendations X.217 and X.227 and in ISO 8649 and 8650.

Commitment, Concurrency and Recovery Service Element (CCRSE)

The CCRSE provides aid for the implementation of distributed transactions in an OSI environment. A distributed transaction is executed with the cooperation of several application processes. The CCRSE may be used to ensure that:

- A sequence of operations of one transaction is not interfered with by the transactions of another application process.

- The operations of one transaction either all terminate successfully or (if successful termination of all operations is impossible) all operations already executed are cancelled. This means that a transaction is executed either in full or not at all.

This ASE may be used to ensure the consistency of distributed data. The CCRSE is specified in ISO 9804 and 9805.

Reliable Transfer Service Element (RTSE)

The RTSE provides for reliable transmission of *Application Protocol Data Units* (APDUs) between two application entities. It ensures that an APDU is transmitted in full, exactly once, or that the application entity is informed of the failed transfer attempt by an error indicator. RTSE is able to survive a breakdown of transmission equipment and of end systems, since the service offered by RTSE uses the reliable transmission provided by the transport layer. Of course, RTSE makes full use of the aid offered by the session layer (for example, the setting of synchronization points).

RTSE is specified in CCITT recommendations X.218 and X.228 and in ISO 9066.

Remote Operations Service Element (ROSE)

ROSE provides services which support the asymmetric joint working of a *client* with a *server*. The server provides a set of operations which the client may execute over the OSI network. Every operation may involve data transfer in both directions. ROSE corresponds very well to the concept of *Remote Procedure Calls* (RPCs) often used in distributed systems.

ROSE describes a formal notation to define the syntax of operations that a client may execute on a server, and specifies a protocol which guarantees reliable transmission in both directions of data belonging to an operation. The implementation of a distributed application using ROSE is based on the formal description of the desired operations and their parameters and on the realization of software which calls the necessary operations on the client and executes the corresponding actions on the server. Program generators already exist for the above formal notation. They generate a skeleton program corresponding to the specifications so only the action routines have to be coded by hand (Rose, 1990). For the transmission of APDUs, ROSE may optionally use the services of the RTSE.

ROSE is specified in CCITT recommendations X.219 and X.229 and in ISO 9072.

Those service elements that are restricted to special standardized applications are termed SASEs. Below, we describe the six most important SASEs already identified. Standardization work for all SASEs is in progress or has been completed.

File Transfer Access and Management (FTAM, ISO 8571)

This enables an application process to read, write to and manage files on a remote system. Transmission of whole files (file transfer) is a subset of this service.

Job Transfer and Manipulation (JTM, ISO 8831/8832)

This permits an application process to initiate data processing on a remote computer (for example, execution of a complicated calculation on a super-computer), to observe, to control and to return the result to the initiator.

Virtual Terminal (VT, ISO 9040/9041)

This enables an application process controlling a local workstation (terminal) to communicate with a remote application, without the need for the type or the manufacturer of the workstation to be known to the application, and without restrictions on the properties of the workstation.

Message Handling Service (CCITT X.400, ISO 10021)

The *message handling service* provided by the message handling system (MHS) permits application processes to exchange messages (Chapters 2 and 9).

Manufacturing Message Service (MMS, ISO 9506)

This defines the format and the meaning of messages exchanged between a control computer in a production line and a programmable device connected to it.

Directory Service (DS, CCITT X.500, ISO 9594)

A directory is a global distributed database which stores data about objects in a communication system (processes, entities, servers, persons, etc.). A directory service is primarily used to map names onto addresses, for example, O/R addresses or PSAP addresses (Section 1.5 and Chapter 2). We discuss standard directory services in Chapter 12.

In the definition of the architecture of the application layer (ISO 9545), it is assumed that most future application processes will be best supported by a type of *building kit of standards* and ultimately by associated implementations conforming to the standards. Thus, most of the SASEs listed above are described as combinations of simpler ASEs and CASEs. The entire set of the ASEs needed for an application and the description of their interaction is called the *Application Context* (AC). The application context also determines the role played by a specific ASE amongst the ASEs needed for an application. For example, the application context for access to the OSI directory consists of three separate ASEs to read, modify and search for entries, together with ROSE and ACSE. Here, the last two play the role of basic services on which the directory-specific ASEs are based. The service available to an application process via the user element is in this case only provided by the functions of the directory-specific ASEs, since these, like a layer within the application layer, are based on ROSE and ACSE. However, we note that according to the current view, the application layer is *not* divided into sublayers. Consequently, the application context describes the services implemented for an AP by the application layer and the dialogue which takes place between two application entities. Thus, it replaces the concept of a protocol, which in the application layer is explicitly only meaningful for individual ASEs.

1.4 The presentation layer

The task of the presentation layer is to provide the application layer with an easy-to-use, universal service interface for the transmission of APDUs. APDUs, unlike the protocol data units of lower layers, are often very complicated data structures; this statement is true both for control information and for user data. For example, in an application involving the electronic exchange of commercial data, APDUs must represent the contents of an invoice in a form suitable for interpretation and processing and must contain statements about all the recipients of the invoice or copies of it. In Chapter 2, we shall discuss examples of APDUs as used in the message handling service. APDUs are presented to the presentation layer as *Presentation Service Data Units* (PSDUs). Thus, in order to obtain an overview of the service of the presentation layer, we must answer the following questions:

- How is the structure of PSDUs described? Clearly, their structure is application-dependent, and there is a set of possible PSDU formats for each application. A specification of the structure of APDUs and PSDUs is called an *abstract syntax*. This only determines the structure of the PSDUs, not their representation.

- How are PSDUs physically represented? PSDUs must be physically stored in both end systems. This means that suitable representations for PSDUs must be found for both the sending and the receiving system. We call these *source* and *target coding*. In many cases the two codings will be different; for example, a text may be represented in ASCII code in one real system and in EBCDIC code in another. Thus, a third coding, the so-called *transfer coding*, which is understood by both systems, is potentially required. Here too the specifications of the three codings are described by the term syntax. The source and target coding are described by a *local syntax*, while the transfer coding is described by the *transfer syntax*.

Figure 1.15 describes the resulting relationships between the entities of the presentation and the application layers.

On establishment of a connection, the entities of the presentation layer have the task of selecting a suitable transfer syntax for the required abstract syntax and both end systems. During the data exchange, they carry out the conversion between the representation according to the local syntax and the transfer syntax. We note here that, firstly there may be a large number of transfer syntaxes for different fields of application and that secondly, more than one transfer syntax may be used for one abstract syntax. For example, a transfer syntax might be designed for the largest possible field of application and in certain circumstances an inefficient

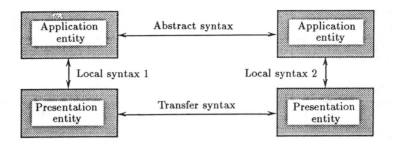

Figure 1.15   Abstract syntax, local syntax and transfer syntax.

coding prescribed in terms of compactness; on the other hand, a transfer syntax for use in real-time systems might be distinguished by a coding which is particularly simple to process.

The following example clarifies the concepts introduced above.

As part of a laboratory experiment, a sensor has to send a sequence of measured integer values to a processing procedure. In this case, the abstract syntax is a sequence of integers. Integers may be represented in the sensor in two's complement, 16-bit format, while a 32-bit one's complement representation is used in the processing procedure (being determined by the processor's arithmetic unit). The appropriate transfer syntax might prescribe that for transmission, integers should be represented as a sign followed by a variable number of decimal digits, followed by an end character.

Specification of abstract syntaxes using ASN.1

Since, as mentioned at the beginning of this section, the data structures to be transmitted are often much more complicated than in the above simple example, a language to describe abstract syntaxes, known as *Abstract Syntax Notation One* (ASN.1), has been developed and standardized within the framework of OSI standardization. This permits a far-reaching formal specification of the structure of PSDUs and APDUs. At the same time, a universal recipe for coding PSDUs (thus, a transfer syntax) has been designed and established as standard. Table 1.1 gives an overview of the different versions of ASN.1.

ASN.1 is a 'Backus-Naur-form'-like context-free language for the definition of abstract syntaxes. It is comparable to the formalism available in popular programming languages such as PASCAL or Ada for the definition of complicated data types. However, ASN.1 is specialized for

Table 1.1   Different language versions for the definition of abstract syntaxes.

Standard/ document	Source	Description
X.409	CCITT 1984 (Red Book)	Specification language for abstract syntaxes with coding rules (with corresponding transfer syntax).
8824	ISO/IEC 1988	Specification language ASN.1 for abstract syntaxes (extended from X.409).
8825	ISO/IEC 1988	Coding rules for ASN.1.
X.208	CCITT 1988 (Blue Book)	Specification language for abstract syntaxes (technically aligned with 8824).
X.209	CCITT 1988 (Blue Book)	Coding rules for X.208 (technically aligned with 8825).

this task and thus has more to offer than these programming languages. In addition to data types, ASN.1 may also be used to declare notations for the specification of values.

An abstract syntax is specified in ASN.1 by a *module definition* (Figure 1.16). Thus, it contains a name, which must be declared, together with the abstract syntax definition, to all the application entities which will use the abstract syntax. Clearly, the names and definitions of all generally valid abstract syntaxes must be internationally recorded so that worldwide connections between application entities are possible without prior bilateral arrangement.

Symbols written in capital letters are reserved and appear thus in the text of the specification (they are terminal symbols). Character strings between quotation marks (") are also terminal symbols. ModuleIdentifier and ModuleBody are non-terminal symbols and are refined by subsequent definitions (also called productions). ModuleDefinition is the so-called start symbol and represents the syntactic unit to be specified. Figure 1.17 gives an example of a complete specification.

```
ModuleDefinition ::=
        ModuleIdentifier DEFINITIONS "::="
        BEGIN
            ModuleBody
        END
```

Figure 1.16   Form of an ASN.1 module definition (schematic).

```
SimpleSyntax DEFINITIONS ::=
    BEGIN
        SimplePDU ::= SEQUENCE OF INTEGER
    END
```

Figure 1.17   Example of an ASN.1 specification.

The abstract syntax **SimpleSyntax** describes PDUs which may consist of a sequence of zero, one or more integers. **SimplePDU** is a newly defined data type.

ASN.1 divides data types into four classes:

- Universal data types (UNIVERSAL) are of general significance. They are comparable with the standard types in modern programming languages. They may be primitive or constructed. Primitive types cannot be further decomposed.

- Application-wide data types (APPLICATION) are unique within an application and distinctive.

- Private data types (PRIVATE) are defined for private use (for example, company-internal or in bilateral arrangements with business partners).

- Context-specific data types (without special identification) are those which only have a meaning within an individual ASN.1 definition.

Every type has a *tag* which consists of a statement of its class membership and a number.

For types of the class UNIVERSAL the numbers are predefined by ASN.1. Table 1.2 shows a selection of universal data types with their numbers.

Constructed types permit the construction of new types from existing universal or self-defined types. For example, a new type **User** may be defined as follows:

```
User ::= SEQUENCE {
    PersonsName       VisibleString,
    OrganizationsName VisibleString,
    IdentificationNr  INTEGER}
```

Values of the type **User** belong to the class UNIVERSAL and are assigned the number 16; in addition, they are constructed and contain as part of their structure the values for `PersonsName`, `OrganizationsName` and `IdentificationNr`, where these values are also assigned numbers in accordance with Table 1.2. The corresponding coding rules, which we consider later, prescribe that the tags should also be laid down in the code. Thus, a receiving entity can decode a coded value (sequence of bits). The need for explicit tags is apparent in the following example; the bracketed numbers represent explicit tags which serve to identify the different members of the SET.

```
User ::= SET {
      PersonsName        [1] VisibleString,
      OrganizationsName  [2] VisibleString,
      Country            [3] VisibleString}
```

Without explicit tags all the elements would be of the type `VisibleString`. Since the coding sequence for the elements of a set within

Table 1.2   ASN.1 universal data types.

Type name Primitive types:	Class	Nr.	Use
BOOLEAN	UNIVERSAL	1	Truth values TRUE and FALSE.
INTEGER	UNIVERSAL	2	Integer values.
BITSTRING	UNIVERSAL	3	Sequence of bits.
OCTETSTRING	UNIVERSAL	4	String of 8-bit bytes (octets).
NULL	UNIVERSAL	5	Representation of the absence of a value.
OBJECT IDENTIFIER	UNIVERSAL	6	Unique name for information objects (such as abstract syntaxes).
OBJECT DESCRIPTOR	UNIVERSAL	7	Representation of a readable (by man) name of an object identifier (as string).
EXTERNAL	UNIVERSAL	8	For modelling data formats not specified or fixed elsewhere.
REAL	UNIVERSAL	9	Representation of real-valued quantities.
ENUMERATED	UNIVERSAL	10	Representation of quantities with a countable (normally small) number of possible values; corresponds to the enumerated type found in various programming languages.

Table 1.2 (cont.)

Constructed types			
NumericString PrintableString TeletexString (T61String) VideotexString VisibleString (ISO646String) IA5String GraphicString GeneralString	UNIVERSAL	18 19 20 21 26 22 25 27	Character strings from various character sets. Character strings may be coded as either primitive or constructed.
SEQUENCE	UNIVERSAL	16	Fixed-length sequence of values with the specified types.
SEQUENCE OF	UNIVERSAL	16	Sequence of zero, one or more values of the same type.
SET	UNIVERSAL	17	Unordered set consisting of a predetermined number of values with specified types.
SET OF	UNIVERSAL	17	Unordered set of zero, one or more values of the same type.
UTCTime	UNIVERSAL	23 24	Various types to represent the time (for example, UTCTime) (Coordinated Universal Time also called Greenwich Mean Time).

a SET is not prescribed, it would be impossible to decode a value of type User without explicit entry of the tags with the numbers 1, 2 and 3 for the context-specific types PersonsName, OrganizationsName and Country.

However, this specification gives an inefficient coding, since, as shown here by example of PersonsName, the value with the context-specific tag 1 actually contains the coding of the VisibleString and thus also an additional tag of class UNIVERSAL with number 26. The directive IMPLICIT may thus be used to specify a type in such a way that, after explicit tagging, the redundant tags in the coding are suppressed:

```
User ::= SET {
        PersonsName       [1] IMPLICIT VisibleString,
        OrganizationsName [2] IMPLICIT VisibleString,
        Country           [3] IMPLICIT VisibleString}
```

Individual elements of a sequence or a set may also be declared to be OPTIONAL, as in the following example for `OrganizationsName`:

```
User ::= SET {
        PersonsName        [1] IMPLICIT VisibleString,
        OrganizationsName  [2] IMPLICIT VisibleString
                           OPTIONAL,
        Country            [3] IMPLICIT VisibleString}
```

A selection of different elements of a data structure may be made using CHOICE:

```
User ::= SET {
        PersonsName [1] IMPLICIT VisibleString,
        Location        OrgOrTown OPTIONAL,
        Country     [3] IMPLICIT VisibleString}

OrgOrTown ::= CHOICE {
        OrganizationsName [2] IMPLICIT VisibleString,
        Town              [4] IMPLICIT VisibleString}
```

Note that in the above example, the use of tags guarantees that the selection made by the sender (`OrganizationsName` or `Town`) can be recognized by the recipient.

Tagging may also be used to derive new uniquely recognizable data types from existing (for example, universal) ones:

```
VersionID ::= [APPLICATION 18] IMPLICIT INTEGER;
```

This defines a new type (different from other types) of the class APPLICATION with number 18, which may be used to represent integer values. It is obvious that a type is only unique application-wide if no other type with the same tag occurs in the same application.

ASN.1 transfer syntax

ISO 8825 (and CCITT X.209) sets down how values, whose structure is fixed in an ASN.1 specification, should be coded. Two types of coding are possible: *definite encoding* and *indefinite encoding*. Definite encoding consists of an *identifier field*, a *length entry* and a *contents field* (see Figure 1.18).

The identifier field contains an entry on the class membership, and the number and indicates whether it is a primitive or a constructed value. The length field specifies the length of the contents field (number of 8-bit bytes).

Identifier field	Length field	Content field

Figure 1.18   Definite encoding according to ISO 8825.

Indefinite encoding does not use a length entry proper, but employs a special pattern in the place of the length entry and a *termination character* (*End of Content*, EOC) consisting of two 8-bit bytes with value 0 (Figure 1.19). This is used, for example, when the sending entity cannot determine the amount of space that will be required by the structure to be coded at a sufficiently early stage.

We thus deduce that a coded value contains at least two or four 8-bit bytes (the identifier field and the length field, in addition to the termination character if necessary). For example, a definitely-encoded value of type BOOLEAN requires three 8-bit bytes; the coding is not particularly efficient in terms of space.

Figure 1.20 shows the coding of the identifier field. Clearly this coding will support a maximum of 32 different numbers per class. Since this is not enough, the reserved value 31 is used to indicate additional 8-bit bytes (successor octets) for numeration (Figure 1.21).

Successor octets with 1 in the highest-order-bit position (position 8) indicate that another successor octet follows. In each successor octet a 7-bit binary representation of the number may be implemented ('x' in Figure 1.21).

A similar means of coding was chosen for the length field. In the *short form*, lengths from 0 to 127 are coded in binary form in the seven lower-order positions of the field. In this case, bit position 8 is 0. Length values greater than 127 (*long form*) are represented as a sequence of 8-bit bytes (octets), where in the first octet, bit 8 is set to 1 and bit positions 7 to 1 indicate the number of subsequent octets (maximum 126; the value 127 is reserved for possible future extensions). The subsequent octets then contain

Identifier field	Length field †	Content field	EOC

†– contains notice of indefinite encoding

Figure 1.19   Indefinite encoding according to ISO 8825.

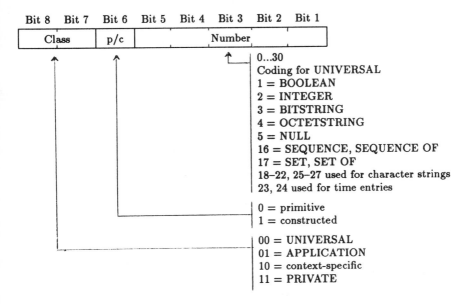

Figure 1.20 Coding of the identifier field.

the length value. Thus, the maximum codable length is $2^{126*8} - 1$ ($\approx 10^{300}$), which is surely a sufficiently large reserve.

Indefinite encoding is indicated by a length field with value 10000000.

Bit 8	Bit 7	Bit 6	Bit 5	Bit 4	Bit 3	Bit 2	Bit 1	
Class		p/c	1	1	1	1	1	first octet

Bit 8	Bit 7	Bit 6	Bit 5	Bit 4	Bit 3	Bit 2	Bit 1	
1	x	x	x	x	x	x	x	second octet
⋮	⋮	⋮	⋮	⋮	⋮	⋮	⋮	⋮

Bit 8	Bit 7	Bit 6	Bit 5	Bit 4	Bit 3	Bit 2	Bit 1	
0	x	x	x	x	x	x	x	last octet

Figure 1.21 Coding of the identifier field for numbers greater than 30.

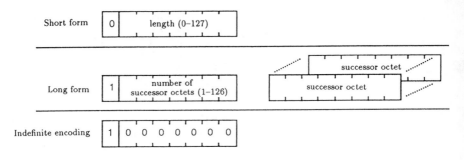

Figure 1.22 Different codings of the length field.

Figure 1.22 summarizes the coding of the length field.

To end this section, we discuss some simple examples of the coding of values of given data types. Here, the index 16 means that the coding is in base 16 (hexadecimal), and thus two numbers or letters together form an octet.

(a) Type BOOLEAN with the value TRUE. FALSE is represented by an octet 0, TRUE is represented by an octet $\neq 0$.

BOOLEAN	Length	Content
01_{16}	01_{16}	FF_{16}

(b) Type VisibleString with the value 'Jones', primitive coding, definite.

VisibleString	Length	Content
$1A_{16}$	05_{16}	$4A6F6E6573_{16}$

(c) Type VisibleString with the value 'Jones', constructed coding, divided into two parts, definite.

VisibleString	Length	Content		
$3A_{16}$	09_{16}	OCTETSTRING	Length	Content
		04_{16}	03_{16}	$4A6F6E_{16}$
		OCTETSTRING	Length	Content
		04_{16}	02_{16}	6573_{16}

(d) Type **VisibleString** with the value 'Jones', constructed coding, indefinite, divided into two definitely coded parts. The two octets of the termination character may be thought of as a primitive value of the class UNIVERSAL with number 0. This gives a fictitious length field with value 0.

VisibleString	Length	Content		
$3A_{16}$	80_{16}	OCTETSTRING	Length	Content
		04_{16}	03_{16}	$4A6F6E_{16}$
		OCTETSTRING	Length	Content
		04_{16}	02_{16}	6573_{16}
		EOC	Length	
		00_{16}	00_{16}	

(e) Type **Name1 ::= VisibleString**, with the value 'Jones':

VisibleString	Length	Content
$1A_{16}$	05_{16}	$4A6F6E6573_{16}$

(f) Type **Name2 ::= [APPLICATION 3] Name1**, with the value 'Jones':

[APPLICATION 3] (constructed)	Length	Content		
63_{16}	07_{16}	VisibleString	Length	Content
		$1A_{16}$	05_{16}	$4A6F6E6573_{16}$

(g) Type **Name3 ::= [APPLICATION 3] IMPLICIT Name1**, with the value 'Jones:

[APPLICATION 3] (primitive)	Length	Content
43_{16}	05_{16}	$4A6F6E6573_{16}$

```
MacroDefinition ::=
    MacroName MACRO "::=" BEGIN
        TYPE NOTATION "::=" TypeNotationDescription
        VALUE NOTATION "::=" ValueNotationDescription
    END
```

Figure 1.23 Definition of a macro.

Macros

The possibility of specifying new notations for types and values in ASN.1 with the aid of *macros* is of particular importance for X.400. Above all X.400 (88) makes frequent use of macros.

The definition of a macro is shown (in schematic form) in Figure 1.23. Here MacroName denotes the name chosen for the macro, while TypeNotationDescription and ValueNotationDescription are place holders for the description of the notation to be used for type definitions and the associated value specifications (respectively). Macros may be used when describing abstract syntaxes to introduce various levels of abstraction which go beyond that which can be achieved solely by structuring in various productions.

A good example of the use of macros is provided by the X.410 (84) macro OPERATION which describes the notation used to specify abstract operations (see Figure 1.24).

Thus, OPERATION is defined as a new type, where in declaring variables of this type, in addition, to the variable names, the arguments of the operation (ARGUMENT), the possible results (RESULT) and the possible error codes (ERRORS) could be given. Note that this type definition specifies

```
OPERATION MACRO ::= BEGIN
    TYPE NOTATION  ::= Arguments Result Errors | empty
    VALUE NOTATION ::= value(VALUE INTEGER)
    Arguments      ::= "ARGUMENT" NamedType
    Result         ::= empty | "RESULT" NamedType
    Errors         ::= empty | "ERRORS" {ErrorNames}
    ErrorNames     ::= empty | IdentifierList
    IdentifierList ::= identifier
                     | IdentifierList "," identifier
    END
```

Figure 1.24 The X.410 (84) macro OPERATION (slightly revised representation).

```
listFiles OPERATION
    ARGUMENT SET
            {directoryName IA5String OPTIONAL,
                -- Default is the current directory
            sortKey INTEGER {filename(0), modifyDate(1)}}
    RESULT fileNames SEQUENCE OF IA5String
    ERRORS {noSuchDirectory, accessDenied} ::= 7
```

Figure 1.25   Example of the use of the X.410 (84) macro OPERATION.

only the syntax of an OPERATION and not the semantics. For example, the fact that the list of names following ERRORS is to be interpreted as possible error codes is only hinted at by the notation (ERRORS).

By way of example, let us consider the abstract operation listFiles which returns the names of files contained in a directory in a specifiable order (see Figure 1.25).

listFiles is an operation with a parameter of type SET, whose components are a character string directoryName and an integer quantity sortKey which may take the value 0 or 1. This definition does not specify that directoryName refers to the name of the directory to be processed nor that a sortKey with values 0 and 1 is used to sort the file names into alphabetical order – we may only deduce this from the choice of identifiers. If successful, listFile delivers a sequence of IA5 character strings by way of result (the file names). In the case of failure, listFile returns the values noSuchDirectory or accessDenied. The end of the definition ("::= 7") specifies that the operation listFile may be identified with the integer value 7 (the operation code). Thus, in ASN.1, the operation listFiles is coded as an INTEGER with value 7. The associated parameters and error codes are also represented according to the ASN.1 coding rules discussed in this section.

1.5 Naming and addressing

The objective of OSI standardization is to facilitate the cooperation of application processes in open systems. Thus, application processes are the primary targets of naming and addressing. Here we shall use the following definitions for names and addresses:

- A *name* is a unique designation for an object in a communication system. In the OSI context, it is principally application processes that must be named.

- An *address* identifies an object with respect to a given coordinate system; thus, an address defines the *location* at which the object may be found.

The targets of addressing in open systems are the entities in the individual layers. An entity in layer $N+1$ is linked to one or more (N)-SAPs (service access points of layer N) at the boundary between layers N and $N+1$; thus, it may be addressed using the address of one of these (N)-SAPs. An (N)-SAP address identifies exactly one (N)-SAP. Applied to individual layers (for example, to the application layer), this means that an application entity may be addressed via one or more PSAP addresses. Similarly, an entity of the transport layer may be selected via one or more NSAP addresses (see below).

An application entity (within the OSI environment) is associated with exactly one application process outside the OSI environment. Thus, we deduce that application processes may be addressed by choosing one of possibly several application entities; these are again addressed with a PSAP address. This shows that an application process may establish an association with another application process if it knows the PSAP address of its partner. Since PSAP addresses are complicated system-specific structures (which may moreover change in the course of time, for example, with the installation of new software or systems) they are best obtained by a directory-service request for information.

A PSAP address consists of the following components (see Figure 1.26):

NSAP address   This is a set of network addresses with which a transport entity is addressed. Note that the NSAP address also specifies the end system in which the application process is to be found.

Transport selector   This identifies the chosen session entity relative to the transport entity.

Session selector   This identifies the chosen presentation entity relative to the session entity.

Presentation selector   This identifies the chosen application entity relative to the presentation entity.

Thus, a hierarchical addressing is used, in which the three selectors have a purely local meaning within the end system selected by the NSAP address. Therefore, they may be freely chosen by the operator of an end system without reference to other end-system users.

On the other hand, NSAP addresses and the names of application processes must be globally coordinated.

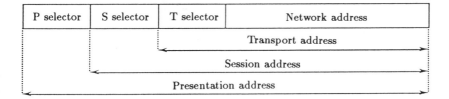

P selector	S selector	T selector	Network address
		Transport address	
	Session address		
Presentation address			

Figure 1.26   Components of a PSAP address.

Figure 1.27 shows how the addressing may be designed in three hypothetical end systems, where system A supports the application FTAM, system B supports MHS and system C supports the applications MHS, FTAM and DS. Here the following assumptions are made:

- The transport entities, and thus, the systems A, B and C are addressed by the network addresses 17600, 18236 and 17657, respectively.

- Because of the relevant standardization, MHS requires an extended session service; FTAM on the other hand only requires a minimal

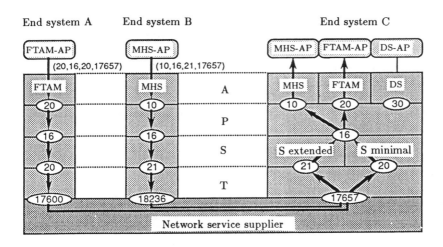

Figure 1.27   Addressing in open systems (example).

Table 1.3 Addresses of application processes (example).

Application process	System	PSAP address
FTAM AP	System A	(20, 16, 20, 17600)
MHS AP	System B	(10, 16, 21, 18236)
MHS AP	System C	(10, 16, 21, 17657)
FTAM AP	System C	(20, 16, 20, 17657)
DS AP	System C	(30, 16, 20, 17657)

session service. However, as an interactive service, FTAM depends on an efficient implementation. Thus, we assume that the operators of the three systems have (optionally) agreed that a session entity with extended functions may be addressed with the transport selector 21 and that an efficiently-implemented session entity, offering only minimal functions, may be addressed with the transport selector 20.

- In all systems the presentation entity is selected with the session selector 16.
- The application entities MHS, FTAM and DS are selected with the presentation selectors 10, 20 and 30, respectively.

Table 1.3 shows the resulting addresses for the application processes.

1.6 Standardization in the OSI context

Since the release of the standard relating to the OSI reference model, standards for all seven layers have been defined. Many of these standards are in the meantime so stable that computer manufacturers and software houses have developed conforming implementations, some of which are already on the market.

It would be going too far to discuss the many standards currently defined or projected. The reader is referred to Appendix B, which gives an overview of the state of OSI standardization.

2

Foundations of message handling with X.400 (84)

2.1   The functional model of X.400 (84)

2.2   The protocol architecture of X.400 (84)

2.3   Management domains

2.4   Names and addresses

2.5   Functions of an X.400 system

2.6   Character sets

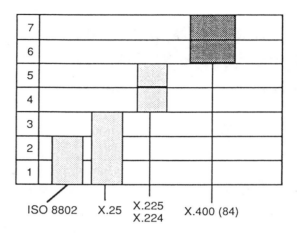

Figure 2.1   X.400 (84) in the OSI reference model.

In this chapter we describe the X.400 standard for message handling (released in October 1984) and the messaging services based on it. We discuss the model of X.400 (84), the address concepts incorporated in it and aspects of the management of a worldwide message transfer system. We shall indicate and describe the most important visible functions as far as the end user of systems which conform to X.400 is concerned.

The role of X.400 (84) in the communications world may be explained with the aid of the embedding in the OSI reference model. X.400 is application oriented and thus should essentially be classified in layer 7. But the 1984 version of the standard also describes service attributes which should be associated with layer 6 (Figure 2.1). We would stress that packet switching, such as that offered by X.25 (layers 1 to 3), has nothing to do with X.400, although at first sight a relationship between these two concepts might be assumed.

X.400 defines two services:

(1) The *message transfer service*. By message transfer, as mentioned in the Introduction, we mean a reliable, connectionless transfer of messages. Messages are sets of information of various types, for example, text, speech, graphics or data and possibly also combinations of these. Reliable transfer means that either a message

is transmitted without errors or that the sender is informed that correct transfer was not possible.

(2)   The *interpersonal messaging service.* This service facilitates the transfer of communications between people and thus, in fact, represents electronic mail. The service is also able to forward communications with components of various types (text, facsimile, speech, graphics – so-called multimedia documents) and to convert these communications if necessary (for example, if an output device is unable to restore a communication to its original form). The interpersonal messaging service is provided by the *Interpersonal Messaging System* (IPMS).

In the recommendations, it is noted that future global *Directory Services* (DSs) should be available which, given the name of a communication partner, would return the corresponding address (Chapter 12).

2.1 The functional model of X.400 (84)

The X.400 recommendations describe a model for message transfer systems and for their accompanying services and protocols. The *functional model* (Figure 2.2) defines the components listed below, which, taken together, represent a spatially distributed system.

The *users* in the MHS environment use these services to send and receive messages. Users in the sense of the MHS may be either people or processes.

The *User Agent* (UA) is an application process which makes the services of the MTS (see below) accessible to the user in an optimal form. A UA may, for example, be realized by a computer program which provides aid for the generation, sending, receiving and even archiving of messages. Every UA, and thus every user, is identified by its address, known in X.400 as the *Originator/Recipient name (or O/R name[1]).*

The *Message Transfer System* (MTS) provides the message transfer service and thus has the task of transferring messages of all types from the sender UA to the recipient UA. It follows from the figure that transfer with interim storage, possibly in many MTAs (store-and-forward transfer), is catered for. Thus, the MTS is based on asynchronous forms of communication.

The *Message Transfer Agent* (MTA) is an application process which forwards incoming messages to the next MTA or to the destination UA.

---

[1]The term 'name' is out of place here, since O/R names give the location of the UA relative to the topology of an MHS and thus are themselves addresses. See also Section 2.5 and Chapter 12.

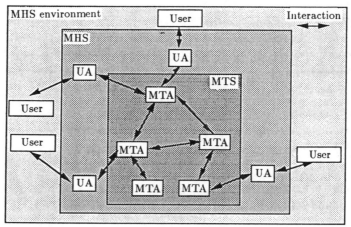

UA: User Agent   MIIS: Message Handling System
MTA: Message Transfer Agent   MTS: Message Transfer System

Figure 2.2   Functional model of an MHS according to X.400 (84).

2.2 The protocol architecture of X.400 (84)

Various mappings of the functional elements onto real systems are possible (Figures 2.3a and b). UAs may be available as application processes on a computer which itself implements MTA functions (system

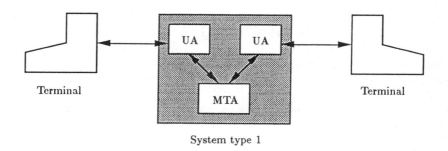

System type 1

Figure 2.3a   One MTA and several UAs in the same real system.

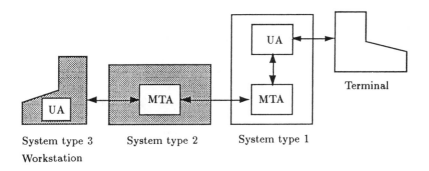

Figure 2.3b   Dedicated real systems (system types 2 and 3).

type 1). This is frequently the case for multi-user systems, which must offer a large number of UAs, and do this in the form of a user-callable command. An MTA may also have a stand-alone implementation (system type 2), as may a UA (system type 3).

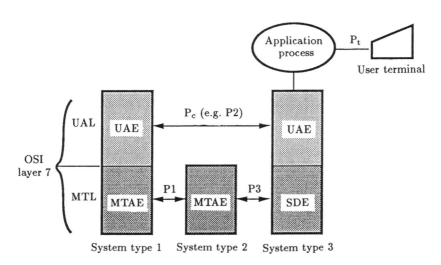

Figure 2.4   Structure and protocols of the application layer according to X.400 (84).

X.400 (84) subdivides layer 7 of the OSI reference model into two sublayers (Figure 2.4): the *UA Layer* (User Agent Layer, UAL) which offers the functions of the UA at its service interface, and the *MT Layer* (Message Transfer Layer, MTL), which, analogously, has a service interface with MTS functionality. The functions supported at the two interfaces are described in detail in Section 2.5.

In OSI terminology, abstract active elements of a layer which cooperate via a protocol are called *entities* (Chapter 1). Thus, the entity which represents the functions of the UAL in a UA is termed the *User Agent Entity* (UAE). Similarly, the term *Message Transfer Agent Entity* (MTAE) denotes any entity in an MTA which carries out the functions of the MTL.

In a system of type 2, the UAL does not contain any entities since the protocols of the UAL are *end-to-end protocols*. In a system of type 3, a *Submission and Delivery Entity* (SDE) carries out the requests of the MTL service interface[2].

The division of the application layer into two sublayers and the various possible types of real systems give rise to four distinct protocols:

Message transfer protocol (P1)

P1 is the protocol of the MTL for the switching and forwarding of messages between MTAEs.

Submission and delivery protocol (P3)

P3 is the protocol of the MTL for the exchange of messages between SDEs and MTAEs; thus, between a stand-alone UA and an MTA.

P_c

P_c represents a *class of application-specific protocols* of the UAL for the exchange of messages between UAEs. X.400 defines a single P_c, namely the *interpersonal messaging protocol (P2)* which in the context of the IPMS is used for interpersonal message exchange.

Interactive terminal-to-system protocol (P_t)

P_t is the protocol between UAEs and the user, in other words the description of the user surface.

X.400 (84) defines P1, P2 and P3 but not P_t. Thus, the interface between user and UA is not controlled in any way; this is certainly in the

---

[2]Since in this case no routing of messages is required, the SDE is simpler than the MTAE.

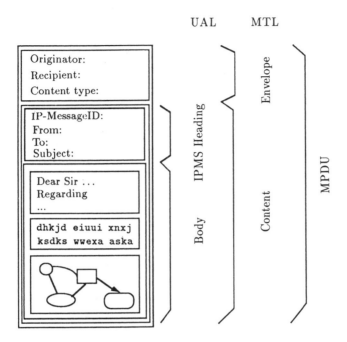

Figure 2.5   Message structure.

interests of the computer manufacturers, the providers of complete solutions and also of the users, who seek a dialogue corresponding to their needs. In a good implementation of an X.400 UA, the user surface of the system will be shaped so that it fits smoothly into the environment (operating system or end-user application), by using the same principles to shape the dialogue.

X.400 (84) with its organization of the application layer, stands in clear contradiction to current notions on the structure of the application layer, as defined, for example, in ISO 9545 (application layer structure) and as described in Chapter 1; see also the discussion of X.400 (88) in Chapter 9.

The protocol architecture described above implies a structuring of messages as shown in Figure 2.5. A message, as transported in the MTS (a PDU in OSI terminology) is called a *Message Protocol Data Unit* (MPDU). It consist of two parts, *envelope* and *content*, where the envelope contains the information required in the switching and forwarding of messages via the MTS. In Section 2.5 we discuss the meaning of the information contained in the envelope.

Two types of MPDU are used: *user MPDUs* are used for the data generated by the user, and *service MPDUs* are used for test purposes *(probe MPDU)* or to transmit system-relevant information *(delivery report MPDU)* (for example, to transmit error messages if a user MPDU cannot be delivered to the desired destination).

The content part of an MPDU is a PDU in the UAL and is thus called a *User Agent PDU* (UAPDU). In the case of the IPMS, we have an IM-UAPDU or an SR-UAPDU; the latter are called *status reports* and (like the service MPDUs) are used to transmit system information. IM-UAPDUs have a largely user-defined content, and are again subdivided into two parts, a *heading* and a *body*. The latter may consist of individual *body parts*, for example, text, telefax documents, encrypted information or even speech sequences. Since incoming communications often only have a comment entry added before being forwarded further, a body part is also defined which can carry whole IM-UAPDUs. A UA can therefore use this to recognize the structure of arbitrary interleaved communications and represent it meaningfully to the user.

The heading of the communication contains control information relevant to IPMS UAEs (Section 2.5).

At this point, we note in particular that the envelope is only processed by the MTS (by the entities in the MTL) and that the heading of a UAPDU is only meaningful in the UAL. The content part of an MPDU is handled as a bit sequence by the entities of the MTL and (except when a conversion of the transmitted information is required) is transmitted unaltered.

2.3 Management domains

The management of a worldwide MHS is a task which can only be successfully accomplished if the large system is broken up into smaller parts. To this end, X.400 provides so-called *Management Domains* (MD) (Figure 2.6). These are domains within which a management authority is responsible for the operation of the system. The following domains are provided:

- *Administration Management Domains* (ADMDs). These are reserved for administrations attached to the CCITT (for example, public organizations such as national PTTs).

- *Private Management Domains* (PRMDs). An organization such as a university or a large company could, for example, form its own PRMD.

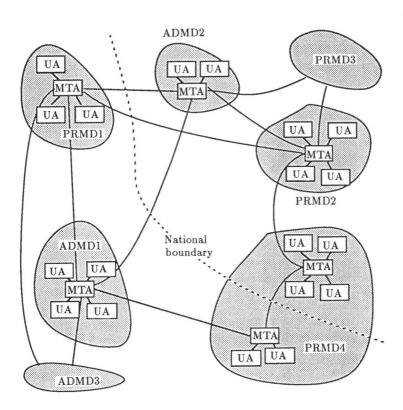

Figure 2.6   X.400 management domains.

According to X.400 recommendations, PRMDs are subordinate to ADMDs, in the sense that PRMDs cannot undertake switching functions between ADMDs.

Various European postal administrations operate or plan to operate ADMDs to which PRMDs could be linked and which in part also offer end-user services (electronic mailboxes) and gateways to the present telematic services (telex, teletex, videotex).

The recommendations provide certain both explicit and implicit advice on structures and associations which are permitted or to be avoided. For example, a narrow interpretation of the text of the recommendations might lead us to conclude that a PRMD which spans one or more national boundaries is not permitted. But just such a case is very likely, since it corresponds to a multinational organization which operates its own MHS. It is noted explicitly that messages which are exchanged between ADMDs should never be switched through a PRMD.

In general, it should be noted that the possibility of operating PRMDs and their embedding depends on the telecommunications legislation of each country and thus is not primarily governed by the X.400 recommendations. However, in our opinion, restrictions on the formation and direct connection of PRMDs, both nationally and internationally, are not to be expected.

Thus, it is not necessary (although it is sometimes sensible) to exchange messages between the PRMDs belonging to different companies via an ADMD. An exchange of messages via ADMDs is certainly advantageous if the traffic volume is small and the cost of maintaining a direct connection is not justified. Thus, ADMDs may serve as reliable mediators between PRMDs and permit immediate wide-area connectivity by a single connection to an international MHS.

Technical and operational regulations are to be expected when a PRMD is attached to an ADMD. Since, according to the X.400 recommendations, 'an ADMD is responsible for the PRMDs attached to it', we must ensure that, for example, a PRMD generates correct message formats and that it delivers messages passed to it with the required reliability. This implies an official authorization procedure for PRMDs which are to be attached to the public MHS. The technical basis for this will be produced by the definition of test sequences which a system must successfully run through and of corresponding test systems. We discuss the testing of implementations in detail in Chapter 13.

2.4 Names and addresses

In communication systems (and elsewhere) a *name* (see also Section 1.5) is a unique designation for an object. In the context of an MHS, it is primarily its users (in other words their corresponding UAs) which must be named.

An *address* also identifies an object, but with respect to a given coordinate system. Thus, an address denotes the *location* at which the object may be found. From these definitions, we deduce that an address is also a name, but not conversely. Moreover an object may have several names but only one address (with respect to the same coordinate system).

For the concept of an address, X.400 misleadingly uses the term *(O/R) name* (see also Section 2.1). O/R names are sets of attributes, that is to say of pairs of the form (attribute type, attribute value), where the attribute types to be used are not conclusively specified in the recommendations. Attribute types are chosen in such a way that an O/R name may be used to determine the location at which a UA is attached to the MTS. Thus, O/R names refer to the architecture of the MHS and are effectively addresses. They contain at least the name of the ADMD, and normally also a PRMD name and the name of a UA within a PRMD. O/R names defined in this way are not particularly user-friendly, since they contain elements of the MHS architecture and are thus difficult to remember and must be changed when the latter alters (or when the location of the user changes). In documenting the role of O/R names, in accordance with X.400 (88), we shall use the terminology *O/R addresses.*

X.400 (84) specifies various forms of O/R addresses.

A first address form, termed 'form 1, variant 1' defines addresses of UAs which are attached to an X.400 system; this represents the normal case (see Table 2.1).

In Table 2.1 attributes in square brackets are optional, although at least one such must be present.

Table 2.1 O/R addresses (form 1, variant 1).

Attribute type	Description of the attribute value
Country name	Two-letter country code as in ISO 3166 (Switzerland: 'ch', Germany: 'de', Austria: 'at', USA: 'us').
Administration domain name	Name of the ADMD to which the UA addressed belongs or to which the PRMD of the UA is attached.
[Private domain name]	Name of the PRMD to which the UA addressed belongs.
[Organization name]	Name of the organization (company name, name of the university).
[Personal name]	Name of the person represented by the UA.
[Domain-defined attributes]	This address component (abbreviated to DDA) may be used for an arbitrary purpose within one or (by arrangement) more domains, for example, if the address components needed for the domain cannot be mapped onto the standard attributes named above. For example, the address of a user of a manufacturer-specific network (DECnet, SNA) could be implemented in this way. As described in Chapters 3 and 4, a different approach is used in the academic world.

Table 2.2 Example of an O/R address (form 1, variant 1).

Attribute type	*Attribute value*	*Meaning*
Country name	= 'ch'	The originator or the recipient of the message is in Switzerland.
Administration domain name	= 'arcom'	Name of the ADMD of the Swiss PTT.
Private domain name	= 'switch'	The hypothetical name of a Swiss PRMD. Represents the operator of the X.400 network.
Organization name	= 'ethz'	Name of the organization ETHZ
Organizational unit name	= 'tik'	Name of a department of ETHZ (for example, 'tik' to denote the informatics department).
Personal name	= 'Bernhard R. Plattner'	This is effectively structured into surname, first name, initials with possible entries for additional first names and a generation (jr., sen.). It is not documented here.

Table 2.2 gives a hypothetical example of an O/R address of an MHS user. Here, we assume that the organization SWITCH in Switzerland operates an MHS, as shown by the value of the PRMD attribute ('switch'). According to ISO 3166, the country code for Switzerland is 'ch'. SWITCH is associated with the ADMD 'arcom' which is operated by the Swiss PTT. We further assume that subscribers in the Eidgenössische Technische Hochschule Zürich (ETHZ) may be reached over the PRMD SWITCH, and that in ETHZ a department may be designated by the address component 'tik'.

Other forms of O/R addresses support the addressing of subscribers to the telex network or teletex users.

MTAs may use all attributes or only a subset for routing. The attributes have no implicit hierarchy, although the meaning of the attribute types imposes such a hierarchy. In fact, in practice, in order to simplify decisions relating to routing in the MTA, it is sensible to define a hierarchy with, for example, country or ADMD or PRMD name at the top.

X.400 (84) also admits other address concepts. Thus, for example, in the address space for a specific company the attribute 'Organization name' may be left out altogether. X.400 (88) is much more specific in this respect, in that a hierarchy is defined according to the attributes of O/R addresses (Chapter 9).

The example in Table 2.2 was specially chosen, in the sense that an attempt was made to give the X.400 O/R addresses the character of names as far as possible. But attributes such as the names of the ADMD or the PRMD clearly do not belong in a 'true' name since they depend on the implementation of the MHS. The use of names in the sense of the initial definition requires the availability of *global directories* of and for MHS subscribers (Chapter 12).

2.5 Functions of an X.400 system

The functions of an X.400 system are defined by a set of services offered at the interfaces to the MTL and the UAL. On this, the recommendations contain a long list of descriptions of *service elements*. Since all X.400-specific service elements are reflected by the presence of corresponding fields in the PDU (MPDU and UAPDU), we discuss below the structure of PDUs and the meaning of the individual fields. Appendix A contains the corresponding complete descriptions of MPDUs and UAPDUs in ASN.1.

The data structure `UMPDUEnvelope` describes the contents of an envelope in the standard data description language ASN.1 (Section 1.4):

```
UMPDUEnvelope ::=SET {
  MPDUIdentifier,
  originator ORName,
  original EncodedInformationTypes OPTIONAL,
  ContentType,
  UAContentID OPTIONAL,
  Priority DEFAULT normal,
  PerMessageFlag DEFAULT {},
  deferredDelivery
  [0] IMPLICIT Time OPTIONAL,
  [1] IMPLICIT SEQUENCE OF PerDomainBilateralInfo
      OPTIONAL,
  [2] IMPLICIT SEQUENCE OF RecipientInfo,
  TraceInformation}
```

The individual fields are used as follows:

`MPDUIdentifier` A unique identification of a message in the MTS, comprising an identification which is unique within a management domain and an identification of the MD.

`originator` Contains the O/R address of the originator.

original   The MTS may convert the format of a message, if the attached UA or MD is not in a position to process the message as it was sent. 'original' denotes the information types (text, telefax, telex, speech, ...) contained in the content part *before* any possible conversion.

ContentType   This denotes the type of the content part, in other words the kind of UAPDU carried in the message. In the case of a UAPDU of the IPMS (protocol P2), this field has value 2.

UAContentID   This is set by the UA on delivery of a message to the MTS. The same value is again handed over to the UA on transfer of a possible delivery report belonging to the same message. Thus, the UA can associate a message with the report. Other mechanisms are also available for this, for example, the IPMessageId of the IM-UAPDU (this possibility is restricted to the IPMS).

Priority   The relative priority of the message (non-urgent, normal, urgent).

PerMessageFlag   A number of Boolean values which are valid for the whole message, for example, statements as to whether a conversion is permitted or as to whether the whole message should be returned if it cannot be delivered to a destination.

deferredDelivery   Specifies a time before which the message must not be delivered.

Sequence of PerDomainBilateralInfo   Contains information from the originating MD which is intended for the MDs through which the message will pass. Typically this field is used for taxation of messages which cross MD boundaries. The field contains the name of the country and of the ADMD and other information not standard in X.400 (but fixed by bilateral agreement) (**BilateralInfo**).

Sequence of RecipientInfo   Contains the O/R addresses of the recipients of the message. Every O/R address is accompanied by a bit, the so-called responsibility flag, which instructs an MTA either:

(a)   to deliver the message to the appropriate recipient;

(b)   to determine definitively that the message cannot be delivered; or

(c)   to transfer the message to another MTA for processing.

In addition, for each recipient, it is possible to specify whether and in which cases delivery reports should be issued.

TraceInformation   Allows the path of a message to be recorded together with statements about the actions undertaken by MTAs.

As one might expect, most of the fields in an envelope are concerned with the forwarding of messages via the MTS. On the other hand, the heading of an IM-UAPDU contains fields which are best known to us from memos and short notes in the normal office environment. The following ASN.1 definition gives the structure of an IM-UAPDU:

```
IM-UAPDU ::= SEQUENCE {Heading,Body}
Heading  ::= SET {
  IPMessageId,
  originator          [0]  IMPLICIT ORDescriptor
                           OPTIONAL,
  authorizingUsers    [1]  IMPLICIT SEQUENCE OF
                           ORDescriptor OPTIONAL,
                           -- only if not the
                           originator
  primaryRecipients   [2]  IMPLICIT SEQUENCE OF
                           Recipient OPTIONAL,
  copyRecipients      [3]  IMPLICIT SEQUENCE OF
                           Recipient OPTIONAL,
  blindCopyRecipients [4]  IMPLICIT SEQUENCE OF
                           Recipient OPTIONAL,
  inReplyTo           [5]  IMPLICIT IPMessageId
                           OPTIONAL, -- omitted if
                           not in reply to a previous
                           message
  obsoletes           [6]  IMPLICIT SEQUENCE OF
                           IPMessageId OPTIONAL,
  crossReferences     [7]  IMPLICIT SEQUENCE OF
                           IPMessageId OPTIONAL,
  subject             [8]  CHOICE {T61String}
                           OPTIONAL,
  expiryDate          [9]  IMPLICIT Time OPTIONAL,
                           -- if omitted, expiry date
                           is "never"
  replyBy             [10] IMPLICIT Time OPTIONAL,
  replyToUsers        [11] IMPLICIT SEQUENCE OF
                           ORDescriptor OPTIONAL,
                           -- each O/R descriptor
                           must contain an O/R name
  importance          [12] IMPLICIT INTEGER {low(0),
                           normal(1), high(2)}
                           DEFAULT normal,
```

```
sensitivity              [13] IMPLICIT INTEGER
                              {personal(1), private(2),
                              companyConfidential(3)}
                              OPTIONAL,
autoforwarded            [14] IMPLICIT BOOLEAN DEFAULT
                              FALSE}
```

Next we discuss the most important fields of a **Heading**:

IPMessageID   Identifies the IM-UAPDU uniquely. It may consist of the O/R address of the originator and an identifier of the communication relative to the originator.

originator   Identifies the sender. Note that an O/R descriptor is used which may contain an O/R address, a name in free-form or both. The O/R address is needed if an answer or confirmation of receipt is required. The name in free-form may, for example, be the full name or an abbreviation used in the normal office environment.

authorizingUsers   Refers to those users who have authorized the sending of the communication (by signature). Note, however, that X.400 provides no security against falsification of any one of these fields.

primaryRecipients   Primary recipients, as opposed to recipients of copies. Normally, primary recipients are expected to react to the receipt of a communication. But a UA treats every primary recipient like a copy recipient, in other words the interpretation of these fields is left to the user or, if need be, to the local functions of the UA.

copyRecipients   Defines the recipients of copies of a communication.

blindcopyRecipients   Defines the recipients of 'blind copies' of a message (primary and copy recipients will not be informed of their existence).

inReplyTo   Identifies an earlier communication which is being replied to by the current one.

obsoletes   Identifies earlier communications which are deemed out of date after the sending of the current message.

crossReferences   Identifies earlier communications which are cross-referenced with the current one.

subject   The subject of the communication.

expiryDate   Defines a time point after which the message is deemed to be irrelevant. The measures to be taken by a UA or by a user when the expiry date is reached are not specified. It is conceivable that a UA may delete an expired communication or specifically advise the user that the communication has expired.

replyBy   Denotes a deadline time for a possible answer. It is left to the user to decide if and when he actually wishes to reply.

replyToUsers   Identifies those users who should receive a possible reply.

importance   The importance of the communication (low, normal, high). This entry may be used by a UA to present communications in various ways; for example, important messages could be highlighted in red lettering.

sensitivity   The entry of a sensitivity (personal, private, confidential) may be used to control the processing of the communication in special cases. For example, a UA should not automatically print an incoming communication with 'personal' or 'private' sensitivity on a printer belonging to the department or to the secretary.

autoforwarded   This denotes a communication which contains a communication which has been automatically forwarded by a UA. This entry obliges a UA not to automatically forward automatically-forwarded communications for a second time, thereby avoiding infinite loops[3].

Doubtless most of the information in the fields described above can easily be given by the user in clear text in a communication. Holding this information in a formal and standardized form in an IM-UAPDU, permits semi-automatic processing of communications in support of users. Examples:

- A UA could report a highly important communication (importance = high) before all others or emphasize it graphically in some special way.

- User convenience is increased in that, if a list of O/R addresses is supplied in the replyToUsers field, an answer from the user will automatically be sent to all these addresses.

- A message archiving system on a UA could display all interrelated communications (using the inReplyTo, obsoletes, and crossReferences fields) in some suitable form when the user presses a key.

- A UA could automatically make its user aware, before the deadline expires, that a certain communication should be answered by a particular time (replyBy).

---

[3]Of course, less restrictive methods of preventing loops may be used, for example, recording the path followed by a communication. X.400 (88) uses this method of suppressing loops in the recursive use of distribution lists in the MTL (Chapter 9).

The types of documents which may be accommodated in a communication are of particular interest to the user. The specification of the type Body provides information about this. A Body consists of a sequence of BodyParts where each BodyPart may have one of 12 predefined types. The type of each BodyPart is uniquely identified by a tag.

```
Body       ::= SEQUENCE OF BodyPart
BodyPart   ::= CHOICE {
           [0]  IMPLICIT IA5Text,
           [1]  IMPLICIT TLX,
           [2]  IMPLICIT Voice,
           [3]  IMPLICIT G3Fax,
           [4]  IMPLICIT TIF0,
           [5]  IMPLICIT TTX,
           [6]  IMPLICIT Videotex,
           [7]  NationallyDefined,
           [8]  IMPLICIT Encrypted,
           [9]  IMPLICIT ForwardedIPMessage,
           [10] IMPLICIT SFD,
           [11] IMPLICIT TIF1}
```

Some of the types provided for BodyPart are not defined in X.400 (84) and are marked as 'for further study' in the recommendations. Despite this, we discuss the different types below:

IA5Text Provided for simple text documents and telex communications, which are represented in the IA5[4] character set. Two different sets of values may be used for characters, namely the full IA5 character set and a restricted set which only includes the characters of the ITA2 telex character set. In both cases, 7-bit coding according to IA5 is used.

TLX Provided for the presentation of telex documents in the ITA2 5-bit code[5]. The precise presentation is 'for further study'.

Voice Provided for the transmission of speech. The presentation to be used is likewise not specified.

G3Fax Provided for the presentation of documents generated by Group 3 facsimile devices.

TIF0 The *Text Interchange Format 0 (TIF.0)* is a text interchange format specified in CCITT recommendation T.73 and used by Group 4 (Class 1) facsimile devices.

---

[4]'International Alphabet No. 5', specified in CCITT recommendation T.50, which corresponds to ISO 646.

[5]'International Telegraph Alphabet No. 2'.

TTX TTX represents a teletex document; in addition to parameters such as the number of pages transmitted, **TTX** contains a sequence of strings of characters from the T.61 character set, where each string represents a page of the teletex document.

Videotex Provided for the presentation of videotex documents; the form of the presentation is not specified.

NationallyDefined A **BodyPart** of this type may be specified on the basis of local agreements in each country. Note that in the type **NationallyDefined** it is effectively possible to declare a set of types (using **CHOICE**) so that there is definitely a loophole for the agreement of private exchange formats.

Encrypted Provided for encrypted information. Not specified in further detail in X.400 (84).

ForwardedIPMessage Represents a communication which is contained as **BodyPart** in another communication. **ForwardedIPMessage** may be used to represent an arbitrary tree structure of forwarded communications (see also Section 9.3).

SFD SFD is an abbreviation for *Simple Formattable Document* and denotes a representation of text documents which, in terms of their graphical form, may be adapted to the available output devices (printer, screen). In an SFD the document contents (for example, the transmitted text) and various formatting parameters (for example, how a section or a page header should be indented) are specified, but the exact appearance of the printed document is not. Thus, an SFD may be properly printed on printers with different page formats and character sets.

TIF1 The *Text Interchange Format 1 (TIF.1)* is a text interchange format which is specified in recommendation T.73 and used by Group 4 (classes 2 and 3) facsimile devices.

Appendix A contains a complete description of the structure of IM-UAPDUs. It provides the interested reader with detailed statements of the different document formats which may be used for **BodyPart**.

2.6 Character sets

Since message transfer systems are to be used in a global context, they must be capable of correctly transferring and representing text documents. This requirement applies both to the format of text documents (the presentation of a text at the destination in a given screen or paper format), and to the ability of the system to present the text at the destination using the same graphic characters used by the originator. That this requirement is not easy to fulfil is clear when we recall that even Roman alphabets include many special characters (from vowels with umlauts to many different accented characters). In addition to this, very differently-structured alphabets (for example, as used for languages from the Asiatic area) must be supported.

For worldwide text communication to be possible the character sets to be used (in other words the available characters and their binary representation) must be standardized with sufficient flexibility, and the real systems used (and above all their computers and their software) must support the appropriate standards. To the dismay of many users, this latter requirement is often not fulfilled.

For message transfer (as is evident from Section 2.5), the character set of the *International Alphabet No.5* (IA5), standardized in CCITT recommendation T.50 and in ISO 646, and the *teletex* character set standardized in recommendation T.61 are relevant.

The 'International Alphabet No. 5' (IA5)

IA5 is based on a 7-bit representation for characters and thus specifies a set of 128 characters (control characters and displayable graphic characters such as letters, numbers and special characters). Every character may be identified both by its 7-bit code and by its position in the character-set table (given by column number/line number[6], Figure 2.7, see also Appendix C).

Columns 0 and 1 contain control characters, while characters 2/1 to 7/14 are displayable graphic characters. The space character (2/0) is classified as both a control and a graphic character and the character 7/15 (DEL) is an additional control character.

In order to accommodate various national needs, the graphical representations of the characters in positions 4/0, 6/0, 5/11 to 5/14 and 7/11 to 7/14 are not rigidly laid down and may be assigned according to national requirements. In addition, positions 2/3 and 2/4 are each assigned two possible graphical representations, one of which may be selected according to national circumstances. National versions of IA5 may be generated, using these options and, if necessary, registered.

An *International Reference Version* (IRV) makes use of the possible options. It is identical with the USA's national version, the ASCII character set (Table C.2 in Appendix C).

The teletex character set (T.61)

As a text-oriented service, the international teletex service specified in CCITT recommendations T.60, T.61, T.62, T.63 and T.73 is subject to

---

[6]The codes for all characters in the same column have the same three highest-order bits.

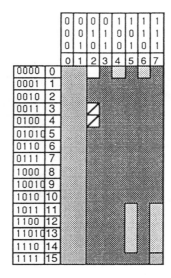

Figure 2.7   Structure of the IA5 character set.

the same demands as message transfer systems. The T.61 8-bit character set for teletex supports international text communication far better than IA5. Use of the 8-bit representation doubles the number of representable characters compared with IA5 (Figure 2.8).

It consists of two sets of control functions (primary and additional columns 0, 1, 8 and 9) and a primary set of graphic characters (space character and 94 other graphic characters, columns 2 to 7), together with an additional set of 94 graphic characters in columns 10 to 15. The occupancy of the positions is shown in Tables C.3 and C.4 in Appendix C.

Column 12, which contains the so-called *diacritical characters*, deserves special mention. These characters are used in conjunction with a character from the Roman alphabet (primary graphic character) to generate characters with accents or umlauts. Diacritical characters are 'non-spacing', that is to say they occupy no space and are prefixed to the corresponding characters. Thus, it is possible to represent many additional character combinations with two consecutive octets. The position 14/12 is a low line (also non-spacing) which may be used to underscore pieces of text.

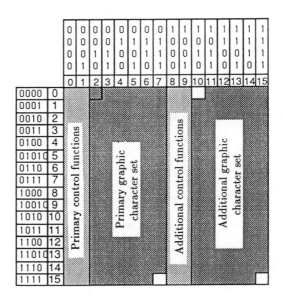

Figure 2.8 Structure of the teletex character set.

Character set extension

A German text containing umlauts, produced using the German national version of IA5, may not be correctly displayed by a recipient whose equipment supports the standard ASCII character set. Special characters appear in place of the umlauts, and while the former may be correctly interpreted by a practised (human) recipient, they are an indication of an unsolved problem.

A satisfactory solution is possible using a standard character set extension. ISO standard 2022 and recommendation T.51 which is based on it, describe various ways of representing additional characters that are not contained in the underlying character set. Primitive formulations also exist for IA5: a character sequence 'O BS /' where BS (backspace) denotes the character in position 0/8 could be interpreted and represented by suitable equipment as Ø. The meaning of such sequences of characters is not standardized in IA5. National versions may produce specifications for this, but this by no means solves the problem of the above user[7].

---

[7]For example, ASCII-conformal equipment will scarcely be able to interpret a foreign national version of IA5 correctly.

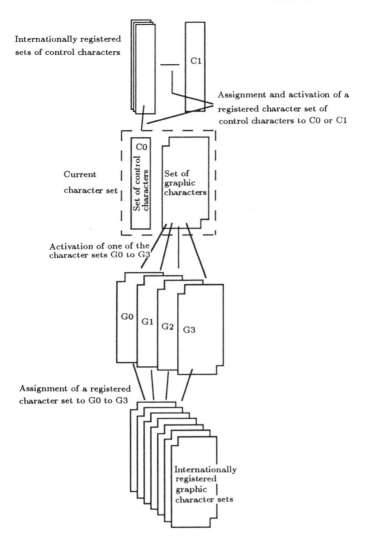

Internationally registered
sets of control characters

C1

Assignment and activation of a
registered character set of
control characters to C0 or C1

C0

Current
character set

Set of control
characters

Set of
graphic
characters

Activation of one of the
character sets G0 to G3

G0

G1

G2

G3

Assignment of a registered
character set to G0 to G3

Internationally
registered
graphic
character sets

Figure 2.9   Character set extension according to ISO 2022 and T.51.

As previously discussed, a second promising solution is offered by
the teletex character set with non-spacing characters.

A more far-reaching solution, which moreover is internationally
standardized by ISO 2022 and T.51, uses the fact that several character
sets may be overlaid on the positions of the underlying code table. We
illustrate this using the character set extensions for the 7-bit environment
of IA5 (Figure 2.9).

The character set table of IA5 has room for one set of control characters and one set of graphic characters. A first step in the extension process involves the fact that an additional set of control characters (C1) and four sets of graphic characters (G0 to G3) may be activated using control sequences from set C0 (C0 is always active). Thus, for example, the character set G3 using the control sequence 'ESC 6/15' may, until further notice, be defined to be the current set of graphic characters. It is also possible to select individual characters from one of the character sets.

In a second step, the character sets C0 and C1 and G0 to G3 may each be assigned one of the many internationally registered character sets[8]. For example, the control sequence 'ESC 2/9 Q' assigns the registered character set 'Q' to the set G1 until further notice. In order to make the characters from Q available, character set G1 must of course be defined to be the current character set.

ISO 2022 and T.51 also give specifications similar to those described here for a 7-bit environment for 8-bit environments such as the teletex character set. In fact, T.61 specifies that character set extensions according to ISO 2022 are possible and classes these as optional functions outside the basic service (in other words, as not belonging to the 'basic teletex service').

Finally, it can be shown that X.400 supports various character sets that could to some extent satisfy the requirements for international text communication. However, this is only advantageous to the user if the system being used implements the various possible functions and character sets correctly.

Thus, we close our discussion of the features of X.400 (84). After studying the first two chapters, the interested reader should be in a position to study the subject in depth using the CCITT standards document (Red Book) (CCITT, 1985).

---

[8]ISO 'International register of coded character sets to be used with escape sequences'. According to ISO 2375 (Data processing – Procedure for registration of escape sequences) character sets may be registered with ECMA in Geneva.

PART II

X.400 in practice: embedding, application and evaluation

In the future, message handling systems conforming to X.400 will contribute substantially to the overall volume of electronic mail, and, in particular, it is likely that X.400 MHSs will be widely used in the academic environment, in industry and in the service sector. Thus, to a large extent, X.400 MHSs will need to be newly introduced, as well as integrated into existing networks.

Here it is important, even in the evaluation phase, to check whether or not an X.400 product may be integrated into an infrastructure (possibly existing), how the connectivity to other X.400 systems and non-X.400 systems can be achieved and what effects the opening of a network to the outside will have on the security of that network.

Since X.400 is an abstract description of protocols and services and does not lay down specific implementation guidelines for corresponding products, the user must be able to classify and evaluate the most important functional subsets of X.400 defined by various bodies together with manufacturers' claims about the features of their X.400 products.

Thus, Chapters 3 and 4 give an initial overview of the possibilities for embedding X.400 MHSs in networks conforming to OSI and in various non-conforming networks. In particular, based on a description of the European academic network RARE MHS, we show how these concepts may be realized in the form of a reliable Europe-wide service.

In Chapter 5, the various definitions of functional subsets of X.400 are discussed and compared. This is relevant to the evaluation of the functionality and possible interoperation of X.400 products. Within this framework, in Chapter 6 we include a guide for practical classification and evaluation of X.400 products, which may be used as a tool for a typical evaluation. Finally, Chapter 7 is concerned with EDI, in other words with the topic of the electronic interchange of documents via X.400.

3

Embedding X.400 in existing and future networks

3.1 What is internetworking and why is it necessary?

3.2 Internetworking in the application layer

3.3 LAN/WAN internetworking

3.4 Security aspects of internetworking

Over a transition period, the interconnection of message transfer systems to a globally accessible communication medium requires connectivity between various types of message transfer systems. This is, in particular, due to the fact that, on the way to worldwide application of X.400, newly-installed public and private MHSs will as a rule conform to X.400, although in addition a large number of systems that do not conform to X.400 exist and will be used. Thus, a successful global migration to X.400 is only conceivable if during this transition phase interaccessibility between users of X.400 systems and non-X.400 systems can be guaranteed.

One important prerequisite for interaccessibility between users is the connectivity of the underlying networks involved. Note that this includes *networks* in several layers of the ISO model, for example, an X.25 network in the network layer and an electronic mail network in the application layer. If a common underlying transport infrastructure is available, connectivity between different message transfer systems (whence in the application layer) must also be achieved.

The aim of this chapter is to describe some aspects of the interworking of various networks in various layers of the OSI model and to discuss some examples. Here, particular emphasis is placed on the effect of network interconnection on electronic message transfer, while security aspects of the interconnection of message transfer systems will be briefly discussed.

3.1 What is internetworking and why is it necessary?

The term *internetworking* denotes the interconnection of computer networks in general. Such a network consists of a number of geographically distributed computers, which are interconnected via a transmission medium and jointly make their services available to users. A network is usually characterized by its provider, its owner, its user groups, and the connection technology or communication protocols used. Based on their geographical extent, computer networks are also subdivided into *Local Area Networks* (LANs), *Metropolitan Area Networks* (MANs) and *Wide Area Networks* (WANs).

For some time, networks from different manufacturers have been offered to users for data communication purposes, partly by private firms and partly also by public postal administrations. With the increasing number of users and with the high degree of networking of offices, management and production environments, the requirement for communication between end users over network boundaries is also increasing. If these networks differ in technical respects (different formats, protocols, services, transmission technologies, etc.), a mapping between the network technologies and their formats and service and protocol elements is needed. Although today this mapping may be realized using special conversion equipment with corresponding loss of performance or functionality, in the short term this unsatisfactory state of affairs cannot be expected to lead to a standardization of existing networks. Only an across-the-board introduction of services conforming to OSI and the migration of widespread services to services conforming to OSI will render the use of conversion equipment superfluous.

In this context, the term *internetworking* denotes the *interconnection of networks* with different technologies, protocols, user groups, administration or accounting.

Existing networks have mostly developed historically and were originally based largely on manufacturer- or operating-system-specific protocols, since there were no corresponding international standards. As far as LANs are concerned, since the first half of the eighties, ISO 8802 has provided, primarily for the lower layers, a uniform standard for the most widespread local area network technologies (token ring, token bus, and CSMA/CD). For WANs, various standards for network services and the corresponding protocols (X.25, ISDN in the future) exist. As far as the worldwide propagation of computer networks is concerned, there is a desire to connect networks of different types (LAN/LAN, LAN/WAN and LAN/LAN via one or more WANs). Since LANs and WANs must satisfy different demands, they provide very different services, so that connection of LANs and WANs will require a mapping between the corresponding protocols, service elements, formats, etc.

3.2 Internetworking in the application layer

When different networks use the same transmission techniques, protocols and services in the lower layers, internetworking only needs to be provided in the application layer. The following subsection describes aspects of internetworking for the application of electronic message handling. A further subsection gives a brief overview of the internetworking aspects of other applications.

Internetworking in the context of electronic message handling

In the academic area and in research there are many different message handling networks with different administrations, user groups, protocols and topologies. Table 3.1 gives a brief overview and includes some comparative statistics.

In addition to these academic and research-oriented networks there are also a number of organization- and company-internal networks which

Table 3.1   Known message handling networks, based on (Quarterman and Hoskins, 1986).

Network	Centre	Cont-inents	Count-ries	Machines	Users	Message protocol	Comms. protocol
ARPA-NET	USA	3	8	2050	not known	RFC 822	TCP/IP
MILNET	USA	2	3	400	not known	RFC 822	TCP/IP
CSNET	USA	4	10	170	not known	RFC 822	TCP/IP, MMDF, X.25
BITNET	USA	1	2	845	not known	RFC 822	IBM RSCS
EARN	Europe	1	17	363	not known	RFC 822	IBM RSCS
UUCP	North America	4	5	> 7000	200 000	RFC 822 UNIX-Mail	uucp
USENET	North America	4	4	> 2500	50 000	Broadcast	uucp,etc.
EUNet	Europe	1	13	896	not known	RFC 822 UNIX-Mail	uucp
RARE	Europe	3	21	380	20 000	X.400	ISO prot, X.25, DECnet, TCP/IP

may be very widely used by a large number of users. There are also commercial message handling services (mainly in North America) such as MCImail or CompuServe which may also have a large number of users worldwide.

Connections between different types of message handling systems are implemented using *gateways*. There are different kinds of gateways and, in practice, combinations of the following gateway types are common:

- Address gateway.
  Address gateways connect networks with different name or address spaces but identical protocols.

- Protocol gateway.
  Protocol gateways connect networks with different protocols by mapping the service elements onto each other and suppressing service elements that cannot be mapped or are not required.

- Format gateway.
  Format gateways map different formats (character sets, sequences of

service elements, etc.) onto each other. Unlike protocol gateways, they do not provide a mapping between the service elements of different networks.

For historical reasons there are very many different electronic message handling systems, which are often organization-, manufacturer- or even operating-system-specific. Examples include UUCP, EARN or the interconnection of the large North American networks such as ARPANET, MILNET and CSNET known as the Internet. As an example, in what follows we describe the mode of operation of an address gateway between the most widespread protocols – Internet mail (RFC 822 (Crocker, 1982)) and X.400[1].

While we have already discussed the X.400 addressing scheme in Section 2.4, for further understanding we must briefly discuss the RFC 822 addressing scheme.

Addressing in RFC 822 is based on the assumption of a hierarchically structured name space, which at its highest level contains a number of units corresponding to large spatially or organizationally related structures (for example, all North American universities or a country's national administration). These units are called *top-level domains* and must be unambiguously named. Within each top-level domain there may be substructured units called *subdomains*, which must be well-defined with the top-level domain or the subdomain in which they are contained. Within a subdomain, all communication partners must be unambiguously identified. This hierarchical model is illustrated by the examples in Figure 3.1.

In the notation of RFC 822, addresses are formed from the name of the local resource, followed by the names of the subdomains up to the top-level domain. Thus, an RFC 822 address is of the form:

Local_part@Domain_specification

where the two parts of the address are formed as shown in Table 3.2.

Table 3.2   RFC 822 addressing scheme.

Local_part:	Local name of a resource according to the domain specification.
Domain_specification:	Address of a resource, listing the subdomains from the inside outwards in the form: {Subdomain.}Subdomain.Top-level domain.

---

[1] *Requests for Comment* (RFCs) are a set of technical memoranda on various technical and organizational questions relating to the American Internet. Some RFC, for example, RFC 822 and RFC 987, function as Internet standards.

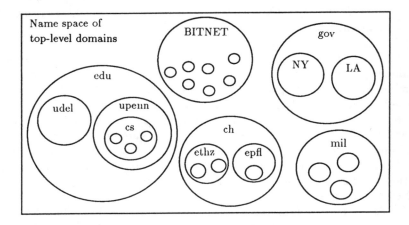

Figure 3.1   Structure of the RFC 822 address space.

This scheme may be used in several variants to represent or conceal organizational structures of the domains concerned. Table 3.3 clarifies this with specific examples.

The Internet standard RFC 987 (Kille, 1986) was defined in order to facilitate internetworking between RFC 822 addressing as described above and X.400 O/R addressing. In addition to prescribing the mapping between RFC 822 addresses and X.400 O/R addresses, RFC 987 specifies the protocol mapping between the RFC 822 and X.400 service elements. However, in what follows, we shall only discuss the address mapping.

Table 3.3   Examples of RFC 822 addressing.

laura@udel.edu	A person at the University of Delaware. The university has no subdomains, or conceals them from the outside.
diane@eng.upenn.edu	A person in the Engineering Department of the University of Pennsylvania.
dennis@ai.cs.upenn.edu	A person in the Artificial Intelligence Project in the Computer Science Department of the University of Pennsylvania.
craig@wk15.ccc.upenn.edu	A user of a workstation in the Campus Computing Centre of the University of Pennsylvania.

For the address mapping, RFC 987 specifies two types of mappings between RFC 822 and X.400. A *standard mapping* which is determined by a fixed set of rules and an *exception mapping* which is controlled by configurable mapping tables. Generally, address conversion using the standard mapping is possible, but some cases require a special transformation using the rules for the exception mapping. Consequently, an initial attempt is made to map an address using the exception rules. If there is no appropriate entry in the exceptions table then the address is converted according to the standard mapping. If however an appropriate entry is found in the exceptions table, the mapping is carried out according to the table entry. If, after this, the address is not completely processed, and if no other entries are found in the exceptions table, the rest of the address is converted according to the standard mapping.

The standard mapping of an X.400 O/R address into RFC 822 is based on the assumption that the X.400 O/R address contains values for at least the standard attributes 'country name' (C), 'administration domain name' (A), 'private domain name' (P), 'organization name' (O) and 'personal name' (PN), and possibly for one or more 'organizational unit names' (OU). All other address forms are handled by the exception mapping. According to the standard mapping, the X.400 O/R address

S=lubich; OU=komsys; O=tik; P=ethz; A=arcom; C=ch

is converted into the RFC 822 address

lubich@komsys.tik.ethz.arcom.ch

The standard mapping of an RFC 822 address into an X.400 O/R address may be carried out analogously in the reverse direction, assuming that a 'local_part', a top-level domain and at least three subdomains are present. The top-level domain is mapped onto the attribute 'country name', and the subsequent subdomains are mapped onto the attributes 'administration domain name', 'private domain name' and 'organization name'. If after this not all the subdomains of the RFC 822 address have been processed, the remainder is mapped onto a sequence of 'organizational unit names'. Finally, the 'local_part' is mapped onto the 'personal name'.

For various reasons, it is possible that addresses may be incorrectly converted by the standard mapping. When mapping RFC 822 addresses, one reason is the existence of top-level domains such as ARPA, UUCP, EARN or BITNET, which do not correspond to a 'country code', but which are semantically incorrectly mapped by the standard mapping onto the attribute 'country name'. Thus, an RFC 822 address of the form

lubich@ethz.uucp

would be mapped by the standard mapping into an X.400 O/R address of the form

S=lubich; A=ethz; C=uucp

This address is clearly incorrect. In addition, the RFC 822 address contains too few subdomains for the attributes 'private domain name' and 'organization name' to be assigned values, as initially required. Thus, the standard mapping is not suitable for the conversion of such RFC 822 addresses into X.400 O/R addresses.

Moreover, in the mapping of O/R addresses to RFC 822 addresses, there is no means of indicating that a specific attribute has no value. This leads to an incorrect retranslation of an RFC 822 address into an X.400 O/R address if the standard mapping is used.

For example, if the X.400 O/R address

S=lubich; OU=komsys; OU=tik; O=; P=ethz; A=arcom; C=ch

is converted into the RFC 822 address

lubich@komsys.tik.ethz.arcom.ch

the information that the value of the attribute 'organization name' is empty is lost, since RFC 822 does not (for example) allow the omission of an attribute value to be shown by two consecutive dots. On retranslation of the RFC 822 address into an X.400 O/R address using the standard mapping, we consequently obtain the incorrect O/R address

S=lubich; OU=komsys; O=tik; P=ethz; A=arcom; C=ch

To obviate this problem, an exception mapping, based on corresponding conversion tables in each RFC 987 gateway, is used. In order to implement the exception mapping in both directions, two tables are required, one for each direction of conversion.

A conversion table consists of a row of entries with which the addresses to be converted are compared for matching of the attribute values. An address may match several entries. In this case, the entry with the strongest match is chosen.

To improve readability, in what follows, we use a variant form of notation for RFC 987 tables which differs from RFC 987 (Grimm, 1987). In this notation, an entry consists of a left and a right side separated by the character **#**. An RFC 822 element within an entry consists of domain names separated from each other by dots. An X.400 element consists of a list of attributes. An attribute consists of the attribute type and the attribute value separated from each other by an equals sign. A semicolon separates an attribute from its right neighbour.

For the case in the above example, with the top-level domain 'uucp' which cannot be correctly converted by the standard mapping, the table for the mapping of RFC 822 addresses into X.400 O/R addresses may, for example, contain the following entry:

```
uucp # C=ch; A=arcom; P=uucp
```

With this entry the RFC 822 address

```
lubich@ethz.uucp
```

would be converted into the X.400 O/R address

```
S=lubich; O=ethz; P=uucp; A=arcom; C=ch
```

where the attribute sequence 'P=uucp; A=arcom; C=ch' in the X.400 O/R message address specifies the gateway at which the message was converted.

For the mapping in the opposite direction, the corresponding table might, for example, contain the inverse entry

```
C=ch; A=arcom; P=uucp # uucp
```

However, the two exception tables need not be symmetric to each other in all cases.

Similarly, the exception mapping can also handle the case of empty attribute values in an X.400 O/R address. For the address in the example

```
S=lubich; OU=komsys; O=tik; P=ethz; A=; C=ch
```

a table entry of the form

```
C=ch; A=; # ch
```

would guarantee the correct mapping into the RFC 822 address

```
lubich@komsys.tik.ethz.ch
```

while an inverse entry

```
ch # C=ch; A=;
```

in the second table provides the correct inverse mapping (with the value of the ADMD attribute omitted) into the original X.400 O/R address.

Further statements on mapping in RFC 987 concern the mapping of 'domain-defined attributes' but we shall not go into that in this context.

The above mappings are not the only ones possible. Every user of a gateway must select the appropriate mappings according to the organizational environment. We return to this issue in Chapter 4.

As illustrated by the example of address mapping between RFC 822 addresses and X.400 O/R addresses, it is in principle technically and organizationally possible to connect different types of message handling systems using gateways, where different types of gateways must be used according to the specific properties of the systems to be connected.

Other forms of internetworking in the application layer

Even today there are a number of other applications conforming to OSI that have non-standard but widely-used counterparts in other networks.

- **File transfer:** Here FTAM is available as a standardized application. The TCP/IP-based 'ftp' is a widespread example of a file-transfer protocol which does not conform to OSI. Corresponding gateways already exist, but because FTAM is not very common they are currently not of great importance.

- **Virtual terminal:** A corresponding OSI draft international standard defines the application VT as an implementation of the function of a virtual terminal conforming to OSI. The TCP/IP-based 'telnet' is a common example of an implementation which does not conform to OSI.

- **Remote job entry:** ISO defines the application JTM as an implementation of the functions of 'remote job entry' which conforms to OSI. The UNIX-based 'uux' is a common example of an implementation of this functionality which does not conform to OSI.

Other services, for example, the currently purely UNIX-based Usenet, will also be converted to OSI-based services in the long term; but it is to be expected that, in a transition period, the use of gateways with corresponding loss of functionality and performance will be unavoidable.

3.3 LAN/WAN internetworking

In talking of *LAN/WAN internetworking*, the term 'LAN' is often equated with a *Connectionless-mode Network Service* (CLNS), while the term 'WAN' is often equated with a *Connection-oriented Network Service* (CONS). This classification corresponds to the current practice whereby in fact in LANs the great majority of services provided are connectionless, while in WANs most services are connection-oriented, although it is not mandatory. Thus, in this section we start from connectionless LANs and connection-oriented WANs, but we also give examples of the implementation of connection-oriented LANs and connectionless WANs.

The choice between a connectionless or a connection-oriented network service in a given environment is strategic and is very important for network management, since it is not easy to convert an existing network and the distributed applications used to the other mode of communication.

ISO 8648 (Internal Organization of the Network Layer) defines a framework for internetworking between subnetworks via various scenarios in which various network protocols are used to connect together different subnetworks and to give the network service a uniform appearance. OSI-oriented connectionless or connection-oriented internetworking determines the choice of *either a uniform connectionless or a uniform connection-oriented network service*, since *interworking units* for CLNS and CONS are not provided. In the same way, there is no provision for the use of the OSI transport protocols between systems with different network services (CONS or CLNS).

The choice between CONS and CLNS corresponds to the conception of the OSI model, which makes a fundamental distinction between *end systems* and *intermediate systems*. Intermediate systems differ from end systems in that they only make use of the functions of the lowest three layers of the OSI model, while end systems take in all seven layers of the model. Consequently, for LAN/WAN internetworking it is assumed that, because of the restriction of an intermediate system to layers 1 to 3, the network layer already provides a uniform (connectionless or connection-oriented) service.

Protocols and services relevant to LAN/WAN internetworking

For a better understanding of the mechanisms of OSI-based LAN/WAN internetworking, we give a brief recapitulation of the protocols and services that are relevant to connection-oriented and connectionless services. The X.25 recommendation is given as an example for the connection-oriented service, while ISO 8802 and ISO 8473 are discussed for the connectionless service. We then list the various classes of transport protocols and their characteristics.

The X.25 recommendation deals with the interface of data terminal equipment to *Packet-switched Data Networks* (PSDNs). The functions required for the connection are spread across the lowest three layers of the OSI model:

- Layer 1 describes the physical interface, in other words the meaning of the lines and the electrical properties of the link (X.21).

- Layer 2 specifies the control procedure for the exchange of data blocks (Link Access Protocol – Balanced mode, LAP-B). The main task of this level is to ensure error-free transmission by the provision of error-correction mechanisms.

- Layer 3 specifies the structure of control information and user data in packets and describes connection set-up, connection release and the use of the connection, in particular the flow control on a link.

In packet-switched networks, two strategies may in principle be used to transport packets through the network (Giese *et al.*, 1985). In the *datagram technique* every packet is transported through the network independently of other packets via the most favourable route at that time (connectionless). In this transmission technique, neither safe transmission nor a given order of the packets is guaranteed. Routing is implemented in each computer involved on the route from the start system to the target system. On the other hand, in the *virtual circuit technique* a connection is set up between the start system and the target system and all the packets for the link are transmitted over this connection (connection-oriented). Here, secure transmission and flow control are guaranteed for each virtual connection. X.25 is based on the use of virtual circuits. Around the world, almost all postal administrations and similar suppliers offer public packet-switched data networks (for example, TELEPAC in Switzerland, Datex-P in Germany, Datex-P and Radio-Austria in Austria) which are interconnected and thus form a common uniform connection-oriented communications infrastructure up to layer 3 of the OSI model.

The ISO 8802 family of standards is concerned with protocols and services in layers 1 and 2 of the OSI model for local area networks, and corresponds to the IEEE 802 family of standards. Five different sections of the standard are relevant to what follows:

- **ISO 8802.5** (IEEE 802.5) describes a ring topology, in which the participating stations control the access to the communications medium by passing on a *token* (token ring).

- **ISO 8802.4** (IEEE 802.4) describes a bus topology, in which the participating stations also control the access to the communications medium by passing on a *token* (token bus).

- **ISO 8802.3** (IEEE 802.3) describes a bus topology in which the participating stations control the use of the communications medium by monitoring the state of the channel, using collision handling in the case of simultaneous access (CSMA/CD).

- **ISO 8802.2** (IEEE 802.2) in conjunction with 8802.3/4/5 describes the link layer protocol (Logical Link Control, LLC). There are two types of logical link control: LLC1 describes a connectionless variant, while LLC2 defines the corresponding connection-oriented protocol.

- **ISO 8802.1** (IEEE 802.1) describes the relationship between the standards of the 8802 family and their precise relationship to the OSI model, together with internetworking and network management aspects.

Since ISO 8802 is only concerned with services and protocols of layers 1 and 2, another standard, ISO 8473 (Protocol for Providing the Connectionless-mode Network Service), defines the connectionless network protocol, which we denote by *ISO IP* in what follows.

Different transport protocols may be used, depending on the (connectionless or connection-oriented) network services offered. In the transport layer there are five classes of transport protocols. They are defined in ISO 8072 and ISO 8073 (CCITT X.214 and CCITT X.224, respectively) and are described briefly below:

- Class 0 was originally defined by CCITT for the teletex service. It has no recovery facility and its use requires a sufficiently reliable network.
- Class 1 corresponds to an improvement on class 0. It has basic recovery facilities but its use requires an underlying X.25 network.
- Class 2 has all the features of class 0 and is able to multiplex several transport connections on one network connection.
- Class 3 is a combination of classes 1 and 2.
- Class 4, unlike classes 0, 1, 2 and 3, does not require the underlying network to be reliable (loss and duplication of messages as well as loss of sequences can be detected and corrected) and is suitable for networks using the datagram technique.

From the definition of the various transport protocols, the class 4 transport protocol (*TP4*) is particularly suitable for a connectionless network, while the other transport protocols (in particular, *TP0* because of its simple structure) are particularly appropriate for use in a connection-oriented network.

Thus, protocols and services of the lowest four layers of the OSI model are defined for both a LAN and a WAN environment. For a connectionless service, ISO 8802 covers layers 1 and 2 of the OSI model, while ISO 8473 defines the connectionless network protocol. For the connection-oriented network service, X.21 and X.25 define layers 1–3. Moreover, in a connection-oriented protocol stack, it is possible to use X.25 in local area networks in accordance with ISO 8881 ('Use of the X.25 Packet Level Protocol in Local Area Networks'). In this case, the LLC2 protocol is used over ISO 8802 technology with the X.25 packet-level protocol on top.

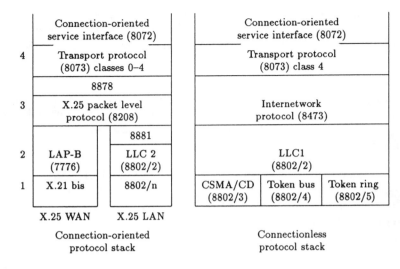

Figure 3.2   Protocols in connection-oriented and connectionless protocol stacks.

A local intermediate layer between X.25 and the transport services is required to provide the CONS over X.25 (ISO 8878 'Use of X.25 to Provide the OSI Connection-Oriented Network Service'). This layer does not define any protocols between systems and has only a local significance.

Thus, we have the two connectionless and connection-oriented protocol stacks as shown in Figure 3.2.

The following paragraphs concentrate on internetworking between connectionless networks based on ISO 8802 and connection-oriented X.25 networks with a common connection-oriented transport service interface. First, we discuss the OSI solution using a uniform network service, then we discuss mechanisms for internetworking without a uniform network layer.

Internetworking via a connectionless or a connection-oriented network service

For the connection-oriented variant of internetworking, we assume that, when using connection-oriented applications, connection-oriented transport and network protocols should also be used (Clyne, 1988). Since X.25 is one of the most common connection-oriented network protocols, the X.25 network relay is implemented between two entities of the X.25 network layer in the LAN and WAN system. Connection-oriented internetworking over

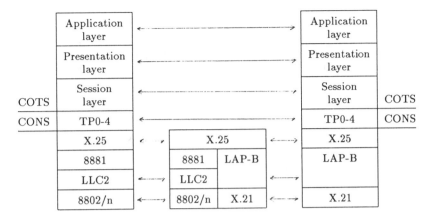

Figure 3.3 Connection-oriented X.25 network relay.

LAP-B (WANs) and LLC2 (LANs) is possible using X.25. The transport protocols are not affected by this so that it is possible to use all five classes of transport protocols. Because of its simple structure, the class 0 transport protocol is normally used. Figure 3.3 shows such a *connection-oriented X.25 network relay*.

In the connectionless variant of internetworking a *connectionless network relay* datagram is sent from a LAN over a WAN to another LAN or to an end system in the WAN (Clyne, 1988). Thus, the connectionless network protocol is implemented in a layer 2 data link protocol (for example, LAP-B in the WAN). Use of the connectionless network protocol implies the use of TP4 for all connection-oriented applications; thus, all end systems in LANs and WANs *must* implement TP4.

Figure 3.4 shows the implementation of LAN/WAN internetworking using a connectionless network relay.

In order to be able to use ISO IP over the layer 2 data link protocol we require an intermediate layer between the layer 2 data link protocol and ISO IP, to support the connectionless mode network service (ISO 8880/3 Provision and Support of the Connectionless Mode Network Service). As Figure 3.4 shows, this intermediate layer does not provide any protocols between the given systems but has a purely local significance.

Thus, LAN/WAN internetworking may be implemented using the network layer internetworking mechanisms described in this section and as intended in OSI. As shown in Figure 3.3, connection-oriented

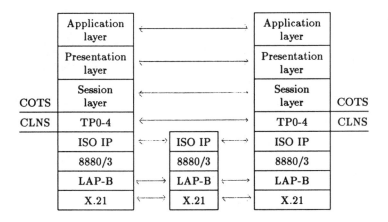

Figure 3.4 Connectionless network relay.

internetworking using X.25 is possible over LAP-B (WANs) and LLC2 (LANs), while connectionless internetworking may be implemented using ISO IP over a layer 2 data link protocol and X.21.

If however a uniform network service is not available, internetworking must be implemented in a higher layer.

Uniform transport service over connectionless and connection-oriented network services

OSI presupposes a uniform network service. If however this is not given or is undesirable, internetworking must be realized at a higher level. As an alternative to creating a uniform network service, the transport layer may be used to provide the higher layers of the OSI model with a uniform service interface for LAN/WAN internetworking. This service interface offers either the *Connection-oriented Transport Service* (COTS) or the *Connectionless-mode Transport Service* (CLTS). A main motivation for this solution is the current lack of realizations of a uniform OSI network service.

If there is no uniform network service, there are in principle two methods of realizing internetworking (Clyne, 1988): the *transport gateway* and the *network converter*.

A *transport gateway* links a connection-oriented WAN service and a connectionless LAN service. As already explained, the different network protocols imply different transport protocols. In the WAN area, the

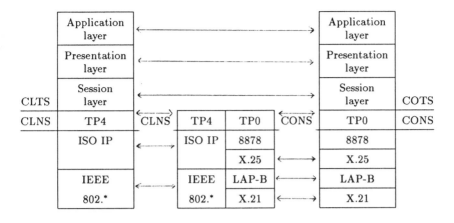

Figure 3.5   Transport gateway.

relatively complicated X.25 protocol already executes complex tasks such as flow control and in this case the connection-oriented TP0 protocol is very simple as far as its functionality is concerned. On the other hand, the class 4 transport protocol contains a complicated protocol for error detection and correction, flow control, etc. Thus, the network protocol may be simple (for example, ISO IP with datagram service). Figure 3.5 shows the realization of LAN/WAN internetworking using a transport gateway. In comparison with other solutions, transport gateways are frequently used for LAN/WAN interconnection. In addition to the transport gateway, which involves layers 1 to 4, there is another method of realizing LAN/WAN internetworking.

The converter between the connectionless-mode and the connection-oriented network service (network converter) shown in Figure 3.6 implements internetworking at the LAN/WAN boundary, in such a way that the connection-oriented network service on the WAN side and the connectionless-mode network service according to ISO 8473 on the LAN side are available.

This requires the use of TP4 in all end systems and the application of ISO 8878 between the network and the transport layer. In addition, ISO 8880/3 must be used between the link layer and the network layer. Figure 3.6 shows the use of such a converter.

Comparison of the methods for LAN/WAN internetworking described in the preceding paragraphs shows that the transport gateway and the connection-oriented X.25 network relay are up to now the

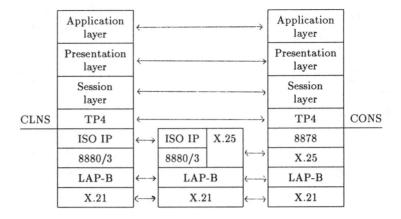

Figure 3.6   Network converter.

most commonly used, while few realizations of connectionless-mode network relays are known (Clyne, 1988). There are to date no known implementations of a connection-oriented/connectionless-mode network converter; however, the problem is currently being studied by ISO. Conceptually, a connection-oriented X.25 network relay is preferred to a transport gateway, however it requires the implementation of X.25 in the LAN environment. This condition is at present not yet met in many LAN realizations, so that transport gateways are normally used.

All in all, it should be said that the use of connectionless protocols as opposed to connection-oriented protocols in the WAN context was not studied in good time by ISO, so that at present there are no corresponding standards and the use of gateways as an interim solution is inevitable.

Finally, we now consider the special facilities of LAN/WAN internetworking for message handling. The most important point is that an intermediate system in the case of this application, involves not only the lower layers, but all seven layers, since X.400 electronic mail assumes a store-and-forward network in which the messages are forwarded within the MTS, possibly via several MTAs, before they reach their destination. Regardless of the architecture used to connect different networks, originators and recipients only use an end-to-end protocol in the layer 7 UAL; thus, end-to-end network connection is not required between originators and recipients but only between two adjacent MTAs in the MTS.

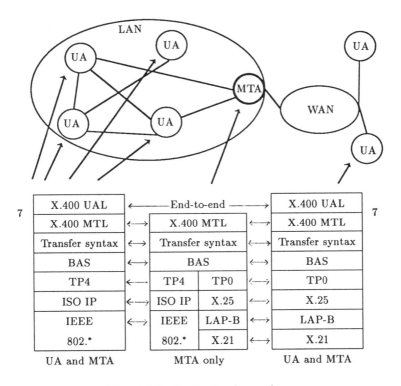

Figure 3.7 Application layer relay.

Figure 3.7 shows a possible topology and a corresponding protocol stack for OSI-conforming internetworking for message handling.

Non-OSI-based LAN/WAN internetworking

For some time, certain manufacturer-specific and operating-system-specific protocol suites, such as TCP/IP, DECnet and SNA, have had a wide distribution. Because of their wide distribution, these protocols must be accorded the status of *de facto* standards. Taking into account the fact that a large number of users make use of services over networks with protocols .of this type, LAN/WAN internetworking must also be provided for these networks. At a later date, it will be possible to carry out a migration to OSI services with the least possible visibility as far as the user is concerned.

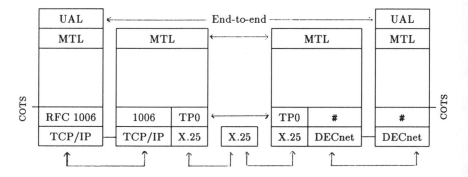

Figure 3.8 Connection-oriented transport service in a manufacturer-specific LAN/WAN environment.

For a common case, namely the use of OSI applications over the TCP transport service, in what follows we show how non-OSI-based LAN/WAN internetworking can be implemented and the effects that this has on message handling.

To facilitate the connection of OSI applications that use a manufacturer-dependent transfer service, the OSI application may in the first instance be ported involving the implementation of specific new protocols above the manufacturer-specific transport service. It is clear that this solution is impractical for a large number of applications and that it does not represent a generally applicable solution. Thus, it is sensible to define a mapping between the OSI transport service and the service of the non-OSI transport network, so that the corresponding transport service interface may be used from the overlying layer as a *Transport Service Access Point* (TSAP) in accordance with ISO 8072, while, as before, the transport layer is based on manufacturer-dependent protocols.

To use the TCP transport service a corresponding Internet standard RFC 1006 (ISO Transport Services on Top of the TCP) is based on the fact that both the *Internet protocol suite* and the OSI model assume the existence of *layers* which perform comparable tasks. RFC 1006 defines how the service primitives and the parameters of the service provided by TCP and the service elements of the class 0 transport service are mapped onto each other. If a corresponding implementation is used over TCP/IP, overlying applications are unaware of the fact that they are using the Internet protocol suite. Figure 3.8 shows such a solution.

What effects does the possibility of non-OSI conforming LAN/WAN internetworking have on electronic message handling? Firstly we note that through the implementation of non-OSI-conforming LAN/WAN internetworking at the transport level, even X.400 systems in non-OSI-conforming local area networks may interoperate with X.400 systems in WANs or LANs that do conform to the standards. The prerequisite for this is the provision of a homogeneous transport service interface. By way of example, Figure 3.8 shows a possible protocol stack for non-OSI-conforming internetworking over manufacturer-specific LAN transport services and a WAN service conforming to OSI.

The internetworking has already been described in the case of use of TCP/IP; similar mechanisms may also be defined for other non-OSI-conforming protocols such as DECnet or SNA, but are not available at the present time. In principle, these protocol suites require the same internetworking mechanisms as described for TCP/IP in RFC 1006; they should be implemented in the DECnet protocol stack at the points denoted by # in Figure 3.8.

LAN/LAN connection

The interconnection of LANs may be implemented in various ways, for example, using a subnetworking concept (possibly involving the definition of one subnetwork per LAN) or using LAN/LAN connections at layer 2. In what follows we shall consider connection at layer 2 in more detail. Layer 2 is divided into two sublayers, the Link Layer Control (LLC) and the Media Access Control (MAC) layers. The 8802.3/4/5 protocols previously mentioned (CSMA/CD, token bus, token ring) are MAC protocols, while 8802.2 describes the LLC protocol. Within a LAN both LLC and MAC are end-to-end protocols, since the network does not contain an intermediate system in this layer. Different LANs may be interconnected via MAC level bridges so that the whole network is uniform from the LLC layer. The various MAC protocols listed above have very similar service interfaces so that when different MAC protocols are used the overlying layers are not affected by this inhomogeneity.

LAN/LAN internetworking using MAC level bridges is however restricted to manageable organizational units, since otherwise uniform network management would be difficult to implement. This is in particular the case for LAN/LAN connections between organizations with different administrations.

3.4 Security aspects of internetworking

Because of various known incidents in large research networks, the protection of computer networks against access by unauthorized users and against illegal reading, modification and deletion of stored data is a very urgent topic, particularly in production and commercial environments.

The fact that applications in different networks are able to intercommunicate gives rise to two questions:

- What additional security problems result from LAN/WAN internetworking as outlined above (in other words from the opening of a company's LAN infrastructure to the outside world)?

- How can applications, and in particular electronic message handling systems, prevent the falsification or unauthorized reading of data while it is being transported through a data network?

In what follows, we give a superficial discussion of security aspects of the application layer with particular reference to electronic message handling. Later, we consider specific effects of LAN/WAN internetworking on the security of the attached networks.

Security aspects in the application layer

A major weak point of the previous version of the X.400 recommendations (1984 edition) was the failure to define security measures. This error was corrected in the new edition of 1988 by the definition of a mechanism for extending X.400, which permits the implementation or omission of optional parts of the functionality. In X.400 (88), one such extension, the concept of *secure messaging*, was introduced to guarantee the integrity, authenticity and confidentiality of messages, together with secure access between components of the MHS. Chapter 11 is concerned with the details of the security aspects of X.400 (88).

When these security mechanisms are used in an X.400 (88) system, they should not be subsequently removed if the partner X.400 system is an X.400 (84) system which does not support this service. In the interoperation of X.400 implementations under X.400 (84) and those under X.400 (88), internetworking with 'secure messaging' is not possible and secure messaging therefore remains restricted to X.400 (88) systems.

These security considerations are similarly valid for other OSI applications. While electronic message handling (X.400) and directory services (X.500) are based on the *authentication framework* defined by CCITT and the services postulated therein, other specific security measures apply for other OSI applications. For example, FTAM defines encryption methods as well as mechanisms to control data access using passwords and mechanisms to check the identity and machine identification of the initiator of an FTAM session. Specific access rights and types of encryption may be specified for each document in the document directory. Moreover, it is possible to determine the identity of the last reader of each document.

Since many applications have similar security requirements, it is appropriate to handle security aspects generally in the application layer. To this end, there is a corresponding proposal for a new CASE which offers security service elements (Nakao and Suzuki, 1989).

Thus, for existing and future applications conforming to OSI we may assume that the necessary security concepts and mechanisms will already be provided for in the definition of the appropriate standard, so that it is also possible to use such applications in a commercial or production-related environment.

Security aspects of LAN/WAN internetworking

When a company's LAN infrastructure is opened to the outside world security problems arise since, in principle, unauthorized people could attempt to access resources in the organization-internal network. The shape and form of this danger is determined by the degree of openness of the local area network. The degree of openness is generally determined by the requirements imposed by each application on the underlying communications infrastructure and should not go beyond that actually required by the application. Here, interactive access or the support of interprocess communication over the network is particularly problematical, since in this case an end-to-end connection in the network or transport layer is required.

In the following, we consider the requirements for electronic message handling. Typically this application will use MTAs via which a message is forwarded from a start system to a target system (store-and-forward). In order to connect an internal message handling system to other wide area systems only one node of the local area network needs to be open to the outside. The MTA at this access node accepts connections from the WAN, draws the messages from the WAN and stores them locally. In a second independent processing step the message is forwarded within the LAN without the originator having influence over this processing. Since there is no need to create an end-to-end connection between the originator's MTA and that of the recipient, the security of the network is guaranteed by equipping an access node with mechanisms for strict access control and logging message traffic. Figure 3.9 shows such a situation.

In the case of electronic mail, on the basis of a local directory service, the local organization may also decide whether the chosen name and address space should reflect the organizational structure or whether this should be partially or completely concealed.

Thus, as far as LAN/WAN internetworking is concerned, electronic mail may be regarded as non-critical to the security of a local area network. Other services may require further opening of the local area network. Thus, for example, FTAM and VT require an end-to-end connection between

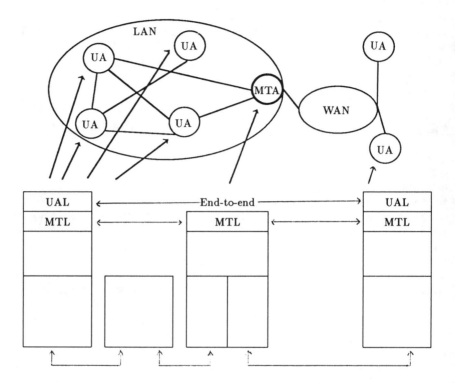

Figure 3.9 LAN/WAN security aspects of X.400.

the start system and the target system, whence unauthorized (interactive) penetration of the network cannot be initially ruled out. Here, on the one hand, care must be taken to protect individual computers in the local area network against unauthorized penetration, while on the other hand activities on the local area network and at the interface to the WAN must be carefully monitored.

Alternatively, within an organization a small isolated network or an individual computer may be opened to the outside in such a way that it is then available for external communication, but does not provide an end-to-end connection to the organization's local area network itself.

Finally, it is clear that it is technically possible to open a local area network to the outside in various ways and that this is not necessarily accompanied by dangers that cannot be countered by careful management. In particular, for electronic message handling it can be assumed that the opening of a local system to the outside does not represent a threat to the security of the local organization, but on the contrary provides an important connection to additional sources of information worldwide, which will be indispensable in the future.

4

RARE MHS: message transfer in the European research network RARE

In Europe, electronic message transfer services have been in use in some countries since the beginning of the eighties (UUCP/EUnet, EARN, HEPNET, etc.), although access to these services was only available to a relatively small number of users. Moreover, unlike the situation in the USA, where organizations such as ARPA (later DARPA or NFSNET) had already ensured the coordination of individual networks by 1969, in Europe, neither coordination between the various transfer services used nor national or international connectivity of the services existed.

The interconnection of existing networks with a view to international coordination, the consistent use of systems conforming to X.400 and the deliberate construction of X.400-based message transfer services in most member states of the European Community and EFTA have eliminated these initial shortcomings and have made it possible to provide a large number of scientists with the opportunity for direct connectivity.

In the first instance, the aim of this chapter is to describe the development and current status of this interconnection of European research networks as far as message handling is concerned and to outline future developments. We use examples to show how the various participating networks, with their different structures and organizations, have connected their infrastructures to RARE MHS, taking into account the particular features of the former.

4.1 What is RARE and how did it come about?

The RARE (Réseaux Associés pour la Recherche Européenne) organization includes the European academic network organizations and their users. Its purpose is to promote coordination between individual networks and to create a standardized network infrastructure in Europe, based on international standards. In addition, RARE also has the task of facilitating and coordinating the connection of this Europe-wide network to other networks outside Europe (for example, the North-American Internet).

The origin of RARE may be traced back to the early 1980s, when a series of working meetings between representatives of the various network organizations took place within the framework of the establishment of the Deutsches Forschungsnetz (German research network, DFN). During these meetings, it soon became clear that efforts should be made as soon as possible to harmonize at a European level the various networks used together with the services and protocols. The concept of a research organization to coordinate existing research networks[1] was formulated on the occasion of one of the first working meetings supported by the

---

[1]We note that the primary purpose of RARE is not to operate networks itself but to ensure the coordination of existing research networks.

Commission of the European Community (CEC), involving between 60 and 70 scientists in Luxembourg in 1985. Subsequently a small central secretariat was established and finance for regular meetings of working groups was made available.

In addition to the planning activities for the European research network as a whole, RARE's activities include operational and technical aspects which are handled by seven so-called 'working groups' (WGs):

WG1 Message handling systems

WG2 File transfer, access and management

WG3 Information services and directories

WG4 Network operations and X.25

WG5 Full screen services

WG6 High-speed communications and ISDN

WG8 Management of network application services[2].

The objectives of the individual working groups are very different and range from the coordination of existing networks to the elaboration of new pilot projects and proposals for standardization in various areas. An annual RARE workshop, first held in 1985, which is increasingly co-organized with other network organizations, provides a forum for members of the different working groups to exchange experiences and an opportunity for taking stock and specification of new objectives for RARE.

In the remainder of this chapter we describe RARE MHS, the project to coordinate the European message transfer networks, in more detail.

4.2 The development of RARE MHS

One important component of the work of RARE is the *RARE MHS* project which is coordinated by RARE Working Group 1 and a RARE MHS project team. The aim of the project is to design a Europe-wide X-400-based infrastructure for the interchange of messages between academic and research institutions and to coordinate its implementation and operation by the national member organizations. In addition, the RARE MHS has the task of facilitating the connection to existing non-X.400-based networks within and outside Europe and of supporting the migration of these networks to the use of products conforming to X.400.

---

[2]A WG7 for the purpose of coordination with the national postal companies and CEPT was provided for but never implemented. The precise descriptions of the areas of work together with reports on the activities of the individual RARE working groups are published in the annual report (RARE, 1989).

Figure 4.1   States participating in RARE MHS.

The RARE MHS project was initiated in 1987, initially for a two-year period (from May 1987 to April 1989), during which time under the leadership of RARE a small project team (MHS project team) was set up at the University of Trondheim computing centre. The task of the project team was to coordinate the European message transfer systems in existence at that time and actively to support the construction of new national message transfer systems in states that did not operate such networks. This was to involve the construction of an X.400-based pilot network which would then be gradually extended and linked to a Europe-wide integrated network. In addition, the project team was to generate a directory and a catalogue evaluating available X.400 products and in particular to investigate interworking with the European public service providers.

From the beginning, 16 states (Figure 4.1) with active representatives in RARE WG1 took part in this pilot project. First, the MHS project team took stock of the existing software and connections. Within the framework of a number of working meetings between WG1 and the MHS project team (the leader of the MHS project team also chaired RARE WG1 from 1987 to 1989), a concept was developed which defined a central MTA in each country for the transmission of X.400 messages abroad. The implementation of this concept now forms the basis for operation of the RARE MHS.

In this scheme, all these central MTAs (well-known entry points, WEPs) can communicate with each other via the public X.25 service of the

European PTTs. Here, the idea is firstly to send messages destined for a subscriber in another country to the central WEP in one's own country, which can then forward the messages directly to the WEP of the target country using the target address. The WEP of the target country is then in a position to forward the messages to the appropriate management domain or organization within that country.

Within the RARE MHS project, the states involved have reached agreements that specify the quality of service and the accessibility of these WEPs. In order to make it possible for states that could not at first achieve this quality of service to participate in the RARE MHS, a distinction was made between experimental and operational WEPs. The task of the MHS project team in this phase was firstly to advise on the construction and operation of X.400 networks and secondly to specify and prepare suitable documentation to define access parameters to each national WEP, appropriate administrative contacts, etc. In addition, simple monitoring of the quality of service of the connected WEPs was carried out during this phase.

One important coordination function performed by the MHS project team involved the definition and coordination of the name and address schemes used in the individual member organizations. Because of the specific national circumstances, it was impossible to define a uniform Europe-wide address scheme. However, the individual national schemes were presented and compared at joint meetings of the MHS project team and RARE WG1. For example, some states specified that certain attribute values, such as ADMD name, PRMD name, etc., should not be used since the corresponding structure is not available. Similarly, for example, these schemes specified whether a PRMD value should be used for all academic organizations within a country or whether each organization should be assigned its own PRMD value. Other organization-specific definitions specify how the X.400 name space is mapped onto the RFC 822 name space (for example, Switzerland has decided not to represent the ADMD and PRMD attributes in RFC 822 addresses). The existence of this experience was a substantial help in the construction of individual X.400 networks, particularly for newly-joining network organizations.

Another problem addressed as part of the cooperation between the MHS project team and RARE WG1 was the provision of connectivity between the RARE MHS and other non-X.400-based systems. In this regard, the connection to the previously described North-American networks played an important role. Based on the RFC 987 mapping mechanism described above, the MHS project team in cooperation with RARE WG1 supported member organizations in the definition of national mapping tables and took on the function of the central distribution point for current table entries, which were subject to frequent alteration, at least during the initial phase. Under this scheme, at predefined times and also after important alterations to their national addressing schemes, all member organizations transmit their current tables to the MHS project team, which then redistributes the tables to those member organizations that operate RFC 987 gateways. Since at the present time, not all member organizations are willing or able to operate their own RFC 987 gateways, the MHS project team and RARE WG1 coordinate the use of existing gateways in some states by foreign states.

In addition to the RARE MHS documentation, which is mainly produced and updated by the MHS project team, the members of RARE WG1 in coordination with the other members of the working group and with the project team have produced a number of documents commenting on various problems in the area of message handling. One important document relating to the operation of RFC 987 gateways is the definition of a minimal profile for the mapping of X.400 standard attributes onto RFC 822 addresses, as used in the North-American research networks (Grimm, 1987), which has been formally adopted by RARE WG1. In addition to the definition of the address mapping itself, this document describes an alternative, easier-to-read notation for the gateway tables together with procedures governing the distribution and use of the table information in the RARE MHS.

This alternative syntax which we have used in this book up to now may, for example, be used as follows to define the mapping of the top-level domain uucp onto X.400 standard attributes in the case of Switzerland:

uucp **#** C=ch; A=arcom; P=switch; O=uucp

The RFC 987 syntax defines the syntax of the same mapping as follows:

O$uucp.PRMD$switch.ADMD$arcom.C$ch#uucp#

Another document formally adopted by RARE WG1 is a recommendation of a short notation for X.400 addresses, such as are used on visiting cards or letterheads (Grimm and Heagerty, 1989). In particular, the key words needed to identify X.400 O/R address attributes are defined together with a hierarchical sequence of the occurrence of these attributes. Examples of valid addresses in this notation are:

C=ch;   ADMD=arcom;   PRMD=switch;   O=ethz;   OU=tik;
OU=komsys; S=lubich

C=ch;   ADMD=arcom;   PRMD=switch;   O=ethz;   OU=tik;
S=plattner; G=bernhard

Together with other RARE working groups and selected experts, members of RARE WG1 and of the MHS project team have worked on a number of studies and reports which form the specification phase of the

European research network Cooperation for Open Systems Interconnection Networking in Europe (COSINE) under the aegis of the CEC. In the final phase of the work on the specification of COSINE, RARE WG1 commented on the technical correctness of the studies relevant to the MHS area.

4.3 Present situation of RARE MHS

According to the original schedule, the RARE MHS pilot project should have come to an end in 1989 to be smoothly replaced by the follow-on project COSINE MHS, the objective of which is to operate the Europe-wide X.400 MHS productively and to drive forward the use of X.400 systems in the states of the European Community. In addition, COSINE MHS is intended to ensure reliable connection to non-X.400 networks and to promote the migration of these networks to X.400.

Because of administrative delays in the implementation of the COSINE research network, the RARE MHS project had to be extended in order to permit a smooth transition between the two project phases without loss of service quality. It is also very important that the two phases should overlap so as to permit the exchange of knowledge between the members of the MHS project team and the operators of the COSINE MHS. Active support for this transfer of knowledge is an important duty of RARE WG1.

In the following we give a brief account of the present position of the RARE MHS. In particular, we describe the present size of the RARE MHS, the products used and current problems that must be resolved in the near future.

Table 4.1, which is based on the RARE 1989 Annual Report, lists the member and associate states of the RARE MHS together with the corresponding numbers of their MTAs (here, it may be assumed that the number of MTAs today is much higher and that most national MHS networks now have operational status).

It is assumed that in the member states at the end of 1989 more than 100 000 users in 350 research institutions were connected to RARE MHS and that this number has increased sharply in the meantime.

Although in the initial phase of RARE MHS on the whole only one X.400 product, the EAN system of the University of British Columbia (Neufeld, 1983), was available for use on UNIX and VMS systems which used domain-defined attributes in the form of RFC 822 addresses (EAN/V1 addressing), since then very many different X.400 products from various manufacturers have been used within the RARE MHS framework on a large number of hardware and operating-system platforms. It is thanks to the active driving forward by the MHS project team of migration to the

Table 4.1 Status of members of RARE MHS.

Country	Number of MTAs	Status
Austria	16	Operational service
Belgium	1	Pilot project
Denmark	9	Operational service
Finland	8	Operational service
France	51	Operational service
Germany	220	Operational service
Great Britain	2	Gateway service
Iceland	1	Pilot project
Ireland	3	Pilot project
Italy	31	Operational service
Netherlands	1	Experimental
Norway	33	Operational service
Portugal	5	Pilot project
Spain	20	Operational service
Sweden	8	Pilot project
Switzerland	62	Operational service
Australia	1	Gateway service
Canada	172	Operational service
Republic of Korea	6	Operational service

use of X.400 standard attributes that this old form of addressing is no longer used. Table 4.2 is a list which was published by the Deutsches Forschungsnetz in mid 1990 of all the X.400 products used in the DFN MHS.

It may be assumed that both in the DFN and in the other states connected to the RARE MHS other products not on the list have since been introduced and are now in use.

Table 4.2   Selection of X.400 products used in RARE MHS.

Product	Manufacturer	Operating system
EAN	UBC	VMS and UNIX
DFN EAN	UBC/DFN (GMD)	VMS and UNIX on VAX, SUN, CADMUS
KOMEX	GMD	BS2000
NOTE400	IBM	VM
PROFS400	IBM	VM
MRX400	DEC	VMS
HP400	HP	UNIX on HP9000
OSITEL/400	DFN (Danet)	UNIX on VAX etc.
DG400	Data General	AOS/VS
UCLAMail/400	DFN (Softlab)	MVS
SUNLINK MHS	SUN	UNIX
TARGON MAIL	NIXDORF	UNIX
MAIL+	INRIA	UNIX on SUN
AKOM	SIEMENS	BS2000
MAIL.X	SIEMENS	SINIX
MAIL/VE	CDC	NOS-VE
GTC 400	GTC	XENIX

4.4 Examples of the connection of national research networks to RARE MHS

Within the RARE MHS framework a large number of very different research networks have been combined into an integrated network. Thus, it is not surprising that connection to the RARE MHS is realized in various ways. In what follows, we use three examples to document various methods of connection to the RARE MHS. We stress that none of the methods described is superior to any of the other methods and that this is not intended as an evaluation of connection methods. Instead, characteristically, RARE MHS connects together a large number of networks with different structures without imposing an organizational structure on the network operators involved which would not correspond to the national situation and therefore would not find acceptance.

SWITCH

SWITCH is both the name of the Swiss national network for research and education and the name of the organization which planned and implemented this network (Plattner, 1988). SWITCH aims to offer its users a range of services based on this network. The electronic message transfer service operated by SWITCH since 1 April 1988 is *SWITCHmail*. SWITCHmail includes the Swiss academic X.400 MHS and also, during a transition period of two to three years, non-X.400-based systems such as the Swiss part of EARN. In the long-term SWITCHmail will be a pure X.400 network, however, one must take into account the fact that at present there are also other message transfer systems based on other technologies which are widely used. Users of SWITCHmail must be able to reach users in these networks and must be reachable from these networks.

The SWITCHmail architecture is based on central equipment (*SWITCH Central System*, SCS), which connects SWITCHmail to other networks and *SWITCH Access Systems* (SASs) as central systems for each subscriber. The subscribers to SWITCHmail include a large number of Swiss academic teaching and research institutions, which we call 'universities' for short. While SASs transport messages between the universities directly, SWITCHmail is also connected to the public X.400 MHS of the Swiss PTT. All SASs and the SCS are linked to each other via a Switzerland-wide communications infrastructure based on public X.25 services and a private leased line network. The latter infrastructure is called *SWITCHlan*. Figure 4.2 shows the structure of SWITCHmail.

Currently there are user groups in some Swiss universities for whom access to an X.400 system cannot be made available because of the non-existence of X.400 implementations for specific computers or specific operating systems. It is however also desirable that these users should be reachable via SWITCHmail. For this reason SWITCHmail had to be based on a naming scheme that allows the inclusion of users of non-X.400 message transfer systems and that conceals any local addressing peculiarities in a uniform name space (Lubich and Plattner, 1989). For this reason, too, the *SAS local gateway functionality* must also be available. Users who are reachable via such SAS gateways are integrated into the SWITCHmail name space. This eliminates one of the main problems of a heterogeneous system visible to the user, namely different name schemes. However, since such installations must be connected via gateways, occasional loss of functionality must be anticipated.

Figure 4.3 shows the resulting structure of an SAS for SWITCHmail.

The Switzerland-wide communication infrastructure connects an SAS with the SCS and with all other SASs. In the SAS, all X.400 messages

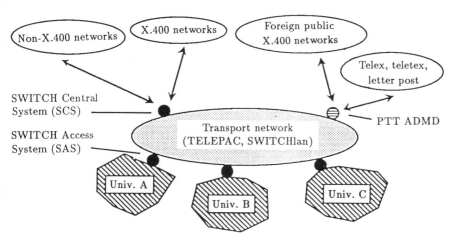

Figure 4.2   Topology of SWITCHmail.

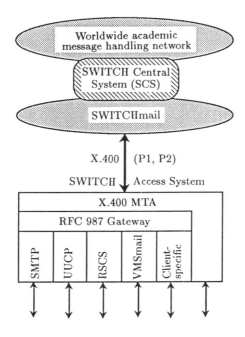

Figure 4.3   SAS functionality.

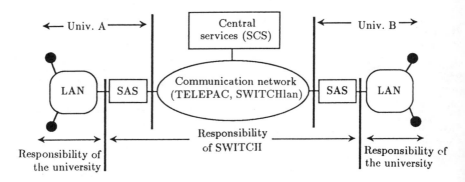

Figure 4.4   Responsibility for SWITCHmail.

are transparently forwarded in both directions, while a number of gateways convert messages into the desired form. For example, if the university attached to the SAS uses VMSmail internally, a message to be forwarded to a recipient at another university will be converted into an X.400 message in the SAS via an RFC 987 gateway. Similarly, an X.400 message to be delivered to a recipient within the university which uses VMSmail is converted from X.400 format to VMSmail format in the university's SAS.

One particular feature of SWITCHmail is the great attention paid to the federal structure of Switzerland, which manifests itself in a precisely defined division of work and tasks between SWITCH and the attached organizations and which depends on close cooperation between the attached organizations and SWITCH. Here, in addition to operational tasks, SWITCH looks after advisory and coordination tasks without forcing decisions against the will of the attached organizations. Figure 4.4 clarifies this division of tasks at the interface between the SWITCH infrastructure and the infrastructure of the attached organizations.

Here, the main point of contact between SWITCH and the attached university is the SAS which physically resides in the university. The university is responsible for providing the infrastructure needed for the SAS and undertakes some of the operational tasks of the SAS. On the other hand, SWITCH is responsible for the technical and organizational integration of the SAS into the communication infrastructure and undertakes tasks involving maintenance and system administration, as necessary.

DFN

The Deutsches Forschungsnetz (German research network, DFN) is the national academic research network in Germany which connects a large number of universities and other research institutions. Formed from its Berlin-based predecessors HMI NET and BERNET, today, under the patronage of the Ministry for Research and Technology, the DFN forms a registered organization with a permanent staff entrusted with its construction and management. The DFN allows its users access to a range of services, namely electronic mail (X.400), dialogue (virtual terminal), file transfer and remote job entry.

The DFN message handling service includes approximately 200 MTAs with around 10 000 attached users who may be directly connected together via an X.25 infrastructure (Datex-P or WIN). However, the DFN message handling service is not a fully meshed network, but depends heavily on central installations to which all MTAs are connected. Because of the growth of the DFN message handling service there has been a recent change to the creation of local access nodes similar to the SAS scheme of SWITCHmail described above. However, unlike in SWITCH, the responsibility for these access systems (and hence for all direct bilateral connections to other universities) lies completely with the individual universities.

Within the framework of the migration to OSI services, even in 1989 nearly all connections between non-X.400 systems (usually leased lines) had been suspended and the systems involved converted to use X.400 products. DFN operates a number of gateway services to foreign non-X.400 networks (for example, to BITNET/EARN and the North-American Internet) which (in the context of RARE MHS) may also be used by arrangement by foreign countries in RARE MHS which are not able or willing to provide such services themselves.

JANET

In 1979 in Great Britain a number of proposals relevant to the services of the British SERCnet (Science Engineering Research Council network, renamed the Joint Academic Network, JANET, in 1984) were designed and implemented. Since each protocol description was assigned a colour, the complete set of protocols is known as the 'Coloured Book' or the 'Rainbow Book'.

The 'grey book' protocol describes the protocol for the exchange of electronic mail between JANET systems which follows the UK *Name Registration Scheme* (NRS) (equivalent to the North-American Internet scheme). The protocol is on the whole equivalent to RFC 822 but the hierarchy of the domains is exactly the opposite:

"In DARPA one writes 'user@vax1.ee.udel.arpa', known as 'little endian' order, while the British write 'user@arpa.udel.ee.vax1' or 'big endian' order, i.e. 'big endians' put the largest, most general or most significant element of the domain first. 'Little endians' use the other order, with the most significant part last. [See Gulliver's Travels by Jonathan Swift: The 'big endian' vs. 'little endian' controversy was the *casus belli* in Lilliput.]" (Kingston, 1984)

In order to connect the JANET systems with all other RFC 822-based systems, JANET operates several format gateways which, whenever messages leave JANET or reach JANET from the outside, invert the sequence of domains in all addresses in the message header.

Although in the process of migration to the use of OSI protocols JANET has shown its readiness to comply with this migration, there are a large number of existing services in JANET with a large number of users (around 1500 interconnected systems), which makes an immediate migration technically and organizationally impossible. Thus, in order to ensure connectivity between JANET and RARE MHS, a central gateway is operated which carries out an address and protocol conversion between the grey book protocol elements and X.400. This gateway is located in a professionally-run computer centre in *University College, London* (UCL) so as to guarantee as trouble free a service as possible.

Comparison of the above methods

We have described three different ways in which national research networks may be connected to RARE MHS. While SWITCHmail consists of a national academic X.400 backbone, with largely homogeneous software and access points in all universities, which is connected with other RARE MHS subscribers via central installations, the DFN message handling service is based on a central service provision together with the almost completely free use of the additional meshed network of individual X.400 systems from many manufacturers. On the other hand, JANET only has the external appearance of an X.400 network, while in reality the connection of JANET to RARE MHS is implemented by an X.400 protocol and address gateway.

All three approaches are tailored to the appropriate national situation. The Switzerland-wide X.400 network constructed in the framework of the activities of RARE caters for a relatively small number of universities which were not previously connected (or were connected only bilaterally) to each other or to other networks. Because of the relatively small number of installations (SAS and SCS), it is in this case possible to use the same software in all the systems of the backbone and to offload a large part of the functionality on to central installations. The use of SASs in every attached university makes it easy to include non-X.400 systems in the universities in a global name and address space. The potential performance bottleneck and the creation of a 'single point of failure' in the central installations may be viewed as potential disadvantages.

In the DFN, on the other hand, from the beginning, emphasis was placed on the use of a large variety of X.400 products, so as to make the migration to universal use of X.400 in German universities as fast as possible. Correspondingly, the connections to non-X.400 systems were dismantled at a relatively early stage. While between universities any direct connections between MTAs are possible, DFN also provides central services (such as gateways to other message transfer systems) and a central point of attachment for MTAs that only require an access point to the DFN message handling service. In comparison with a backbone approach, this scheme reduces the danger of potential bottlenecks in the MTS.

In the JANET approach, the existence of an extensive operational network with productive services which would be subject to at least temporary loss of functionality in a migration to X.400 was taken into account. Moreover, at that time, not all the services provided by JANET were available as OSI services. Thus, to facilitate access to the other networks reachable via RARE MHS a central gateway solution was implemented in JANET. While this essentially solves the problem of mutual accessibility it forms a potential bottleneck in view of the large user group. Moreover, operation of the pure gateway solution may slow down the migration to a solution conforming to OSI, since the immediate need is no longer directly visible.

In addition to the three solutions described, there are many national variations that reflect the current needs of particular network users and network providers. We again stress that none of the above methods of connection can be classified as generally superior to any of the other methods.

It is in principle advantageous that no overall (and therefore necessarily artificial) network structure and management has been implemented within the RARE MHS framework. Instead we find a combination of various networks and network operators which allows all those involved to migrate to complete use of X.400 systems while taking account of their own handicaps and requirements. However, this additional degree of freedom must be worked for with the emphasis on coordination, as shown by the MHS project team.

4.5 Cooperation of RARE MHS with other services

In addition to the coordination of the national research networks included in RARE MHS, the MHS project team has the job of ensuring and coordinating the connectivity to other message handling systems both within and outside of Europe. Because of the fact that connection to the North-American research networks is increasingly important it is crucial to provide gateway services according to RFC 987 between RARE MHS and the RFC 822-based networks and to coordinate the operation of existing gateways. This coordination task is currently carried out by central collection and distribution of RFC 987 mapping tables by the MHS project team. The RARE MHS gateway services themselves are operated by several gateway installations within RHS member organizations. In the medium term this task will be carried out by a corresponding COSINE service which will be implemented either by a central European gateway service or by a small number of Europe-wide accessible gateways in individual member states.

Interoperation with the European X.500 pilot project now becomes an important task which is coordinated by RARE WG3. On the one hand, it is intended to include the end-user data of MHS subscribers in the directory, while on the other hand, the directory is also to be used to store and make available RARE MHS operational data. Here it is firstly a question of administering the information needed to interconnect the MHS WEPs (namely technical administrative information such as TSAP identifiers, X.121 addresses, telephone/telefax numbers of the administrators, etc., collected centrally until now by the MHS project team) in the directory. Moreover, even the RFC 987 mapping information currently held in static tables may be stored and administered in the directory. At the present time, this information may be used to generate the static tables in the gateway. After the introduction of a corresponding RARE directory service with the appropriate reliability, this storage in the directory offers the additional possibility of completely dispensing with static mapping tables and of specifically retrieving the information from the directory whenever an address mapping is carried out.

In addition to maintaining the consistency of RFC 987 mapping information in an X.500-based directory, coordination of other representations of the same information must be ensured by RARE MHS. In particular, in the North-American research networks attempts are now being made to store RFC 987 mapping information (amongst other things) in a separate directory, the DNS (Domain Name System, RFC 1034/1035). This means that, on the one hand, the consistency of the data in the two directories must be maintained and on the other hand that procedures to input and output some or all of the table information must be defined and coordinated.

In addition to contacts with other message handling networks, coordination with other pilot projects and communication networks within the European Community (COSINE in particular) is important for RARE MHS. This includes firstly the Europe-wide X.25 service IXI (International X.25 Interconnect) defined by RARE WG4 and implemented in a COSINE project, and secondly the X.400 network Y-NET which is currently under construction and which is intended to provide access to X.400-based message handling to researchers in commercial and academic fields. While IXI has been available as a pilot service since the beginning of 1990 and has to some extent been used to transfer messages between the RARE MHS WEPs, Y-NET is currently not yet operational. The coordination between Y-NET and

RARE MHS via RARE WG1, on the one hand, and via the corresponding COSINE project group (COSINE Project Management Unit, CPMU), on the other hand, is however guaranteed and ensures the direct coordination of both X.400 networks.

Finally, the MHS project team has the job of supporting coordination with the operators of ADMDs in the member states. Since the attached countries have different telecommunications legislation and since until now only a relatively small number of European ADMDs are connected to one another, coordination is still restricted to the passing of information about the situation in all countries to all ADMD providers. In the future, however, we may assume a far greater connectivity of the European ADMDs. In this case, it is (amongst other things) the job of the MHS project team to coordinate when subscribers to RARE MHS (or its follow-on project) should be directly connected to each other (PRMD to PRMD) and when a connection over one or more ADMDs should be used.

4.6 Future developments

In the near future the present RARE MHS will be superseded by the follow-on project COSINE MHS in such a way that continuity of the service is guaranteed. Independently of this a number of tasks must be undertaken in future research and pilot projects. Firstly, there is the problem of the introduction of X.400 systems based on the new version of 1988 and of the interworking between the different systems (see also Chapters 9 and 10). Moreover, it will be increasingly important for users of X.400 systems in the research field to be able to handle not only text information but also graphical information, speech, etc. via X.400. This new form of multimedia message handling with X.400 is still the subject of research, but will lead to first pilot projects in the medium term. Participation in the definition of relevant standards and in the coordination of such pilot projects is an important duty for COSINE MHS which will enable it in the future to provide an increasing number of users with a service that is equally reliable, interesting and of a high technical quality.

5

Profiles and functional standards

5.1 The organizations

5.2 Profiles and functional standards for
     X.400 (84): an overview

5.3 Profile contents

In Chapter 2 we introduced the services of a message handling system. Recommendation X.400 (84) subdivides the services into *basic services* and *optional services*. Basic services are functions that facilitate the exchange of electronic mail between the users of a message handling system. As far as the optional services are concerned, users may select (like from a building kit) the services that they want to use for daily mail traffic. Thus, they can optimally tailor the system to their own needs and requirements.

The reality is somewhat different. The user has access to an implementation of the X.400 (84) recommendations on a computer, which provides the basic services and certain optional services. Thus, it necessarily follows that different manufacturers have implemented different optional services. The authors of the recommendations intended this. However, it also clearly gives rise to some problems.

What happens when implementations with disjoint sets of optional functions or different concrete realizations of these services wish to exchange electronic mail? It should be apparent that an implementation may behave in an undefined way. In specific cases (for example, interruption of service), failure of some X.400 implementations is conceivable.

To counter this problem, rules have been agreed that precisely describe the *minimal behaviour* of an implementation. It does not necessarily follow that all implementations support the same optional services. Instead, the rules specify the minimal support required for each service. Thus, it is possible for all those involved (implementors, operators, and users of X.400 systems) to assess how an implementation (either their own, or that of a partner) would behave. These specifications are particularly interesting for all those who have to implement an X.400 system; they are known as *implementation recommendations* and are widely used in practice (see also the statements on *conformance* in Appendix D).

Use of the terms *profile* and *functional standard* to designate implementation recommendations has caught on. A profile or a functional standard is defined gradually. The interim results of this process are specified in profiles. When a profile is formally confirmed by one of the organizations listed in Section 5.1, this profile is subsequently called a *functional standard*.

This chapter contains an overview of the development of profiles and of the definition of functional standards by the organizations involved (Section 5.1) and discusses the profiles and functional standards relevant to X.400 (84) (Section 5.2). The chapter ends with an introduction to the structure and content of a profile (Section 5.3) and with a comparison of the contents of the latter.

5.1 The organizations

The international standardization of communication protocols and services is largely carried out by two organizations, namely the *Comité Consultatif International Télégraphique et Téléphonique* (CCITT) and the *International Standardization Organization* (ISO).

The CCITT consists of all national post and telephone companies. The members of ISO are the national standardization bodies, for example, SNV (Schweizerische Normenvereinigung (Switzerland)), ANSI (American National Standards Institute) and BSI (British Standards Institution).

The task of these organizations is to normalize standards and recommendations proposed by their members for formal release as a standard or a recommendation. ISO and CCITT are in particular also responsible for the specification of communication services and protocols. Proposals for new communication services and protocols come not only from the members of these two organizations, but are also introduced by organizations representing various interests in standardization work (for example, the *Electronic Industries Association* (EIA), the *European Computer Manufacturers Association* (ECMA), the *Institute of Electrical and Electronic Engineers* (IEEE)). The final definition as standard or recommendation is often preceded by lengthy consultations to discuss and consider all the various interests. This is surely a reason for the much-criticized over-generality of standards. In order to tackle this problem, many national and multinational associations and organizations have generated implementation recommendations. This section attempts to give some order to the myriad of organizations who define or have defined profiles and functional standards for X.400 (84).

In Europe, the development of profiles involves primarily the *Standards Promotion and Application Group* (SPAG), the *Comité Européen des Administrations des Postes et des Télécommunications* (CEPT) and the *Comité Européen de Normalisation, Comité Européen de Normalisation Electrique* (CEN/CENELEC). SPAG has published its profiles in a 'Guide to the Use of Profiles' (SPAG, 1987). CEPT and CEN/CENELEC base their work on the results of SPAG. Only CEN/CENELEC is authorized to define functional standards. These are known as *European Norms* (EN) or *European Prenorms* (EPN) (see also Section 5.2). To exclude unnecessary differences and incompatibilities between the profiles and functional standards, CEPT and CEN/CENELEC have set up a special group, the *Information Technology Steering Committee* (ITSTC). This is intended to act as a mediator between the two organizations.

In the USA, the *National Bureau of Standards* (NBS), renamed the *National Institute for Standards and Technology* (NIST) in 1988, deals with X.400 profiles. These are contained in the report *'Stable Implementation Agreements for Open Systems Interconnection Protocols'* (NIST, 1988). The profiles of the NIST are called *stable implementation agreements*.

The NBS (NIST) and CEN/CENELEC have also tried, on an informal level, to make their profiles compatible. Recently, coordination work was institutionalized, and on the CEN/CENELEC side, the *European Workshop for Open Systems* (EWOS) was tasked to exchange with NIST all information needed to ensure profile compatibility.

For the sake of completeness, we also mention the following organizations. In the area of automation, technical and office there are several other implementation recommendations: *Manufacturing Automation Protocol* (MAP), and *Technical and Office Protocols* (TOP). The *Government Open Systems Interconnection Profiles* (GOSIP) define a uniform protocol architecture based on OSI standards which is important for governmental procurement of communication devices in Europe and in the USA. GOSIP are not new protocols but are based on existing ones.

5.2 Profiles and functional standards for X.400 (84): an overview

Many X.400 implementations are involved in the realization of the 'electronic mail' service. Operators of an X.400 system may include PTTs which are usually responsible for operation of the ADMD, businesses that form their own PRMD, and departments that have access to their own MTA. A message from the originator to the recipient will usually pass through the following interfaces:

- The message is transferred from one MTA to another MTA within a PRMD.

- The message is sent from one PRMD to another PRMD or to an ADMD.

- On the way to its destination the message is passed between ADMDs.

The X.400 (84) recommendations are not concerned with the interfaces between MDs. To close this gap and to ensure reliable exchange of electronic mail over these interfaces, SPAG, CEN/CENELEC and NIST have defined corresponding profiles. Figure 5.1 and Table 5.1 show the profiles associated with each interface.

The profiles and functional standards are as follows:

- ENV 41 201 Private Message Handling System: User Agent and Message Transfer Agent: Private Management Domain to Private Management Domain.

- ENV 41 202 Protocol for Interpersonal Messaging between Message Transfer Agents Accessing the Public Message Handling Service.

- A/311 Message Handling Services: UA + MTA: PRMD to ADMD (P2 + P1).

- A/3211 Message Handling Services UA + MTA: PRMD to PRMD (P2 + P1) Long-Term Full Service.

- NBS X.400 SIG Functional Standard for Message Handling Systems based on the CCITT X.400 Series (84) encompassing: PRMD to PRMD; PRMD to ADMD; ADMD to ADMD.

The profile A/311 and the functional standard ENV 41 202 also define the functionality between ADMDs. In profile A/323 'Private MHS: Interpersonal Messaging MTA to MTA (Intra-PRMD)', SPAG defined the functionality of the interface between MTAs in a PRMD. We mention this profile for the sake of completeness; because of its minor importance we do not discuss it further in this chapter.

The user is particularly interested in the functionality defined by a profile and what part of that is realized in the X.400 implementation to which he has access. Manufacturers advise on the latter in their product descriptions (Appendix D: List of X.400 products); however, this only indicates the profiles to which their implementation conforms. As we shall show in this chapter, this does not enable us to deduce what else is actually implemented. For, as we have already stated, profiles define only a minimal functionality. An implementation may (and in specific cases will) have a greater capability. These statements only serve as a criterion for the fact that an exchange of messages is possible with implementations of the same profile. The problem of conformance with the regulations is thus not solved (see Chapter 13). It is clear from the collected information given in Appendix D that almost all X.400 manufacturers' implementations conform to several of the profiles listed in Table 5.1. This immediately raises the question as to whether the functional standards and profiles are mutually compatible. An answer to this question is important, since an implementation cannot recognize whether it is exchanging messages with

Table 5.1   Profiles for X.400 (84).

	PRMD – PRMD	*PRMD – ADMD*	*ADMD – ADMD*
CEN/CENELEC	ENV 41 201	ENV 41 202	
SPAG	A/3211	A/311	
NBS	NBS X.400 SIG		

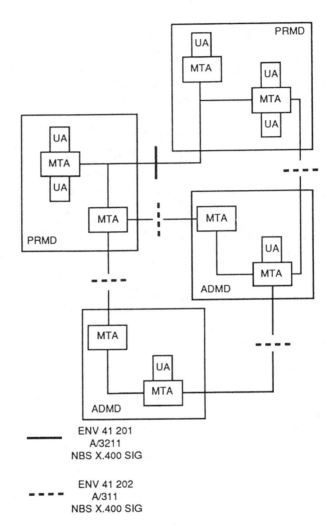

Figure 5.1 X.400 (84) profiles for the interfaces between MDs.

an implementation that conforms to ENV 41 202 or NBS X.400 SIG. We look into this question in the next section in the paragraph headed 'Comparison of X.400 (84) profiles'.

5.3 Profile contents

Profiles describe the functionality of an X.400 implementation that is made available to its users and other X.400 implementations at the interfaces. Overall, the functionality consists of:

- The communications infrastructure that links the X.400 implementations and ensures an error-free exchange of messages.

- The services offered to users of a message handling system (*interpersonal messaging service*) and the services offered by sublayers of higher layers (*message transfer services*).

- The PDUs exchanged between X.400 implementations.

Abstracted from the communications infrastructure, the message transfer layer, namely the part of an X.400 system that realizes the message transfer service, defines the lowest layer of the hierarchy. Within the MTL the MTAEs implement the MT services by exchanging P1 PDUs. Thus, the interfaces between the MDs (Figure 5.1) may be equated with the P1 PDUs. A similar approach holds for the UAL, which represents an abstraction of the interpersonal messaging service. The UAEs in the UAL, which coordinate their actions by exchanging P2 PDUs and perform the messaging service, define a logical interface between individual X.400 systems. The user and UA, and UA and MTA interact at each interface by calling services.

The content of an X.400 (84) profile largely defines how these interfaces (services and protocol elements) must be supported by an implementation. In addition, every profile contains statements on:

- The status of the document.

- The changes made to it since the last version.

- Any other important profiles and functional standards and the extent to which they agree with the given profile.

- The scope of application for which the profile is defined.

- The conformance requirements for implementations of this profile (a statement as to when an implementation may be considered to conform to the profile (Chapter 13)).

- A list of the relevant basic documents (which are the ISO standards, CCITT recommendations and other profiles).

As in Chapter 2, it is clear that the services of an X.400 system divide into those which are directly accessible to the user (IPM services) and those which support message transfer (MT services). We stress that for IPM services a basic distinction is made between whether a service is provided by an originator or by a recipient. In many cases (optional services) an implementation may make a service available to an originator, although it need not. On the other hand, an implementation must process a received message associated with the provision of an optional service in some way, even if this should suppress the services to be provided. In contrast, all messages, whether received or to be sent, must be correctly processed by an MTA. This requirement follows immediately from the observation that an MTA in an MD may be involved in the *transfer of messages* of arbitrary origin (even from other MDs and for an ADMD from all attached PRMDs).

In the case of the services defined in the X.400 (84) recommendations a profile contains at least the following statements:

- Requirements in respect of support for origination.
- Requirements in respect of support for reception.
- Requirements in respect of support for transmission.

As already mentioned in Section 2.5, the services of an X.400 system may be mapped onto the P2 and P1 protocol elements. From this narrow association between services and protocol elements it follows that, analogously to the definition of the requirements for the support of services in a profile, requirements for the manipulation of protocol elements are stipulated. For protocol elements, distinction is made between requirements for:

- The generation of a protocol element.
- The processing of the protocol element by the recipient.
- The processing of the protocol element on transmission.

These requirements cannot be expressed in terms of a yes/no matrix (yes corresponds to 'to be implemented', no corresponds to 'not to be implemented'). Instead, there are fine gradations of the extent to which an implementation must and may support a service or a protocol element.

Classification of services and protocols

Before we go into the details of the classification of services and protocol elements we clarify the problem with examples of several cases.

Examples

By way of example, we consider the 'deferred delivery' service. 'Deferred delivery' is one of the optional MT services which, according to recommendation X.401 (84), may be offered to a UA. 'Deferred delivery' allows a user of an X.400 system to attach a time to the message he originates, before which the message should not be delivered to the recipient.

As previously noted, 'deferred delivery' is an MT service and as such is not directly accessible to the user. Thus, a UA must make this service available to a user in an appropriate way. The UA may deliver the time specified by the user to the MTS in a parameter of a service primitive. The 'deferred delivery' protocol element in the '**UMPDUEnvelope**' (Section 2.5) may be used to transmit the time to remote MTAEs.

'Deferred delivery' may be implemented in the following ways:

- The originating MTA waits to transmit the message until the time specified by the user is (or is almost) reached.

- The receiving MTA waits to deliver the message until the time specified by the originator is reached.

- A combination of both the above procedures, where the MTAs involved in transferring the message are jointly responsible for the provision of the service.

In the first case, the provision of the service is a matter for the X.400 system used by the originator. In the remaining two cases, the service can only be properly provided if the MTAE of the originator, all the MTAEs involved in the transfer, and the MTAE of the recipient support this service. This is shown in Figures 5.2a–5.2d.

Figure 5.2a shows the case in which the 'deferred delivery' service is implemented by the X.400 system of the originator. The X.400 systems

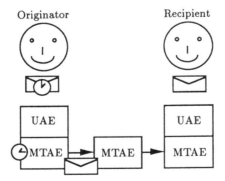

Figure 5.2a   First procedure with support for origination.

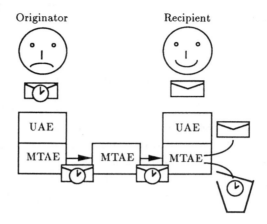

Figure 5.2b   Second procedure without support for reception.

tasked with the message transfer and the X.400 system of the recipient are not made aware of the fact that 'deferred delivery' was stipulated.

In the case shown in Figure 5.2b, the recipient receives the message ahead of time. Since the X.400 system of the recipient does not support the 'deferred delivery' service, the message is delivered to the recipient immediately it is received. The time in the 'deferred delivery' protocol element is ignored.

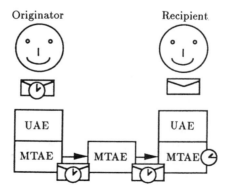

Figure 5.2c   Second procedure with support for reception.

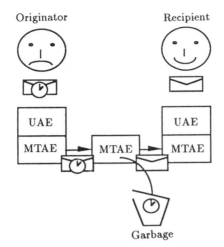

Figure 5.2d   Third procedure without support for transmission.

Figure 5.2c shows a different case. The MTAE implementation of the X.400 system of the recipient waits to deliver the message to the UAE until the time is reached after which the message may be brought to the attention of the recipient.

Figure 5.2d shows the case in which one of the X.400 systems that transfers the message *en route* from the originator to the recipient does not support the 'deferred delivery' protocol element. The information contained in this element is deleted from the P1 PDU. Consequently, none of the subsequent MTAEs nor the MTAE of the recipient are made aware of the fact that the message should not be delivered before the time specified.

In the following we describe the linguistic rulings of the profile to classify the services and the protocol elements. The classification specifies how each service and each protocol element should be supported by an X.400 implementation. With this knowledge, the user may assess how his message will be processed by his own X.400 system, by the X.400 systems involved in the transfer and by the X.400 system of the recipient. At the end of this section, we again consider the examples and discuss the effects of the profile specifications in these cases.

Classification of the services

Before we consider the classification of the services, we must introduce a number of terms. In the following, we talk of the service provider, the service user and the user. In Figures 5.2a–5.2d MTAE is a service provider. The services it offers are used by a UAE and made accessible to a user of the MHS over an interface.

Beginning in the UAL, the service provider is a UAE, and the service user is, for example, an interactive interface to the user.

In Section 2.5 we alluded to the possibility that, in message processing, the user may be supported by the system. This statement was explained by means of an example. The arrival of a highly important message could be immediately indicated by an acoustic signal or this could be graphically emphasized on a list of incoming messages. In the next paragraphs, when we refer to 'appropriate actions' we mean these possibilities.

In the classification of services we distinguish between (ENV 41 202)[1]:

- SUPPORT = S (supported). This basically means that

  (1) The service provider makes the service accessible to the service user.

  (2) The service user makes the service accessible to the MHS user, or, should this not be possible, flags the corresponding information.

  Support for origination means that

  (1) The service provider makes the service available to the service user.

  (2) The service user makes the service available to the MHS user on generation of a message.

  Support for reception means that:

  The service provider makes the information associated with the service available to the service user.

- NON-SUPPORT = N (not supported). This means that the service provider need not make the service available to the service user. The service provider should not interpret the occurrence of the corresponding protocol element in a received PDU as a protocol error. A transfer system should forward such communications transparently (unaltered).

- NOT USED = NU (not used). This means that although the service is defined by the OSI standard it is not used in the functional standard.

- NOT APPLICABLE = NA (not applicable). This service is not applicable in the given context.

---

[1]The statements here also hold for ENV 41 201, the SPAG profiles and NBS X.400 SIG. We discuss the most important differences at the end of the section.

Classification of the protocol elements

In the classification of protocol elements, we distinguish between (ENV 41 202):

- UNSUPPORTED = X. The protocol element may be generated. Neither the transfer system nor the X.400 system of the recipient of the message should be expected to process the protocol element in any form. It may be assumed that the transfer system forwards such messages transparently. In the transfer system and in the X.400 system of the recipient, no importance should be attached to the absence of the protocol element.

- SUPPORTED = H. The protocol element *may* be generated. Appropriate actions should be taken in the transfer system and in the X.400 system of the recipient.

- GENERATABLE = G. Implementations must be able to generate and process the protocol element, even if it need not occur in all PDUs. Appropriate actions should be taken in the transfer system and in the X.400 system of the recipient. The functional standard defines the conditions under which the protocol element must be generated.

- REQUIRED = R. Implementations are required to generate the protocol element in all PDUs. The absence of the protocol element in a received PDU does not represent a protocol error since there may be other implementations in which this protocol element is not *required*. Appropriate actions should be taken in the transfer system and in the X.400 system of the recipient.

- MANDATORY = M. This protocol element must occur in every PDU. If it is missing this is a protocol error. Appropriate actions should be taken in the transfer system and in the X.400 system responsible for the delivery.

ENV 41 202

The following tables (Tables 5.2–5.6) show excerpts from the classification of the ENV 41 202 services and protocol elements. In a final discussion of the previous example, we indicate the sense of the classification.

Unlike the X.401 (84) recommendation, ENV 41 202 specifies that an X.400 implementation need not support the 'deferred delivery' service. As a limitation of this classification, ENV 41 202 stipulates that the provision of the service is solely a matter for the local X.400 system of the originator. This corresponds to an implementation of the service according to the first procedure in the previous example.

In the following, we must therefore assume that the originating X.400

Table 5.2 Support for the UA services.

Service	Origination	Reception
...	...	...
Importance indication	N	S
...	...	...
Subject indication	S	S
...	...	...

Table 5.3 Support for the UA services which stem from the MTS.

Service	Origination	Reception
...	...	...
Deferred delivery	N	NA
...	...	...

Table 5.4 Support for the MT services.

Service	Remark
...	...
Deferred delivery	N
...	...

Table 5.5 Classification of the P2 protocol elements.

Protocol element	Class	Restrictions	Notes
...	...	...	...
Subject	G	Max. 128 characters. In T.61 coding, max. 256 octets.	Generated if subject indication called.
...	...	...	...
Importance	H		
...	...	...	...

Table 5.6   Classification of the P1 protocol elements.

Protocol element	Class	Restrictions	Notes
...	...	...	...
Deferred delivery	X		
...	...	...	...

system waits to start the transfer until the time is reached after which it may begin to send the message. Since 'X' is set for the 'deferred delivery' protocol element, all systems involved in the transfer of this message from the originator to the recipient will forward this message unaltered (at least as far as the 'deferred delivery' protocol element is concerned). Thus, it follows that the failure mode of an X.400 system illustrated in Figure 5.2d is excluded.

As already stated in the introduction to this chapter, the functional standard defines the minimum behaviour of an X.400 implementation. Deviations from this minimum are of course the rule. In all cases, an X.400 implementation will permit users to inform it of their assessment of the importance of the message to the recipient, in the same way that one is accustomed to with the various forms of letter post (registered, express). This corresponds to the following classification (Table 5.7) for the 'importance indication' service.

Comparison of X.400 (84) profiles

To end this chapter, we compare the contents of the functional standards and profiles introduced above. The comparison is restricted to showing which profiles are compatible. This is summarized in Table 5.8.

Table 5.7   Classification for 'importance indication'.

Service	Origination	Reception
...	...	...
Importance indication	S	S
...	...	...

Table 5.8 Profile compatibility matrix for X.400 (84).

	PRMD – PRMD		PRMD – ADMD ADMD – ADMD		
	ENV 41 201	A/3211	ENV 41 202	A/311	NBS X.400 SIG
A/3211	=				(1)
A/311			=		(1)
NBS X.400 SIG	(1)		(1)		

=   The functional standard and the profile have an identical content.

(1)   The NBS X.400 SIG profile largely covers the functionality defined by the A/311 and A/3211 profiles and the ENV 41 201 and ENV 41 202 functional standards. An implementation which conforms to the A/311 and A/3211 profiles or to the ENV 41 202 and ENV 41 201 functional standards may exchange messages with an NBS X.400 SIG if the following restrictions are observed:

—   No protocol elements should be generated that are defined in ISO MOTIS but not in X.400.

—   The only 'body part' to be supported is of type IA5Text. NBS X.400 SIG implementations may generate body parts with an identification number greater than 30.

—   For P1, restrictions on the number of recipients per message and on the maximal length of the bitstring for 'encoded information types' are defined. Absence of the 'original encoded information types' field has another meaning.

—   For R-OPEN (in the RTS) the value defined by NBS for the application layer protocol must be used.

The above list shows that the differences in the protocols are more of a technical nature and should be noted by an implementor. They are of minor importance to the user.

For practical application, this means that the conformance of a specification to one of the X.400 (84) profiles is sufficient 'to guarantee' a reliable message exchange. For the user, it is much more important to know which services are implemented. To determine this, a user has only to ask the manufacturer of the X.400 implementation.

The above overview of the compatibility of the X.400 profiles concludes this chapter. The classification of services and protocol elements is described in somewhat less detail in the recommendations. In Chapter 13 we build on this classification of the recommendations.

Our description will allow the user to classify and compare the collected information on conformance given in Appendix D (List of X.400 products). With the knowledge provided in this chapter, the reader will be in a position to read and interpret the relevant profiles.

6

A guide for the evaluation of X.400 products

Regrettably, incantation of the magic formula 'X.400' is not in itself sufficient to achieve universal connectivity for asynchronous communication. In the previous chapters it emerged that the attainment of X.400-based communication requires a balanced and coordinated selection of many options defined in X.400 (see also Chapter 5). Not for the last time, we stress that in order to realize message handling systems, real systems in the sense of OSI (in other words implementations of X.400) must be available. In view of the complexity of the X.400 standard, it is not self-evident that independently-developed implementations can intercommunicate. We discuss this subject in detail in Chapter 13. In this chapter, we concentrate exclusively on important aspects of implementations that are not specified in the recommendations, but which are relevant to the selection of X.400 products for use in a given environment. This is directed above all towards readers who are faced with the task of setting up an X.400-based message transfer system in a company or a department and of evaluating products for it. Here we may distinguish between the following cases:

(1) The X.400 services are implemented by connecting the individual users to an *X.400 system operated by a third party* (a PRMD or an ADMD). This solution is sensible if the users are occasional or the organization does not have or cannot obtain staff to operate its own system.

(2) An individual PRMD is implemented in which one or more *dedicated systems* are created and operated for this service. Such systems normally offer the functions of an MTA and of UAs and may be accessed from display terminals or personal computers with terminal emulation. This solution is suitable if the organization does not have sufficient computing power of its own (mainframe or departmental computers). The operation of such a system requires trained personnel.

(3) In organizations that are already well-equipped with computers, it is often most advantageous to provide the existing computers with software conforming to X.400. This may come either from the computer manufacturers themselves or from third parties. If computers of different types and possibly from different manufacturers are used within an organization, it will frequently be necessary to use various X.400 products. The operational cost of this solution is the highest of all three cases considered; at the same time, it is the easiest to use since it can offer the users an X.400 system embedded optimally in their normal working environment.

In the following, we present a checklist that may be used to characterize X.400 products and which may serve as a basis for rating an announcement or an evaluation of proposed products. It is above all applicable in case 3 (above), but may provide valuable advice in the other cases. The checklist may be easily rewritten as a questionnaire directed towards the manufacturers and suppliers of X.400 products.

Appendix D contains a list of X.400 products which are described using this checklist.

Underlying version of X.400

Is it an implementation of X.400 (84), X.400 (88) or ISO 10021?

Functionality

As explained in Chapter 2, the various functions of an X.400 system may be combined in various ways in a real system. A product may offer only MTA functions or MTA and UA functions for the interpersonal messaging service, or it may even offer non-standard services. It is also of interest to know whether stand-alone UAs are possible, in other words, whether P3 (X.400 (84)) is implemented.

Some products do not provide stand-alone UAs, but a user interface to a UA, which is remote from a central system. The user interface is in this case typically realized by an application program on a workstation computer. A manufacturer-specific protocol is usually used between the UAs in the central system and this application program.

If this is an implementation according to X.400 (88), the protocol variants implemented must be specified (Chapter 9).

Hardware configuration

The hardware configuration required for installation and operation of the system (including the type of the central processing unit) should be stated. The required sizes of the main memory (possibly also the size of the virtual memory) and of the backup memory are also of particular importance. In systems with UA functionality, guide figures for the memory requirements as a function of the number of registered and simultaneous users should be given.

Operating system

Since X.400 implementations make heavy demands on the services of the operating system, it is conceivable that a given product is not compatible with all operating systems available on a computer. It should be stated on which operating systems and from which revision or version number the product may be operated.

Additional requirements for application or auxiliary software

Often X.400 implementations are not available as stand-alone products, but must be used in conjunction with other application software offered by the manufacturer. Mostly, this concerns office automation products which have been available for some time; it is also conceivable that a database management system may be required for message archiving.

In certain circumstances, an existing office automation product must be updated for use with X.400 (a new version must be installed). This could be a problem for the client if it is not straightforward to combine the new version with his non-X.400-based office application.

Network services supported

As described in Chapter 3, X.400 products may be based on various protocols in the lower layers or more precisely on the services realized by these. The internationally standardized protocols CCITT X.25 for WAN and ISO 8802 for LAN environments are naturally to the fore. An implementation that supports both protocols may serve as a *Well-known Entry Point* (WEP) into a company-wide LAN-based network.

In certain circumstances, it is also of interest to know whether the product in question can support *de-facto* standards such as TCP/IP or manufacturer-specific network solutions. A yes to this question could be very important for the integration of X.400 into an existing distributed system (Chapter 3).

Additional requirements for communication products

Some X.400 products are delivered as a package together with the implementations of the underlying layers (in particular layers 4, 5 and 6). This means that it is possible to build directly onto the supported networks, without other conditions.

In other products, the installation of additional communication products is essential.

User interface

The introduction of X.400 in an environment in which electronic mail is already used (for example, using a manufacturer-specific system) is not without problems. Since, in particular, the addressing used in X.400 is different from all address schemes previously used, the users will generally have to adapt themselves to a new application program and thus to a new user interface. One of the best arguments for a new user interface is the superior functionality and quality (thus, the ease-of-use) offered to the user.

When making a selection, particular attention should be given to the ease-of-use of the user interface of an X.400 product. For the user 'easy-to-use' generally means that a new program requires the same style of user interaction as the other application programs used on the same computer.

X.400 user interfaces may be line oriented, they may offer full-screen menus or they may work in a fully graphical environment with windows and a mouse.

It is conceivable that, instead of a special X.400 UA user interface, that of the manufacturer's present office automation system may be offered, extended if necessary by a facility to specify X.400 addresses.

Programmer interface

Company-specific auxiliary functions may in principle be implemented by the development of special application software which accesses the X.400 services. This gives rise to the question of the availability of a programmer interface which is accessible to the programmer and documented. There should be a statement of the X.400 services that may be accessed (message transfer service, interpersonal messaging service) and the programming languages that are supported. A collection of utility routines should at least permit the management, coding and decoding of the data structures for P1 and P2.

Note that access to the MTS in principle permits the realization of any applications based on asynchronous communication. However, it must be borne in mind that in a heterogeneous environment a new application of this type must be implemented on various computers; MTS-access must therefore be granted to all the computers in question. Thus, a future standardization of programmer interfaces would be very important.

Gateway functions

If systems for electronic mail, or similar services that do not conform to X.400, are operated, the question arises as to the gateway functions supported by the X.400 product. We must distinguish between gateways to and from manufacturer-specific systems and gateways to and from widespread telematic services. If the latter are required, but are not supported by the product in question, public services may if necessary provide a solution.

It is in principle possible to develop one's own gateway if the necessary programmer interfaces are available. However, the reader should note that comprehensive gateway functions are expensive to implement. Minimal solutions are often quickly implemented, but scarcely satisfactory in the long term.

Conformance

Every product should satisfy one or more of the profiles discussed in Chapter 5. Since these profiles only declare a partial functionality to be obligatory, 'conformance to profile xy' only means that the underlying functions (such as the interchange of text in the IA5 character set) are guaranteed.

Detailed statements on conformance may be obtained if it is possible to get sight of the test reports which were generated when the corresponding test suite was executed with a recognized test system. However, we stress that the evaluation of test reports requires specialist staff.

Some manufacturers list systems from other manufacturers with which their systems can interoperate successfully. It is also of interest to the purchaser to know whether the system in question is actually being used in conjunction with one of the public ADMDs emerging in various countries[1].

Network management

We cannot stress strongly enough that the operation of a PRMD which consists of a large number of MTAs and which has many users, is costly and can only be successfully sustained with trained personnel. Thus, the following management functions must be supported by appropriate utilities:

- The management and distribution of routing tables.
- User administration, including the allocation of names and addresses, the registration, alteration and deletion of user names, and the assignment of rights (for example, international access and maximal message length).
- Event flagging for system monitoring, fault diagnosis and generation of statistics for planning purposes.
- Performance monitoring.

Ideally, network management may be carried out from a central point. Utilities for the management of a heterogeneous system (using various X.400 products) can only be expected when the running standardization of network management functions converges and the corresponding products are implemented.

Auxiliary functions

In addition to the X.400 services, many products offer a large number of auxiliary functions. These include:

- Directory services (local/distributed, manufacturer-specific/X.500 compatible). Often alias names (short names) are used locally instead of complicated O/R addresses.

---

[1] Individual European postal administrations plan or operate experimental ADMDs to which PRMDs that use implementations from various manufacturers may be connected.

- Message archiving and retrieval.

- Automatic output of messages on a local printer.

- Distribution lists. These are a local function in X.400 (84) and standardized in X.400 (88), but optional for an implementation.

- Authentication of users, encryption and electronic signature of messages (Chapter 11).

7

EDI/EDIFACT: Electronic document interchange

7.1 What is EDI/EDIFACT?

EDI (*Electronic Document Interchange*) is the electronic interchange of documents in all possible areas of business. The aim of EDI is to replace the numerous paper documents used in the course of business by electronic forms. Such documents include orders, delivery notes, consignment notes, customs declarations, receipts, invoices and money orders. From ten to a hundred paper documents may be exchanged in the course of a single deal.

Electronic document interchange has considerable advantages over the use of paper documents:

- Faster transmission and thus faster completion of business.

- Procedures may be automated.

- Cost reductions.

- Avoidance of errors in data entry, since paper documents are only entered once in the computer.

However, the use of EDI is not purely advantageous. The main disadvantages include:

- The provision of additional computer hardware and software implies investment costs, which are not unimportant for the smaller and the smallest companies.

- Technical problems in the EDI system may slow business procedures down or bring them to a complete halt.

- The authenticity of electronically transmitted documents is not guaranteed (at least by the EDI systems available today).

In order to ensure the interoperability of EDI systems from different manufacturers, international standardization of the electronic representation of all possible document types is under way. At an early stage such a standardization was initiated by the United Nations Economic Commission for Europe and by ISO and other standardization committees. The current standards and proposed standards are collectively denoted by EDIFACT (*Electronic Document Interchange for Finance, Administration, Commerce and Transport*).

This standardization involves both the format of the information to be transmitted and its coding. In the OSI world, the use of ASN.1 transfer syntax for the coding would be obvious; for historical and practical reasons (use of existing text-oriented transmission media such as telex, teletex, SMTP mail), a text-oriented format is used.

The syntax of EDIFACT messages is described in detail in Section 7.3; the possible content of an EDIFACT message is illustrated in Section 7.4

using the example of an invoice. Section 7.2 describes the use of various transmission services, in particular X.400, to transmit EDIFACT messages.

EDIFACT is a very new application and the standardization work is still in progress. While the work is almost fully completed in the area of message syntax, only a few message-content types have been developed to the extent that they may be used in practice. Section 7.5 gives an overview of the status of standardization and of current work. Section 7.6 describes the current position of the use of EDIFACT. The last section, Section 7.7, contains concluding considerations and a view of the future.

7.2 Relationship to electronic mail

Data transmission services are needed to transfer electronic documents. In principle, any service that is able to transmit the data with sufficiently high reliability is suitable; for example, telex, teletex, X.400 MHS (84 or 88 version), other electronic mail systems, and FTAM or file transfer with manufacturer-specific protocols via modem and switched telephone network.

For larger amounts of data, and when dialup lines are being used, it is no longer sensible to establish a direct connection from the originator of the document to the recipient. In this case we work with an X.400-like architecture (Figure 7.1) where the message switching nodes corresponding to the MTAs are called *Clearing Centres* (CC) and *terminals* correspond to the UAs. Typically, clearing centres are interconnected by dedicated lines; EDIFACT terminals only use the lines to connect to the nearest clearing centre.

When using X.400 or other electronic mail systems, it is unnecessary to install separate clearing centres, since the MTAs of the X.400 system take on their tasks. However, in order to meet the particular requirements that EDIFACT imposes on an electronic mail system (for example, large amounts of data or guaranteed minimum availability), separate clearing centres will still be used for EDIFACT in the future. In addition, clearing centres may also offer gateways between different data transfer services.

As a consequence of the state of standardization and the increasing spread of X.400 message transfer systems, X.400 MTS is expected to be used as the primary data transfer service for EDIFACT messages in the future; like P2/IPMS, a new X.400 message type has been defined for EDIFACT. The structure of this new message type has not yet been fully specified: as we show in Section 7.3, as far as the underlying message transfer system is concerned, EDIFACT messages are simply a sequence of characters. The introduction of new service elements in X.400 (88), and in particular the possibility of sorting and retrieving messages in a message store (see

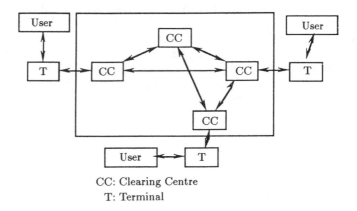

CC: Clearing Centre
T: Terminal

Figure 7.1 Structure of an EDIFACT network.

Chapter 9) according to certain criteria, suggested that EDIFACT messages should also be provided with a heading and that the important fields of the message should be duplicated in the header.

The few EDIFACT implementations available today follow a pragmatic route; under X.400, they generate a P2-formatted content, the body of which contains the EDIFACT message to be transmitted.

7.3 Syntax of EDIFACT messages

The smallest logical unit in an EDIFACT message is the *data element*; this corresponds to a document data field, such as an identification, a number or a price. A distinction is made between character strings and numerical values (including both integers and decimal numbers).

Several closely-related data elements may be combined into data element groups, such as date and time.

Several data elements or data element groups are combined into a *segment*. The first data element of a segment, the *segment identifier*, specifies the type and thus the structure and nature of the information contained in the segment. For example, a NAD segment contains the name and address of a business partner. The role of the partner involved is given in another data field in the segment or may be deduced from the position of the segment within the message.

Sequences of segments that describe the same real-world object are combined into *segment groups*. If more than one object is to be described, the segments of the group appear repeatedly. Nesting of segment groups is also possible.

The segments belonging together to the same document form the *EDIFACT message*. Each message is of a specific *message type* (for example, INVOIC) and for each message type there is a specification for the sequential ordering of the segments and the formation of segment groups on the one hand and for the logical content of the segments on the other. There is a common specification for the first and last segments of all messages. The first segment of every message is of type UNH and contains, amongst other things, the message type. The last segment of a message is of type UNT and contains check information such as the total number of segments in the message.

For efficiency reasons, EDIFACT messages are often bundled into transfer files before they are transmitted. Several messages to the same destination and of the same message type may be combined into a *functional message group* to facilitate efficient handling of the message traffic in the clearing centres. The beginning and the end of a message group are marked with the segments UNG and UNE. However, the message groups are optional.

Several individual messages or message groups are combined into a *transfer file*. The beginning and the end of a transfer file are marked with the segments UNB and UNZ. The UNB segment contains, amongst other things, a statement about the EDIFACT standard used and its version.

Optionally, a UNA segment may be placed before a transfer file to permit the definition of data delimiters other than apostrophe, plus, colon and question mark; however, this redefinition facility is rarely used.

Figure 7.2 shows an overview of the structure of a transfer file.

Thus, EDIFACT messages have a hierarchical structure. Within an OSI application, use of ASN.1 transfer syntax to code this structure during the transfer would obviously be appropriate. However, for historical reasons a purely text-oriented method is used to code messages:

- Data elements within the same data element group are separated from each other by the special character ':'(colon).

- Data elements or data group elements within a segment are separated from each other by the special character '+' (plus sign).

- The end of a segment is marked by the character '' ' (apostrophe).

- If one of the above special characters occurs in a data field it must be prefixed by the reset signal '?' (question mark) so that the special character loses its control function. The same applies to the question mark itself.

This structuring is illustrated in Figure 7.2. Figure 7.4 gives an example of such a message.

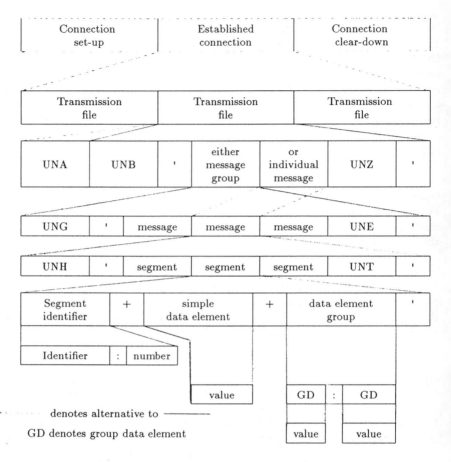

Figure 7.2 Structure of an EDIFACT transfer file.

The following two basic types of character sets are used for EDIFACT messages:

- Level A. Only capital letters, numbers and a selection of special characters from IA5 (T.50); no print control characters. This character set is mainly used for telex transmissions.

- Level B. Complete IA5 character set (T.50) including non-printable characters (these are used as data delimiters). Other character sets (teletex, etc.) may be used by mutual arrangement.

Firma Meier AG
Electronic Components
EinbahnStrasse 101
8021 Zürich

Herrn
Hans Muster
Zehnderweg 559
8021 Zürich

INVOICE Nr. 999123   28th February 1990

Part number	Description	Quantity	Price	Amount
123-1071	Transistor BC 107 A	20	0.50	10.00
137-3553	Transistor 2N 3553	10	6.40	64.00
118-7400	IC TTL 74LS00	50	0.90	45.00
Postage and packing				6.50
Total			SFr.	125.50

Payable within 30 days net to
Giro account number 80-11111-7

Please note: Company holidays from 9th to 20th April 1990.

Figure 7.3   Example of an invoice.

7.4 Content of an EDIFACT message illustrated by the example of an invoice

The content of an EDIFACT message is best illustrated by an example. Figure 7.3 shows an invoice in paper form; Figure 7.4 shows the resulting EDIFACT message. In the interests of clarity, every segment of the example is broken into one or more separate lines; in principle, however, line breaks may occur at arbitrary points (such as in the middle of a data element) or may be omitted completely.

The segments used in the example are described briefly below:

UNA   Segment to define data delimiters. The usual delimiters for character sets of level A are defined.

UNB   Header segment of the transfer file; contains a statement on the standard and which version of it is used (UNOA : 1 for UN/EDIFACT, explained in Section 7.5), EDIFACT system-specific source and destination addresses (126401 and 126981, respectively), date and time at which the file was generated (900228 : 1503 for 28th February 1990, 15.03 hours) and an identification (REF701).

UNH   Message header segment; marks the start of an individual message. Contains the originator's message reference number (INV001), the message type (INVOIC : 1) and a sequence number (1).

BGM   Basic data of the invoice; contains the code for commercial invoice (380), the invoice number (999123) and the date of the invoice (900228 = 28th February 1990).

RFF   Reference entries; contains references to other documents relating to this invoice (PO = order; reference number was 90003) and their dates (004 = date of order; 900103 = 3rd January 1990).

NAD   Name and address of the buyer (BY in the first NAD segment) and the seller (SE in the second NAD segment) together with their reference (126981/126401) and origin numbers (91 = assigned from seller; 92 = assigned to buyer). This is followed by the name, address, town and post code of the partners involved.

```
UNA:+.?'
UNB+UNOA:1+126401+126981+900228:1503+REF701'
UNH+INV001+INVOIC:1++1'
BGM+380+999123+900228'
RFF+90003-T001: P0+004:900103'
NAD+BY+126981:91++HANS MUSTER+ZEHNDERWEG
559+ZUERICH++8021'
NAD+SE+126401:92++FIRMA MEIER AG+EINBAHNSTR
101+ZUERICH++8021'
UNS+D'
LIN++123-1071+20:21:PC+0.5:CA:1+20+10'
LIN++137-3553+10:21:PC+6.4:CA:1+10+64'
LIN++118-7400+50:21:PC+0.9:CA:1+50+45'
LIN++999-9901++++6.5'
UNS+S'
TMA+125.5'
UNT+13+INV001'
UNZ+1+REF701
```

Figure 7.4   Example invoice in EDIFACT format.

UNS+D This marks the start of the listing of the individual items of the invoice.

LIN Invoice item; every item corresponds to one or more segments. Contains the article number (123–1071), the quantity ordered (20 : 21 = statement that this is a quantity ordered; PC = unit of measurement is a number of items), price per price-unit and size of the price-unit (0.5; CA = according to catalogue; 1 = size of the price unit), number of price units (20) and price of the whole item (10; zeros after the decimal point are suppressed).

UNS+S Marks the end of the list of the individual items of the invoice.

TMA This gives the total value (125.5) of the invoice.

UNT Message end segment; contains the message identification (INV001) and the number of segments (13).

UNZ End segment of the transfer file; contains the same file name (REF701) as the corresponding UNB segment.

In this example, the EDIFACT message contains the absolute minimum of information. The definition of the invoice message is universally framed so that all statements that appear in invoices (for example, the bank account of the originator of the invoice, the terms for payment, or product descriptions associated with order numbers) may also be incorporated in the electronic form. Even the notice about company holidays, given in the example, is electronically codable as a general notice.

7.5 State of standardization: current work

Relevant standards

Currently, various international, national and industry-specific standards and standard series exist for EDIFACT. The most important series of standards, which is increasingly beginning to replace the others, is UN/EDIFACT, which was jointly developed by the United Nations (UN) and the International Standardization Organization (ISO). UN/EDIFACT systems are in the main specified by the following four standards:

- *UN/EDIFACT syntax rules*, technically in agreement with ISO 9735. This specifies the syntax rules which we described in detail in Section 7.3. The standardization process for this document is complete.

- *UN Trade Data Element Directory* (TDED), technically in agreement with the draft standard ISO DIS 7372. For all data elements that may occur in a message, this specifies their format, their exact meaning, the format of data group elements and code lists to be used in each case. Work on existing data fields is largely complete; new data elements are constantly being added with the incorporation of new business branches in UN/EDIFACT.

- *UN Electronic Document Segment Directory* (EDSD); specifies the possible types of segments and their structure. Segments are defined in such a way that they may be used as universally as possible. This document is still being worked on; the definitions of most of the segment types are stable.

- *UN Electronic Document Message Directory* (EDMD); specifies the possible message types and their construction from segments. Only *invoice* and *purchase order* message types have been released as (stable) standards; other types will follow in the next two years. This is discussed in detail in the following paragraphs.

The standardization process

At international level, the standardization of UN/EDIFACT is driven forward by WP4 (*Working Party 4 on Facilitation of International Trade Procedures*) of the United Nations *Economic Commission for Europe* (UN/ECE) together with the *International Standardization Organization* (ISO). The responsibility for the standardization of new message types rests within WP4 with the *Group of Experts 1* (GE1) '*Data Elements and Automatic Data Interchange*'. Most Western European countries are represented within this group by the *EDIFACT BOARD*; Eastern Europe and North America are also represented by international organizations.

Within the EDIFACT BOARD, new message types are being developed in the *Message Development Groups* (MD). Currently the following MDs are active:

MD1 Trade

MD2 Transport

MD3 Customs

MD4 Finance (formerly MD4B)

MD5 Construction

MD6 Statistics

MD7 Insurance (formerly MD4A)

MD8 Travel, tourism, leisure

MD9 Health, pharmacy (proposed)

The same division is also found in the national EDIFACT syndicates formed by all interested partners (software manufacturers, network operators, users).

Standard message types

As previously mentioned, standardization work for the various message types is by no means complete; only the *invoice* and *purchase order* message types have been released as standards. Table 7.1 gives an overview of the status of the development of the various messages types (status at October 1990).

Table 7.1   UN/EDIFACT message types.

Message type	Description	Status
INVOIC	Commercial invoice	2
ORDERS	Purchase order	2
CONTRL	Control message	1
CREADV	Credit advice	1
CREEXT	Extended credit advice	1
CUSDEC	Customs declaration	1
CUSRES	Customs report	1
DEBADV	Debit advice	1
IFT...	International forwarding and transport message framework (7 messages)	1
PAYEXT	Extended payment order	1
PAYORD	Payment order	1
QALITY	Quality data	1
REMADV	Remittance advice	1

Explanation of status codes:

2   UNSM standard.

1   Draft accepted by UN/ECE WP4 for formal trial.

0   Draft document released by MD.

In addition to the message types listed in Table 7.1, there are 19 messages having status 0 and 37 candidate messages (under development by MD, but no draft released).

7.6 Use of EDI today

In parallel with the UN/EDIFACT standardization work, projects have been started in various countries of the world to introduce EDIFACT at a national level. Particularly noteworthy in this respect are England and the USA, where the standards UNTDI and ANSI X12 are stable and the infrastructure needed to use these standards (message transport networks, systems for clearing centres and terminals) has been created. In both these countries, the number of companies making practical use of EDI is correspondingly high. However, in other European countries such as Belgium (ICOM), Germany (SEDASS), Finland (CCC), France (ALLEGRO), the Netherlands (TRANSCOM) and Austria (ECODEX), national EDIFACT systems are already in use. Most of these systems, like the English system TRADACOM, rely on network components from specific manufacturers and are therefore not 'open' systems.

In addition, numerous companies with an industry-specific reliance on EDI have jointly decided to realize such systems. Here we mention ODETTE (automobile industry; since 1988 based on UN/EDIFACT syntax and TDED), CEFIC (chemical industry), EDIFICE (computer industry), RINET (reinsurance societies), COST 306 (transport industry) and DOCIMEL (European national railways; in development). CEFIC and COST 306 were experimental systems which have been replaced by various other networks for productive operation.

In addition, numerous firms are now already using EDI, both internally and in conjunction with their most important partners; often company- and manufacturer-specific solutions are in use on these systems.

7.7 Outlook

At the beginning of this chapter, we listed the advantages that could accrue from the use of EDI. Industry interest is correspondingly high. In Europe alone, in mid 1989 approximately 2000 firms were connected to the various national EDIFACT systems and by mid 1990 that may rise to 3000. International connectivity is possible as industry-specific and national systems are adapted to UN/EDIFACT, and the attraction of EDIFACT again increases. Thus, over the forthcoming years, EDIFACT will become a supporting pillar of the modern economy; at the same time EDIFACT will become an increasingly important application of X.400 systems.

PART III

New approaches

8

A critical assessment

8.1   Shortcomings of X.400 (84)

8.2   Problems of application and practice

We begin Part III by summarizing the problems exposed explicitly or implicitly in the two preceding parts. The reader will have noticed that there is a gap between theory and standardization, as described mainly in Part I, and practical experience as described in Part II. In fact, many aspects of the practical use of message transfer systems cannot be logically deduced from the theory; this is actually to be expected, since the practician is often confronted with an initial situation that is not adequately covered by the standards documents. In general, it must be said that the discrepancy between standardization and day-to-day data communication is not a temporary phenomenon. The coexistence of systems conforming to OSI and systems based on *de facto* standards or manufacturer-specific systems (including gateways), together with a continuous 'migration to OSI' will always be necessary. The reason for this lies in the observation that research and development are prerequisites for the generation of technically advanced standards. It follows that there will always be products or prototypes available that are technically superior to the standards and which (particularly in the academic world) are quickly accepted and used. There are many examples of such phenomena; here we mention just two typical and very different examples:

- The current international standard for the technology of local area networks with bus topology and CSMA/CD access method (ISO 8802/3) is based on research work carried out by Xerox at the end of the seventies. Standardization was not based on this work, but on a *de facto* standard for *Ethernet* postulated by a consortium of manufacturers (Digital Equipment Corporation, Intel and Xerox). Before the release of the ISO standard, which differed in certain details from the Ethernet specification, there were already dozens of products and thousands of installations operating in accordance with the latter. Thus, the problems of coexistence and migration described above still exist today.

- ISO standard 8571 (File Transfer, Access and Management, FTAM) was released in 1988 (see also Chapter 1). FTAM, which could certainly form the basis for a development of standardized file servers, has met strong competition from Sun Microsystems' *Network File System (NFS)*.

   Since the introduction of Sun workstations and the (deliberate) disclosure of its architecture and protocols, the distribution of NFS has increased dramatically; there are now implementations for products from many other manufacturers. It is uncertain whether FTAM can take over the role of NFS. It is also conceivable that, like Ethernet as far as international standardization is concerned, NFS will receive an ISO stamp of approval.

One might object to a standard being developed without there being a model in the form of a successful product. This would imply increasing *prospective standardization*, in that, new technologies, of which in certain circumstances there was little or no practical experience, would be standardized. This is clearly the opposite of *retrospective standardization*, as was the case with Ethernet versus 8802/3. Prospective standardization is advantageous in the case of complicated systems which can only be implemented by industry at great expense, when at the same time no equivalent competing technology dominates the field and thus where there is a good chance that the standard and systems conforming to it will be widely accepted by industry and by users. This type of standardization implies a periodic revision of the standards documents as a result of experience with conforming implementations. In the nature of things, the first revision will involve large changes and a stable state will be attained asymptotically with subsequent revisions.

X.400 is a classical case of prospective standardization. As previously mentioned, electronic mail is not new. Technically, X.400 goes beyond this, in that electronic mail is viewed as one of many applications of message transfer services. The only increasingly serious competitor, the *Simple Mail Transfer Protocol* (SMTP), developed in the context of ARPANET (Postel, 1982), has until now been used almost exclusively in the research environment and has conceptual shortcomings (for example, the purely text-based message-exchange format). In addition, it lacks the very sensible division into a message transfer service and an electronic mail service. The many existing manufacturer- and service-specific systems have not prevented X.400 from achieving acceptance; on the contrary, they themselves have generated a major requirement for a uniform approach to asynchronous data exchange.

Even in the Introduction, we prepared the reader for the fact that there are two conceptually different versions of X.400, namely the first release X.400 (84) and the revised version X.400 (88). In this chapter, we have shown that the reason for the existence of two different versions of X.400 lies in the 'nature' of X.400 as a prospective standard. In the remainder of this chapter, we comment briefly on the shortcomings of X.400 (84) and raise some earlier application- and practice-related problems. Most of these problems are discussed in Part III of the book.

8.1 Shortcomings of X.400 (84)

Shortly after its release, X.400 (84) was criticized on the grounds that while it provides support for the delivery of messages to different destinations, *it does not actually lay down a concept for group communication*. Aids to group communication support those forms of communication in which a group of participants discusses a common theme. Naturally, individual participants may leave the group and new participants arrive during a discussion. Many existing systems, including *bulletin-board systems* and systems such as EuroKOM and USENET, support group communication. Distribution lists (which we discuss in detail in Part III) are a very simple, but functionally restricted aid.

For broad commercial use of X.400 systems, in particular for communication between organizations, *security services* are indispensable. Technically, in this area, X.400 (84) has nothing to offer, except for the remark 'for further study' which appears as a comment at the point where a body part is described as being of 'encrypted' type. Here, security does not only mean security against unauthorized reading or modification of communications. It incorporates an overall notion of the security of all everyday sequences of events in a modern office environment (including the ability to sign communications, the ability to prove that a communication has been sent or received, etc.). Chapter 11 describes the X.400 (88) concept of security in detail.

Stand-alone user agents are supported in X.400 (84) by the submission and delivery protocol (P3). Neither P3 nor the functions of the MTA provide for the archiving of messages or the interrogation of message archives. This means that the user of a stand-alone UA must use local message archives, which is acceptable so long as he is working with the same physical UA (for example, his stand-alone workstation). As soon as the user processes messages on other computers he will be confronted with the problem that the messages are archived on different systems and thus are not available where they are required.

Another problem with the X.400 (84) approach is associated with the fact that the memory capability of the MTS is (rightly) considered to be limited. This is problematic for users of personal computers that function as stand-alone UAs, since a message that cannot immediately be delivered is in principle deemed to be undeliverable; if the UA is not continuously switched on, this may lead to error messages (non-delivery reports). An optional service element, known as 'hold for delivery', may (if available) be used by the UA to arrange for limited temporary storage in the MTA. To overcome this problem, additional storage for messages would have to be provided; while extended storage in the MTS would be possible, it would not necessarily be advantageous, since MTAs are specialized devices for message forwarding. The X.400 (88) *Message Store* (MS) is used to archive messages and communications; it is an elegant solution to both the problems discussed above.

In Chapter 4, we discussed the use of X.400 to implement an electronic mail service in an academic environment. A large part of the work involved the development of a *naming scheme* to permit the unambiguous naming of subscribers, and the mapping of this onto the existing X.400 *address structure* (O/R names). The alert reader will have noticed that great trouble was taken in an attempt to satisfy the different requirements of a user-friendly naming scheme and an addressing scheme (where the latter involves O/R names). In the end, this problem may be traced back to the overall lack of directories. Solutions to both problems are discussed in detail in Part III.

Chapters 3 and 4 were devoted to the problem of the interconnection of X.400 systems with existing systems providing similar services using different technology. The need for gateways to other systems also exists elsewhere other than in the academic world; in fact, gateways to traditional or new telematic services such as telex, teletex, telefax, etc. are almost a must in a modern company. Chapter 9 shows that this problem is now being taken into account, even conceptually.

At first sight, the fact that X.400 (84) is no longer in harmony with the OSI standardization in the layers 6 and 7 is only theoretically a problem. A solution is required, since future OSI products, which up to and including layer 7 implement a basis for application-independent communications, should also be usable with X.400. X.400 (88) therefore has a new structure which conforms to the OSI application layer standards. However, we stress that this change, together with the modifications to the protocols (particularly P1) implied by the previous paragraphs, raises a new interworking problem (between X.400 (84) and X.400 (88)) which must be solved. This is discussed in Chapter 10.

8.2 Problems of application and practice

Next, we list some of the problems arising from the discussion in Parts I and II:

- It was mentioned that user interfaces to X.400 systems are not standardized. When we consider the fact that public X.400 services which are accessed by traditional means (telephone, public data networks) or by ISDN could become widespread, there arises the obvious question as to the desirability of a *generally binding standardization of user interfaces* to X.400 services.

  One particular type of user interface is the format of the representation of O/R names on visiting cards and letterheads. Since, in the medium term (until the widespread introduction of directory services) this rather informal channel is the most important way of exchanging addresses, specification of this format is of some importance. Without going into further details, we refer to the publication by Grimm (Grimm and Heagerty, 1989), which contains a practical proposal accepted by the academic world.

- Since it is anticipated that one day many applications will be based on a message transfer service, the question arises as to the portability of programs that implement such applications. A standardized logical programmer interface to the MTS and/or to the IPMS with facilities for various current programming languages (PASCAL, COBOL, FORTRAN, C, C++, etc.) would be an appropriate means of providing better protection for large investments in application software. In fact, in Spring 1989, an initiative to standardize an 'Application Program Interface (API) for X.400' was launched by a group of software developers and computer manufacturers.

- Communications protocols may be inexactly or incompletely defined by international standards or protocols – the development of implementations conforming to standards is always a very difficult and error-prone activity. This applies in particular to complicated application-layer standards and implementations of them. Thus, a method is needed to define the term 'conformance to standards' and techniques are required to test implementations for 'conformance to standards'. We discuss this problem in Chapter 13.

- The tasks of an operator of a message transfer system (an ADMD or a PRMD) are only outlined in part in the standards. For example, solutions must be found for the registration of ADMDs, PRMDs and subscribers, and thus also for the allocation of names and addresses. Likewise, plans and facilities are required for monitoring the distributed system for the purposes of error detection, collection of traffic data for performance evaluation, long-term planning (statistics on traffic volumes), etc. In addition, routing tables, which contain entries about the forwarding of messages within and outside a management domain, must be maintained. This immediately leads to questions as to the number of staff needed to manage a system and as to which of their activities may be automated. Since there are no standards in this latter area, new problems may result in an inhomogeneous environment (use of X.400 systems from different manufacturers in the same PRMD or ADMD), for example, because traffic recordings are partially incomplete or in different formats.

- X.400-based MHSs operate according to the store-and-forward principle, whereby incoming messages are temporarily stored in the MTA or forwarded to a UA or to another MTA. Based on the O/R addresses in the message and on locally held *routing information* an MTA determines the MTA to which a given message is to be forwarded. This mechanism is comparable with the routing mechanism used in packet-switched networks, except that in the case of MHSs, the routing is based on messages and not on packets. Thus, the question arises as to whether dynamic routing should also be used, where applicable, as in the case of packet-switched networks (in other words, whether the routing information should be automatically adapted to the current state of the system). This would facilitate optimization, in that, for example, overloaded MTAs could be avoided by selecting a different route or a cost function could be used to determine an optimal route.

We note, however, that the background to the use of the store-and-forward principle in the application layer differs from that in the case of packet-switched networks. We may assume that data exchange between MTAs is not carried out over dedicated lines, but that the end-to-end network service (connectionless-mode or connection-oriented) is used over layers 6, 5 and 4. Thus, there are two major reasons against dynamic routing:

— Direct associations between the MTAs are technically possible; interim storage in more than two MTAs is not imposed by a predetermined network topology (the physically available lines), as is often the case in packet-switched networks. It may often be traced back to other causes (for example, the WEP concept – see Chapter 3) and thus dynamic routing is not sensible.

— A uniform distribution of the load across the available resources is already provided for by the appropriate network-layer mechanisms. The same also applies to the transmission-bandwidth resources, but not to the processing capacity of an MTA.

These arguments should not hide the fact that capacity bottlenecks and thus blockages do in fact occur. However, these are not so much the result of normal variations of the traffic volume as of structural problems (for example, a chronically overloaded WEP) or breakdown of system components (hardware or software). In the first case, only a longer-term resolution of the structure will help; in the latter case, automatic detection and temporary rectification of the problem (with an alarm to the system administrator) would actually be desirable. The reaction times for the treatment of problems are of the order of minutes, unlike in packet-switched networks where intervention must take place within tenths of seconds. We deduce that the automation of routing in MHSs will be an important task of future *network management systems*.

Based on the knowledge that MTAs may also, in principle, have direct associations, another solution offers itself. This is based on the principle that an MTA accepts a message from an originator UA and passes it directly to that MTA which will deliver it to the destination UA. This solution is not practical with static routing, since the routing tables required are too large and would be difficult to manage. It may however be automated with the help of a directory service (see Chapter 12). For this, for each recipient of messages, the directory must contain a statement specifying the MTA to which messages for this recipient should be delivered. This information may be used to enable the originator UA to transfer a message directly to the destination UA. Currently this solution is not yet usable:

— There is no convention for the information to be stored in the directory.

— It is to be expected that, for this solution, interrogation of the directory service would be necessary for a large fraction of all messages. The directory service would have to be equipped to meet this requirement and be able to respond to queries in a short time. In addition, the directory should support the mutual authentication of MTAs either using passwords (simple authentication) or by certification (strong authentication).

— At present, the initial configuration of MTAs, which enables them to establish associations between each other, is a rather complicated and fault-prone procedure. It is normally carried out by highly-qualified specialist staff. Automation of this would at the same time imply substantial simplification.

The solution described above could be attractive, particularly for large PRMDs for which the problems are easier to rectify than in an international context.

A model of this solution exists. The *Simple Mail Transfer Protocol* (SMTP) used in the US (and recently worldwide) Internet, supported by the Internet *Domain Name System* (DNS) may be used as described above.

9

Introduction to X.400 (88)

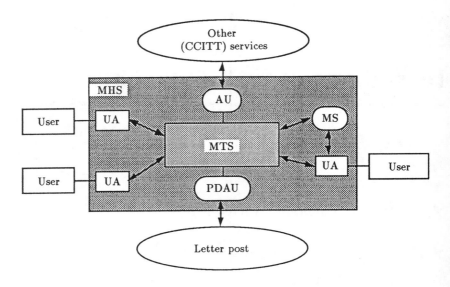

Figure 9.1   Functional model of MHS (88).

9.1 The functional model

The functional model of X.400 (88) is essentially very similar to that of the 1984 recommendations. However, its description and, in general, the specification of X.400 has become more formalized, although a strict and verifiable formal description has not been chosen. The MHS is represented as an *object* which contains other objects (for example, the MTS and UAs) (Figure 9.1). The MTS offers the other objects of the MHS *abstract services* for message *submission*, *delivery* and *administration*. From the point of view of the MTS, all other objects of the MHS are *consumers* that make use of a service. Consequently, the MTS has the role of a *supplier*. The service it supplies is specified in an abstract form in the recommendations.

The *Access Unit* (AU), and, as a special case of this, the *Physical Delivery Access Unit*, (PDAU) are new objects in the MHS. They represent gateways to other telematic services (telex, teletex) and to letter post; it is also conceivable that AUs may be used as gateways to non-X.400 systems (academic research networks such as the American *Internet* or manufacturer-specific systems). A gateway to letter post is, however, for the moment, only provided for in one direction, namely from the MTS to letter post.

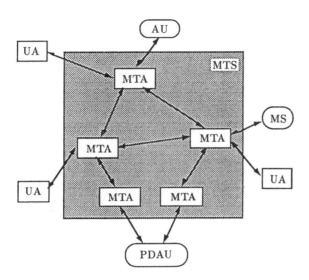

Figure 9.2   Functional model of the MTS.

The object *Message Store* (MS) is also new; we discuss the motivation for this in Section 9.3.

In turn, the MTS also contains objects, namely the MTAs (Figure 9.2). MTA objects offer one another the abstract *transfer* service, which provides for reliable message transfer.

The interpersonal messaging service is described in the same way as the services of the MTS and MS, as an abstract service which is offered by the *Interpersonal Messaging System* (IPMS).

9.2 Alignment with application layer standardization

As noted in Chapter 2, the previous subdivision of the application layer into two sublayers (UAL, MTL) contradicts the current standardization of the structure of the application layer. Moreover, in 1984 the properties of the presentation layer and the CASEs, and in particular RTSE and ACSE, were not yet defined. Thus, X.400 (84) also included aspects of the presentation layer. In fact, in 1984, a forerunner of the ASN.1 description language and

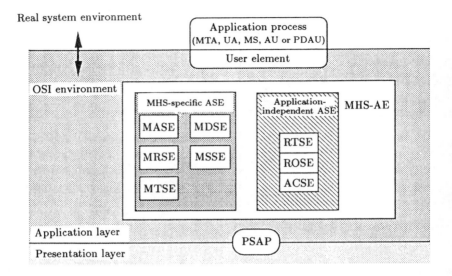

Figure 9.3   Structure of the application layer for an MHS according to X.400 (88).

the corresponding encoding rules were standardized with the X.400 series of recommendations as X.409 (84). In the 1988 release of the CCITT recommendations, ASN.1 has rightly found a place in the X.200 (88) series (X.208 and X.209) and has thus become independent of X.400 (88). ASN.1 and X.208 are used generally in X.400 (88) to describe ASEs.

Thus, in X.400 (88) a great deal of effort has been taken to align the new recommendations with the current OSI standards. The services of the MTS and the corresponding protocol building blocks are newly and rigorously described in the form of application service elements (ASEs).

Figure 9.3 shows the structure of the application layer, as it is used for an application entity in X.400. In addition to the application-independent ASEs (ACSE, ROSE and RTSE), five MHS-specific ASEs are defined. A specific application context is defined by a choice of the available ASEs (see below). The MSE-specific ASEs consist of the following functions:

Message Administration Service Element (MASE)

Permits the registration of consumers (UA, MS, AU) with a supplier (MTA, MS) and the exchange of data for authentication.

Message Delivery Service Element (MDSE)

Contains operations for the delivery of messages and reports and for control of the delivery process.

Message Retrieval Service Element (MRSE)

Permits access to the message store through operations such as *summarize, list, fetch, delete, register* and *alert*. The latter is used by the MS to signal the arrival of a new message.

Message Submission Service Element (MSSE)

Contains operations for the submission of messages and reports and for control of the submission process.

Message Transfer Service Element (MTSE)

Contains operations to establish associations and to transmit messages, probe messages and reports between MTAs.

The objects UA, MS, AU, PDAU and MTA in the functional model of X.400 (88) represent application processes in the sense of the OSI model. The communications aspects of these are modelled by application entities; thus, protocols which realize the services offered by the entities must be defined between the application entities. The following protocols are defined in X.419:

- The *MS access protocol (P7)* for access of a UA to the MS. The UA is in all cases the initiator of an association with the MS and so the MS cannot actively initiate a connection with the UA.
- The *MTS access protocol (P3)* for access of an MS or a UA to the MTS. MSs and UAs are always consumers (thus, P3 is an *access* protocol); both the MTS and an MS or a UA may initiate an association.
- The *MTS transfer protocol (P1)* controls communication between MTAs. The association between two MTAs is symmetric.

Figure 9.4 illustrates the possible applications of the different protocols. It is assumed here that the objects involved are implemented in different physical computer systems.

In line with the principles introduced in Chapter 1, the protocols P1, P3 and P7 are described in terms of application contexts, which themselves involve an appropriate selection of ASEs. Effectively, several application contexts are possible for each protocol. Use is made of the

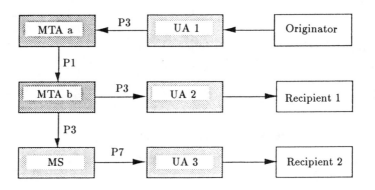

Figure 9.4   Use of protocols in X.400 (88).

X.400-specific ASEs (MASE, MDSE, MRSE, MSSE, MTSE) introduced above and the application-independent (supporting) ASEs (ACSE, RTSE and ROSE) discussed in Chapter 1. Table 9.1 gives an overview of the various application contexts and the associated ASEs.

Application contexts designated by 'forced' are used if the MTS may occur as initiator, in other words when it is able to 'force' the delivery of a message to the consumer (UA, MS or AU). The designation 'reliable' implies that reliable message transmission is guaranteed using the RTSE.

The protocol P7 is not contained in X.400 (84). The protocol P3 provided in X.400 (84) was not implemented (or at least not widely implemented) because of its limited applicability. Thus, when the application contexts for these two protocols were defined, little or no consideration had to be given to earlier standards or even to existing implementations. In this respect, the picture for P1 is somewhat different; as can be seen from Appendix D, there are a number of implementations of P1 and thus also of the kernel of X.400 (84). This means that at least one application context for P1 must take account of the past, since compatibility with 'old' MTAs is guaranteed. Table 9.2 shows the possible application contexts for P1.

The AC 'mts-transfer-protocol-1984' uses the protocols specified in X.400 (84) (P1 according to X.411 (84), using the RTS protocol according to X.410 (84)). It follows that implementations according to X.400 (88) must support this AC if they are to interoperate with older implementations.

Table 9.1 Overview of the application contexts for P3 and P7 and the ASEs used.

Application context (AC)	X.400-specific ASEs				Supporting ASEs		
	MSSE	MDSE	MRSE	MASE	ROSE	RTSE	ACSE
ACs for P3:							
mts-access	C	C	-	C	x	-	x
mts-forced access	S	S	-	S	x	-	x
mts-reliable access	C	C	-	C	x	x	x
mts-forced-reliable-access	S	S	-	S	x	x	x
ACs for P7:							
mts-access	C	-	C	C	x	-	x
mts-reliable access	C	-	C	C	x	x	x

Key x: ASE used   C: Consumer appears as initiator
      -: ASE not used   S: Supplier appears as initiator

The AC 'mts-transfer-protocol' uses the same protocol architecture as 'mts-transfer-protocol-1984', but supports additional functions which were newly added with X.400 (88). This is shown by the fact that both the MTSE according to X.400 (88) and special versions of RTSE and ACSE compatible with X.400 (84) are used.

Table 9.2 Application contexts for P1.

Application context	X.400-specific ASEs MTSE	Supporting ASEs	
		RTSE	ACSE
mts-transfer-protocol 1984	1984 subset	-	-
mts-transfer-protocol	x	X.410-1984	X.410-1984
mts-transfer	x	x	x

Finally the AC 'mts-transfer' represents the 'new' protocol P1 itself. The above discussion is clearly relevant to the question of the interworking of X.400 (84) and (88) implementations. We shall discuss this question in detail in Chapter 10.

9.3 The message store

At the beginning of this part of the book we identified two basic problems associated with the operation of stand-alone UAs and the corresponding standardization in X.400 (84). X.400 (88) introduces a new object outside of the MTS, the *Message Store* (MS) which helps resolve the problem of archiving and that of timely delivery of messages.

The MS in X.400 (88) represents a message archive. Access to the MS is via a new protocol, the *Message Store Access Protocol* (MSAP, P7). Its main function is to support operations that interrogate the message archive. In addition, P7 may be used to submit messages, so a stand-alone UA can manage with this protocol. The previous P3 is still present and is used to transfer messages between the new MS and the MTAs. It is sensible to implement a message store in such a way that it provides high availability; as a rule, it will provide a 24-hour service and be able to accept and archive incoming messages on its own.

As provided for in X.400 (84), P3 may also be used to connect a stand-alone UA (without MS).

Naturally, an MS may also be implemented in the same physical system as an MTA, so that the use of P3 between MTAs and MSs is restricted to the case of a stand-alone MS.

Figure 9.4 illustrates the use of the various possible protocols between the different objects.

The data model of the MS assumes that a set of *entries* is stored in an MS. Entries consist of a set of attributes which consist of an attribute type and an attribute value. A first class of attributes relates to data structures that occur in a message envelope (for example, the originator and the recipient of the message). The second class of attributes is content-specific, in that the attributes involved are derived from the data structures that occur in the contents of a message. If it is a message carrying an IPMS communication (in other words, an IM-UAPDU), the subject of the communication or its importance, could, for example, be stored as an attribute in the MS. In search and read operations, interrogation (based on attribute-type and attribute-value pairs) may be used to find the desired messages or communications and retrieve them from the MS.

IM-UAPDUs represent a particular problem because they may contain forwarded communications (**MessageBodyPart**, previously called **ForwardedIPMessage**). On the one hand, the relation expressed in the

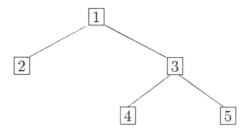

Figure 9.5   Hypothetical structure of nested forwarded communications.

nesting must be conserved, while on the other hand, it should be possible to search in fields of the IPMS heading of a forwarded communication. The tree structure of nested communications is represented in the MS by an entry for each communication (even when it is a forwarded communication) and the use of special attributes in the tree as pointers to a *parent* or a *child*. Figures 9.5 and 9.6 illustrate this solution.

Figure 9.5 shows a communication 1, which contains communications 2 and 3 as forwarded communications; in turn, communication 3 contains communications 4 and 5.

Figure 9.6 illustrates how this tree structure is represented in the MS by several entries. This representation enables a user or a process to navigate through the tree of forwarded messages in order to find the desired information.

9.4 Distribution lists

As a new option, X.440 (88) provides a form of group communication based on *Distribution Lists* (DL). Distribution lists are well-defined lists of subscribers (the *members* of the list). Messages sent to a distribution list are passed to all members. The procedure by which messages are passed to the members is called *expansion.*

Distribution lists allow authorized subscribers to reach all group members of a given distribution list using a single address. There immediately arises the question of the rules governing the use of distribution lists.

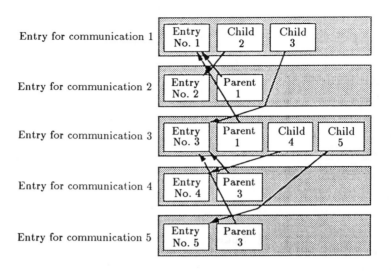

Entry for communication 1

Entry for communication 2

Entry for communication 3

Entry for communication 4

Entry for communication 5

Figure 9.6 Representation of the tree structure of Figure 9.5 using special attributes in entries.

Since it is often not desirable for every subscriber to be able to send a message via a distribution list, there is a facility to define for each distribution list a set of subscribers that have the right to distribute messages via the list. This may be used to restrict the use of distribution lists to a *closed user group* and may protect against bulk transmissions, which might possibly be made by the advertising industry when it discovers the new medium.

The *owner* of the distribution list is a special user. He has the right to manage the list (thus, to add and delete members). The OSI directory (X.500, see Chapter 12) may be used to implement the storage and management of distribution lists.

A distribution list may be a member of another nested distribution list. This enables the generation of hierarchical forms of organization; for example, the distribution of information in a company may be organized in such a way that each department has a distribution list with an appropriate name and all the members of the department as its members. Messages to all departments, and thus to all the staff of the company may then be distributed via a single distribution list containing the distribution lists of all the departments as members. Clearly, this approach also has the disadvantage that it imposes a strong hierarchical organization which sometimes fits badly with the existing structures.

Since a distribution list may appear more than once in a nested structure, messages may be *duplicated* (a message transmitted once may be received several times by one or more recipients). A UA or the MS may (optionally) recognize duplicates (using the unique message identification) and remove them.

Nested distribution lists involve the risk of recursion and thus of infinite loops, in that messages which are sent via one or more distribution lists may be re-sent to a distribution list by which they have already been expanded. Technical measures in the protocol between MTAs (in the protocol P1) permit the detection and *control* of loops, see also Chapter 10. These mechanisms are also useful if loops arise as a result of faulty entries in routing tables.

The address of a distribution list is an O/R address in which the value of the attribute 'common name' may be freely chosen. Since this attribute may also be used for other purposes, a distribution list cannot be recognized *a priori* by its name. However, the originator may use the service element 'DL Expansion Prohibited' to instruct the system not to distribute a given message via distribution lists.

The address of a distribution list also defines the place and thus the MTA where the expansion takes place (*DL expansion point*). Note that, in principle, expansion at the location of the originator would also be conceivable; however, this would require evaluation of the information about all possible nested distribution lists when a message was sent.

The expansion of a distribution list by an MTA requires the latter to check whether the originator has the necessary authorization; then all the members of the distribution list are copied onto the list of message recipients and the message is forwarded (multiply, as required) to the recipients. Naturally, the recipients are able to recognize that a message has reached them via one or more distribution lists.

9.5 Security

Also new in the 1988 version is a model for secure message transfer. This consists of a set of *security services* and a construction kit of *security elements* which may be used to implement the security services. The importance of this extension, as far as the successful use of X.400 in commercial areas is concerned, cannot be over-stressed. We discuss this in detail in Chapter 11.

9.6 Name and address scheme

The development of an OSI standard for directory services, simultaneously with some of the changes described above, led to a revision of the X.400 name and address scheme. It is generally recognized that user-friendly message handling systems may only be realized by providing global directories, in which the addresses of subscribers are stored. Thus, the revised recommendation specifies how an MHS should be used by a directory service and what information should be stored in it for MHS applications. Since it will be some time before directories are broadly introduced, the use of this service is optional and local directories may take on the role of the distributed OSI directory.

It was recognized that the O/R names of the 1984 version are actually O/R addresses and a new scheme for O/R names was introduced. O/R names in the new version consist of a *directory name*, or an *O/R address*, or both. If the O/R address is contained in the O/R name, the MHS will use it to address the subscriber. If only the directory name is present, the directory service will first be interrogated to determine the corresponding O/R address. If both components are included, the message will be sent using the O/R address; if it comes to light that the O/R address is invalid, the directory service will be consulted in a second step to (hopefully) find a correct O/R address.

The new O/R addresses may have one of four forms: *mnemonic, numeric* or *mail* form, or *terminal identification*. A mnemonic address identifies the subscriber according to his position in a professional work environment (within the organization to which he belongs). Numeric addresses use a number to denote a UA within an MD, while mail addresses largely correspond to the addresses now used for letter and parcel post. Terminal identification consists (amongst other things) of a network address of one of the conventional telematic services (X.121 address or telex number).

Table 9.3 lists the attribute types which occur in O/R addresses and advises about their use in the various address forms.

The new attribute type 'common name' is used to denote distribution lists and roles in an organization (for example, director, head of purchasing).

A considerable number of new attribute types is needed to address messages to letter post subscribers (via PDAUs).

The new standard also gives guidelines relating to possible hierarchies within the attribute types.

9.7 Extension of protocols

A new mechanism has been defined to extend the functionality of the protocols. This mechanism is based on the fact that the specification of the data formats at various places (for example, in a message envelope, in O/R addresses and in the heading of an IPMS communication) allows for additional fields in which protocol extensions could be implemented. The mechanism used in principle permits arbitrary extensions, whereby each

Table 9.3 Forms of X.400 addresses in X.400 (88).

Attribute type	mnemonic	numeric	mail formatted	mail unformatted	terminal
General attributes					
Administration domain name	M	M	M	M	C
Common name	C				
Country name	M	M	M	M	C
Network address					M
Numeric user identifier		M			
Organization name	C				
Organizational unit name	C				
Personal name	C				
Private domain name	C	C	C	C	C
Terminal identifier					C
Terminal type					C
Attributes determining the mail route					
Physical delivery service name			C	C	
Physical delivery country name			M	M	
Postal code			M	M	
Attributes for mail addressing					
Extension postal O/R address components			C		
Extension physical delivery address components			C		
Local postal attributes			C		

Table **9.3**   (cont.)

Attribute type	Forms of O/R addresses				
	mnemonic	numeric	mail formatted	mail unformatted	terminal
Physical delivery office name			C		
Physical delivery office number			C		
Physical delivery organization name			C		
Physical delivery personal name			C		
Post office box address			C		
Poste restante address			C		
Street address			C		
Unformatted mail address				M	
Unique mail name			C		
Domain-specific attributes					
Domain-defined (one or more)	C	C			C

Key   M: mandatory
      C: conditional
      empty: not applicable

protocol extension may consist of an arbitrary type and a value of this type. By way of example, we consider the specification for extension fields in a message envelope, which has the following (somewhat simplified) form:

```
ExtensionsField ::= SEQUENCE {
      type [0] EXTENSION
      criticality [1] Criticality
      value [2] ANY DEFINED BY type }

criticality ::= BITSTRING {
      for-submission (0),
      for-transfer (1),
      for-delivery (2) }
```

   type defines the type of the extension (the **EXTENSION** macro, not listed here, prescribes how this type should be specified, see also Section 1.4

on macros) and `value` contains the corresponding value. Since the presence or absence of an extension may enable or prevent certain operations, the entry `criticality` is used to indicate the criticality or non-criticality of the corresponding extension for the operations of message submission, transfer or delivery. If an extension is denoted as being critical for an operation, the operation should not be executed if the extension is missing. An example of this problem is given in Chapter 11.

Clearly, the use of extensions requires good coordination if problems associated with the interworking of different variants of the same protocol are to be avoided. Thus, in many cases, including also for extensions of the envelope, only standard extensions are permitted. Since, moreover, the main purpose of the extension facility is that later changes to the standard should be easy to specify and have locally-restricted effects, future extensions will be standardized in the form of appendices to X.400. This implies that extensions are not thought of as loopholes for private and bilateral modifications of X.400.

One extension already standardized involves the representation of attribute types and values in O/R addresses. These may be represented as before as PrintableString or in the new version as PrintableString *and* TeletexString. This extension has led to X.400 (84) and X.400 (88) interworking problems (Chapter 10).

9.8 Changes to the interpersonal messaging service

As a consequence of the new structure of the application layer, the previous end-to-end protocol P2, which resulted from the division of the application layer into two, is no longer formally present; however, the structure and the meaning of the messages transferred in the IPMS context are standardized as before (X.420), and have taken on the character of a *document architecture*. X.420 (88) has been completely rewritten (although the physical alterations to X.420 (84) are not large) and is much more voluminous than X.420 (84). This has less to do with the systematic and formal nature of the representation with its various levels of abstraction, but is mainly a result of the fact that many omissions and inaccuracies of the old release have been included and corrected. Thus, the recommendation contains, for example, a statement on the conformance requirements for implementations of the IPMS.

Since the message store can also store IPMS communications, which it makes accessible via IPMS-specific attributes, Appendix C of X.420 (88) specifies how the contents of the fields of the IPMS heading should be referenced in interrogation.

With the omission of the UAL and the MTL, the somewhat artificial *Submission and Delivery Entity* (SDE), introduced in X.400 (84) for stand-alone UAs, is also dropped.

One important change from the old recommendation is the fact that a similar extension mechanism for arranging new fields in the heading is provided, as previously described in Section 9.7. This will simplify future extensions of the standard, which is particularly important for the IPMS, which may potentially be used for the most varied applications.

In many instances, new and clearer notation has been introduced for the information objects. This also applies to the possible body parts which are specified as follows:

```
BodyPart               ::=  CHOICE {
ia5-text               [0]  IA5TextBodyPart,
voice                  [2]  VoiceBodyPart,
g3-facsimile           [3]  G3FacsimileBodyPart,
g4class1               [4]  G4Class1BodyPart,
teletex                [5]  TeletexBodyPart,
videotex               [6]  VideotexBodyPart,
nationally-defined     [7]  NationallyDefinedBodyPart,
encrypted              [8]  EncryptedBodyPart,
message                [9]  MessageBodyPart,
mixed-mode             [11] MixedModeBodyPart,
bilaterally-defined    [14] BilaterallyDefinedBodyPart,
externally-defined     [15] ExternallyDefinedBodyPart }
```

It is noticeable that the body parts TLX (for telex) and SFD (simple formattable document) have been dropped. The job of TLX may easily be taken over by ia5-text, if the ITA2 telex character set is used. SFD is more than replaced by teletex. The two new body parts bilaterally-defined and externally-defined meet the requirement for a facility to define new body parts for special or private applications. They physically replace the body part nationally-defined, which is only retained on compatibility grounds. The externally-defined body part differs from nationally-defined and bilaterally-defined in that, in addition to the value, the type may be given in the form of an 'object identifier' (a pointer to the specification of the syntax of the body part). This is a convenient way of conveying a specification of the structure of a privately defined body part together with its value. Use of the externally defined body part for this purpose is therefore encouraged

9.9 New organization of standards documents

Table 9.4 gives an overview of the organization of the recommendations of the X.400 (88) and ISO 10021 series.

Table 9.4   Overview of the recommendations of the X.400 (88) series.

CCITT	ISO	Title	Short description
X.400	10021-1	System and service overview	A non-technical overview of the system architecture of MHSs, the services and functions offered. The text is easy to read and mostly covered in this book.
X.402	10021-2	Overall architecture	A refinement of X.400 and ISO 10021-1. Goes into much technical detail, but does not give formal specifications.
X.403	N/A	Conformance testing	Defines the conformance testing of X.400 (84) implementations.
X.407	10021-3	Abstract service definition conventions	Describes the concept of 'abstract services' used in the standard and defines the way in which these are described. Important for an understanding of the other recommendations/ parts, in particular X.411 and ISO 10021-4.
X.408		Encoded information type conversion rules	Rules for the conversion of documents of the various standardized types, which arise in the content part of messages.
X.411	10021-4	Message transfer system – abstract service definition and procedures	Semi-formal description of the service and the functions (including parameters and data structures exchanged) of the MTS. In particular, this part covers the description of message structures.
X.413	10021-5	Message store – abstract service definition	Semi-formal description of the service and the functions of the MS.

Table 9.4 (cont.)

CCITT	ISO	Title	Short description
X.419	10021-6	Protocol specifications	Description of the application contexts for the various MHS protocols (P1, P3, P7).
X.420	10021-7	Interpersonal messaging system	Semi-formal description of the service and the functions of the IPMS, including the structure of communications.

The recommendations of the F.400 series describe the application of X.400 in public MHSs (Table 9.5). For understandable reasons, no corresponding standards were developed by ISO.

Table 9.5 Recommendations of the F.400 (88) series.

CCITT recommendation	Title
F.400	System and service overview
F.401	Naming and addressing for public message handling services
F.410	Intercommunication with public physical delivery services
F.420	The public interpersonal messaging service
F.421	Intercommunication between the IPM service and the telex service
F.422	Intercommunication between the IPM service and the teletex service

10

Interworking between X.400 (84) and MHS (88)

After the publication of X.400 (84) it took almost four years before the first commercial X.400 products reached the market in any sizeable number. Although such a long period before the market introduction of corresponding systems is not expected in the case of MHS (88), for the moment a widespread further introduction of X.400 (84) systems must be reckoned with. Above all, the suppliers of public services will over the next few years use predominantly X.400 (84). In parallel, the manufacturers will bring MHS (88) systems to the market at the beginning of the nineties, in particular because X.400 (84) does not incorporate several features (for example, security mechanisms) which are important to the industrial and service sectors, and because the use of directory services, which is important for the construction and operation of large MHSs, is not defined in X.400 (84).

Because of the simultaneous use of MHS (88) systems and X.400 (84) systems during a transition period and in view of the desire for connectivity between the individual user groups, there is a need to investigate the extent to which X.400 (84) and MHS (88) systems can interoperate, since the functional scope of MHS (88) is a major extension of that of X.400 (84).

In its Appendix B, ISO 10021-6 (and X.419 (88)) describes rules for interworking between MHS (88) and X.400 (84) systems. Moreover, initial studies of this topic have already begun. The following sections provide a summary of this interworking problem based on ISO 10021 and on a study by RARE (Craigie, 1988).

In order to understand the problem in question together with the proposed solution, it would be advantageous for the reader to be familiar with the ASN.1 definitions of the X.400 (84) P1 and P2 protocols given in Appendix A.

10.1 Properties of MHS (88) relevant to 84/88 interworking

Relevant new functionality in MHS (88)

MHS has a number of new service elements that were not present in X.400 (84). Thus, it is necessary to define what happens to these service elements when they occur in a message which is forwarded from an MHS (88) to an X.400 (84) MTA. Below we briefly list the new services of MHS (88) relevant to interworking:

- Introduction of distribution lists.
- Use of X.500 directory services.

- Security elements.
- Additional content types.
- Delivery to an *access unit* (mapping of a message onto another medium).
- Newly defined protocol stack.

Extensions of loop detection

A new service element, *internal trace*, indicates the route of a message over MTAs within a domain, in order to facilitate the detection and elimination of loops. However, MHS (88) does not specify how this information should be evaluated and which activities are needed to detect a loop. Since a potentially-standard mechanism designed to detect and eliminate loops using trace information must be very general, it is likely that a (possibly *ad hoc*) solution can also be realized with the standard mechanism.

Most of the problems of interworking between MHS (88) and X.400 (84) discussed below are the result of differences in the evaluation of trace information by MHS (88) and X.400 (84) systems.

Requirements on the underlying layers – differences between ISO and CCITT

ISO 10021 and X.400 (88) place different requirements on the underlying OSI layers for the protocol P1. While X.400 (84) could not make use of the complete OSI stack but defined the RTS service as part of X.400 (84) (termed *X.410 transfer mode* in the following), the services of a newly structured application layer (see also Chapters 1 and 9) are now available. In particular, there is a new definition of the RTS service (ISO 9066) which, among other things, supports the *normal mode*. This mode is characterized by the use of ACSE to set up and release a connection and by the use of the service elements of the OSI presentation layer. While in ISO 10021 *normal mode* RTS is mandatory and X.410 *transfer mode* is optional, the converse is true in X.400 (88). Correspondingly, ISO 10021 defines three types of MTAs with different capabilities:

- **MTA type A** supports only 'normal mode RTS' and satisfies ISO 10021.
- **MTA type B** supports 'normal mode RTS' and also 'X.410 transfer mode'.
- **MTA type C** supports 'normal mode RTS' and 'X.410 transfer mode' and has facilities for mapping messages in the MHS (88) format into the form needed for X.400 (84) when possible (*downgrading*).

Table **10.1** Interworking between ISO 10021 and X.400.

CCITT MOTIS ISO 10021	X.400 (84)	X.400(88) only X.410 'transfer mode' (minimal)	X.400(88) both transfer modes (complete)
MTA type A	No	No	Yes
MTA type B	No	Yes	Yes
MTA type C	Yes	Yes	Yes

Yes: interworking possible   No: interworking not possible

Table 10.1 shows the interworking table for X.400(84) and X.400 (88) systems, as given in ISO 10021, for these types of MTAs.

CCITT's intention to support 'X.410 transfer mode' in any case, results from the desire to achieve connectivity between the old X.400 (84) systems and MHS (88) systems as easily as possible. This leads to the problem seen in Table 10.1 where X.400 (88) systems that only support the 'X.410 transfer mode' and ISO 10021 systems of type A cannot be directly connected together. However, this potential problem will not have severe effects, since many X.400 (88) systems will be extensions of X.400 (84) systems and thus will support both RTS modes. Moreover, pressure is being exerted on CCITT from various sides to remove this difference in the next revision of X.400 (1992) so that 'normal mode RTS' (the ISO version) is declared to be mandatory by both organizations. CCITT has already announced its willingness to comply with this requirement. The announcement of this intention will influence the manufacturers of X.400 products; thus, the spread of minimal X.400 (88) systems is not envisaged. The removal of this difference between CCITT and ISO is thus a mere formality.

To guarantee the connectivity between X.400 (84) and MHS (88) systems, in X.400 (88) CCITT requires that all X.400 (88) MTAs support *downgrading*, while this facility is optional for ISO (type C MTA). While provision of downgrading facilities will certainly not be sensible and necessary in every MHS (88) system, the placement of type C MTAs depends largely on the MHS topology offered. We consider this topic further in Section 10.2.

As far as the use of the MTA access protocol (P3) and the message-store access protocol (P7) is concerned, ISO and CCITT are agreed on the common use of P7 over ROS (ISO 9072) and 'normal mode presentation' and (respectively) on the use of ROS over RTS.

Extension mechanism

In order to facilitate the implementation of extensions of MHS (88), MHS (88) defines a generally-applicable *extension mechanism*. Most extensions of MHS (88) over X.400 (84) are already defined using this mechanism. This mechanism greatly simplifies the migration from X.400 (84) to MHS (88) and from MHS (88) to future extended MHSs, since it is possible to define core functions which every MTA must support and since additional functionality may be introduced in the extensions. If an extension present within a message can be supported by the target system, it will be appropriately mapped; if it cannot be supported then a decision must be taken as to whether to delete the extension or not to forward the message. In MHS (88), an extension may be marked as CRITICAL, in which case the message should not be forwarded. In Section 10.3 (Interworking with X.400 (84)) we discuss the special case of 'downgrading'.

10.2 Migration topologies

In view of the fact that, in a message from an MHS (88) system to an X.400 (84) system, either MHS (88) extensions are lost or the message cannot be delivered, it follows immediately that the possible connection of MHS (88) systems over one or more X.400 (84) systems (*transit systems*) should be avoided. However, because of the expected growth in the distribution of MHS (88) and the simultaneous removal of X.400 (84) systems, it would not be advisable to require every MTA to have type C capabilities (with the possibility of interworking with arbitrary MHS (88) systems and with X.400 (84) systems). Instead, the introduction of type A systems should be the urgent goal, while type C MTAs with the facility to downgrade messages should always be used where a connection to X.400 (84) systems is still required. Correspondingly, it must be ensured that, for their part, operators of management domains migrate to MHS (88) as soon as possible and if necessary provide several SAPs for the different MHS types. If the operator of a management domain (for example, an ADMD) is not yet in a position to provide the appropriate functions, both direct and international connections between MHS (88) management domains must be assumed during a transition phase.

Overall, during this migration phase, when a domain or an individual MTA is connected to an MHS, care should be taken to match the capabilities of the MTAs involved, so as to avoid undesired effects such as, for example, loss of information due to available downgrading. Here coordination and forward planning are required at organization-wide, and national and international levels. However, the details of such a coordination are heavily dependent on the local circumstances.

10.3 Interworking with X.400 (84)

In this section we shall discuss the specific mechanisms for the interworking between MHS (88) and X.400 (84) systems, as defined in MHS (88).

Mixed operation of MHS (88) and X.400 (84) within a domain

ISO 10021-6 and X.419 (88) define a set of rules for conversion of a message from MHS (88) form to X.400 (84) form. This procedure is known as *downgrading* and must typically occur when a message leaves an MHS (88) domain and is sent to an X.400 (84) domain. These rules say nothing about the use of different types of MHSs within a domain. This restriction of 'downgrading' to domain boundaries contradicts practice, since, as a rule, MHS (88) MTAs in an existing X.400 (84) domain are integrated, and no new domain within a domain is introduced for MHS (88) systems.

In order to guarantee a uniform behaviour of X.400 (84) systems with respect to MHS (88) systems in a domain, it is firstly necessary to ensure that the use of the trace information to detect and eliminate message loops is uniform across all X.400 (84) systems.

While a number of *profiles* talk about the evaluation of 'internal trace information' by an X.400 (84) system in order to avoid loops, different profiles define different and not always mutually compatible methods for handling trace information. We cannot therefore assume the existence of appropriate implementations of X.400 (84) with MHS (88) compatible algorithms to *detect* and eliminate infinite loops. Thus, Craigie has proposed an extension of Appendix B of ISO 10021-6/X.419 (88) involving a mapping between MOTIS 'internal trace information' and 'internal trace' in ISO 10021/X.400 (88) ((Craigie, 1988), Appendix A).

During a transition period, it will not be possible to avoid mixed domains of this type in all cases; however, this should be avoided as far as possible.

Generation of O/R names for MHS (88) from X.400 (84)

While most extensions in MHS (88) are optional or have correspondingly sensible default values, so that downgrading by omitting an extension usually causes few problems, several special cases must be taken into account in the case of the mapping of O/R names – the new *common-name* attribute, 15 new attributes for addressing *physical delivery* recipients and the possibility of coding all printable character strings (PrintableString) in the teletex character set (T.61).

The 'common-name' attribute removes a weak point in the X.400 (84) naming scheme, namely the fact that the attributes defined there are not suitable for the syntactically correct naming of roles and *distribution lists*[1]. On the basis of the powerful concept of distribution lists in MHS (88) it is to be expected that MHS users in an X.400 (84) domain might also wish to address corresponding roles and distribution lists in an MHS (88) domain. Craigie has proposed an extension of Appendix B of ISO 10021-6/X.419 (88) which, when implemented, would allow users of X.400 (84) systems to use the 'common-name' attribute ((Craigie, 1988), Appendix B). Specifically, he proposed that in an X.400 (84) system a *Domain-defined Attribute* (DDA) should be used in such a way that the type of the DDA is set to the value 'common-name' with its value field representing the value of the common-name attribute. This ruling requires firstly that in the X.400 (84) system DDAs are available even at the UA user interface and secondly that there is a facility to map this DDA to the 'common-name' attribute in the MHS (88) system which carries out the conversion at the boundary between the X.400 (84) domain and the MHS (88) domain. None of the profiles defined for X.400 (84) requires support for DDAs and not all conversion-MTAs will support this form of mapping; thus, a number of X.400 (84) implementations will not be in a position to use this form of addressing.

A similar DDA-based mechanism would have to be used in order to make use of the 15 previously mentioned additional attributes for addressing 'physical delivery' recipients, where in this case also the same conditions apply as for the use of a DDA of type 'common-name'. However, the need to support 'physical delivery' will be far less important, since many of the X.400 (84) systems in existence today will already have been replaced even before PDAUs (*Physical Delivery Access Units*) are widely used.

In the case of the alternative coding of printable character strings in T.61, the solution involving the use of DDAs is not available, since DDAs are themselves defined as 'PrintableString' in X.400 (84). One solution might be to map the T.61 characters into characters of the 'PrintableString' character set; however, this solution would not be user friendly. As an alternative and recommended solution, it must be possible when using an MHS (88) system to generate and accept, by way of alternative, attribute values coded in each of the two character sets. This procedure is also to be recommended since it is likely that not all MHS (88) systems will be able to generate teletex coding.

Use of distribution lists

Assuming that a user of an X.400 (84) system is able to address an MHS (88) *distribution list* using the given DDA mechanism, use of an MHS (88) distribution list by a user of an X.400 (84) system will be possible. In the same way, users of an X.400 (84) system may be members of an MHS (88) distribution list. However, because of downgrading of messages, so

---

[1] For example, the mapping of such recipients onto the attribute 'surName' is common but semantically incorrect.

much information may be lost that X.400 (84) systems may fail to deliver messages from a distribution list to the recipient, and may instead delete the messages as a result of their mechanism for detecting and handling infinite message loops. Moreover, an X.400 (84) system does not send delivery and non-delivery reports to the hierarchy of distribution lists or administrators defined in MHS (88) but directly to the originator of the original message sent to the distribution list.

Additionally, there are a number of other problems associated with the downgrading of messages between an X.400 (84) user and an MHS (88) distribution list which may lead to individual messages from an MHS (88) distribution list not being accepted by an X.400 (84) MTA. However, if the downgrading mechanism is changed so that these messages may be received by an X.400 (84) MTA, so much information may be lost that loops, and in particular loops over several distribution lists or loops involving the rerouting of messages, may no longer be detectable by an X.400 (84) system.

One possible solution would be to extend the MHS (88) distribution-list mechanism to explicitly identify entries that point to users in an X.400 (84) domain, in order that messages to such a subscriber may be specially handled. However, this may lead to loop problems when another distribution list is reached via an X.400 (84) domain, in other words when an X.400 (84) system has to forward messages between two MHS (88) systems. However, as previously discussed, this case (an X.400 (84) transit domain between two MHS (88) domains) should be avoided if possible, in which case this solution would be practicable. Craigie has proposed a corresponding extension of ISO 10021-6/X.419 (88) ((Craigie, 1988), Appendix C).

Use of security mechanisms

Since X.400 (84) systems contain no equivalent to the security mechanisms defined in MHS (88) and since the corresponding attributes are marked as CRITICAL, messages that contain these attributes cannot be mapped onto X.400 (84) messages and consequently will not delivered.

Interworking in IPMS

MHS (88) says nothing about the downgrading of an IPMS communication since, according to the relevant ISO and CCITT committees, this is a matter only for the recipient of a communication. Moreover, it is assumed that the MTS is transparent as far as transported communications are concerned, whence the content of a communication is unaltered (although this is already violated by the introduction of the *content conversion* service elements). Craigie has proposed an extension of ISO 10021-6/X.419 (88) to include mapping rules to convert an MHS (88) IPMS communication into the X.400 (84) P2 format using an MTA of type C ((Craigie, 1988), Appendix D). If the content type of such a communication has the value

'22' (not defined in MHS (88), intended meaning 'not conforming to X.400 (84)'), according to these rules the extension element in the header of a P2 communication and the syntax element in the videotex parameters of a communication content should be deleted whenever they are present. If the content of a communication contains externally-defined content types then the corresponding identification number (tag) should be altered from the value '15' (*externally defined*) to the value '14' (undefined in MHS (88)); however, the content should not be converted[2]. When the conversion is finished, the content type of the corresponding message is changed from '22' to '2' (that is, to the value 'conforming to X.400 (84)').

The problem of conversion of content types and of agreement to use certain content types also arises between MHS (88) systems, since it is not in all cases guaranteed that all MHS (88) systems support all currently-defined '*encoded information types*' and moreover, new 'encoded information types' may be defined. This problem is not a result of the migration from X.400 (84) to MHS (88) and will remain even when only MHS (88) is used. One possible solution involves recording all the 'encoded information types' accepted by a recipient in a future directory service, which would then be interrogated by a sender before a message is sent. Moreover, the sender may automate the evaluation procedure by stating what should happen to his message if it contains 'encoded information types' which (according to the entry in the directory service) the recipient does not support. For example, he might specify that the message should nevertheless be delivered unaltered, that it should not be delivered or that it should not be delivered if it cannot be converted. We discuss the use of directory services in detail in Chapter 12.

10.4 Conclusions

The problem of interworking between MHS (88) and X.400 (84) is a temporary problem which may be resolved by coordination between operators of management domains and the individual MTA administrators and by a rapid migration to MHS (88) systems. It is above all important to coordinate the topologies of message handling systems, so as to avoid messages being transported between MHS (88) systems via one or more X.400 (84) systems.

In addition to eliminating X.400 (84) systems, the migration aims to move as quickly as possible to the exclusive use of MHS (88) systems

---

[2]The handling of externally-defined content types is outside the scope of definition of MHS (88). The above conversion rules only enable such a content type to be sent to an X.400 (84) system and do not convert the content, so that the recipient must use his own tools (not specified in more detail) to decode and analyze this content type using the ASN.1 specification in MHS (88) for an 'externally-defined body part'.

corresponding to ISO 10021 (which communicate via the complete OSI stack using 'normal mode RTS'). This ISO 10021/X.400 (88) interworking may also lead to problems in a transition phase, since, as mentioned, ISO 10021 and X.400 (88) differ in several details. As in the case of the use of 'normal mode RTS', on the one hand differences will be eliminated by the standardization bodies themselves, while on the other hand it is hoped that common profiles and implementation guidelines will be generated. Moreover, as far as the second important interworking problem is concerned (different 'encoded information types'), a proposal to use directory services and statements of actions following evaluation of a directory service entry by the sender has already been put forward.

11

Security in electronic message handling systems

11.1 Introduction

Wherever information is transmitted the communication partners expect the information transmitted to arrive unaltered. Security features are important prerequisites for a message handling system which is intended to transmit contracts, documents or even electronic bank transfer orders. Such security features include guaranteed *integrity* of transmitted messages, verification of originator, verification of submission and receipt and also *confidentiality* of transmitted messages and protection against loss or duplication of messages. Even the transmission of simple notes or a greeting requires some minimal security; a simple note which is diverted during transmission by a hacker to another destination may lead to confusion. In short, a totally insecure message handling system is only of limited use.

To achieve security means defending a system against threats. Section 11.2 describes possible threats against an electronic message handling system. Section 11.3 discusses the fundamental cryptographic principles of the security elements; Section 11.4 deals with the use of certificates for public key security. Section 11.5 discusses the security elements provided in X.400 (88), while Section 11.6 goes into other important aspects of secure message handling. Section 11.7 gives examples to describe the use of security elements against potential threats, and Section 11.8 rounds off this chapter with some general considerations.

11.2 Possible threats against an X.400 MHS

In order to make a system secure the possible threats must first be analyzed.

There are many reasons why people may attempt to attack an electronic message handling system and misuse it to their own advantage. These reasons range from simple curiosity, through espionage, to deliberate disruption of company-internal communications or alteration of electronically transmitted instructions. Even regular users of the system may behave illegally by denying having sent or received a message in order to avoid the legal or social consequences of that message.

Attacks may be directed against any components of the message handling system, both against computer systems and application programs running on them and against connections between computers. It is irrelevant whether the attacker himself has authorized access to the system and to the connecting lines (for example, as administrator), or whether he has obtained access illegally using a weak point of the system in question (for example, as a hacker). Figure 11.1 shows possible points at which a message handling system might be attacked.

Attacks against a connection involve reading or modification of

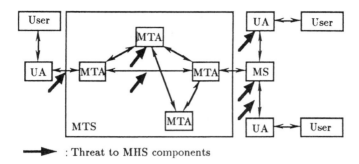

──► : Threat to MHS components

Figure 11.1   Possible points at which a message handling system might be attacked.

data packets on the link or interruption of the link. Attacks against a system typically involve reading or alteration of stored messages or management information. One possible attack which comes between these is the *masquerade*. Here, an attacker might, for example, attempt to set up a connection from his system to the MTA of the company Alpha, announcing himself on this connection as MTA Beta, in order to steal or introduce messages. Even end users may attempt to send or receive messages under false names.

Once an attacker has penetrated a system or a connection, there are various methods of attack open to him. He may, for example:

- Restrict or totally halt the operation by disrupting individual systems and connections.
- Forward messages illegally.
- Read messages.
- Alter or delete messages or introduce his own message. Alterations to a message are not restricted to the contents, but may also involve control information.
- Delete, duplicate or alter the sequence of messages.
- Deliver messages marked for 'deferred delivery' ahead of time (*preplay*).

In the past, numerous examples have shown that such threats exist and should be taken seriously:

- *The Internet worm.* A worm is a program which, once started on any computer, copies itself independently over a network into another computer, where it starts up in the same way. On 2 November 1988, the computer operations of numerous computers connected to the US Internet were disrupted for days by such a program. Amongst other things, the program used weak points in the implementation of a message handling system to penetrate hitherto-unaffected computers.

- On 1 April each year, the worldwide UNIX bulletin board system USENET, which has a great deal in common with an electronic message handling system, is plagued by a large number of joke messages. Since these messages are mostly fed in under illegal originator names, it is difficult to determine their origin.

- Several years ago, a group of hackers succeeded in smuggling an electronic banker's order worth several millions into the network of an English bank. However, the false instruction was discovered, since that bank's internal guidelines required telephone confirmation for orders involving large amounts of money.

11.3 Fundamental cryptographic principles

Symmetric cryptosystems

All security elements in X.400 (which are discussed in detail in Section 11.5) are based on the use of cryptographic methods to protect messages and parts of messages against attack. In simple words, the sensitive components are encrypted and thus protected against illegal reading or alteration; only legitimate recipients who know the secret key are able to decrypt these components.

In *symmetric coding systems* the same *key* (to be kept secret) is used for *encryption* and *decryption* by all the partners involved (Figure 11.2). Coding systems of this type have been well known for some time; their main disadvantage is the fact that both the sender and the recipient must know the secret key. This leads to the problem of *key distribution*, since the keys must be distributed over secure channels. In addition, one must have full confidence in the *communication partner* in that he is expected not to give away or misuse the key. Moreover, electronic signatures are not possible. On receipt of an encrypted message, the recipient knows the sender, since apart from himself only the latter knows the key. However, he cannot prove this to third parties, since he can generate and encrypt any message himself.

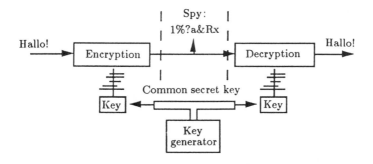

Figure 11.2   Symmetric cryptosystem.

Asymmetric (public key) cryptosystems

In contrast, in *asymmetric cryptosystems*, different keys are used for encryption and decryption (Figure 11.3). The two keys are generated at the same time; according to their purpose, one of the two keys, the *public key*, is made accessible to all interested parties, while the other key, *the secret key*, is known only to a single communication partner, the key holder. Once separated, it is only possible to deduce the secret key from the public key at excessive costs (for example, several weeks or months of computing time on several supercomputers working in parallel).

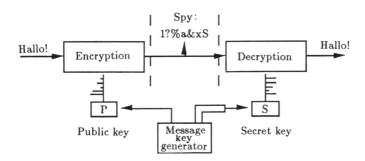

Figure 11.3   Asymmetric cryptosystem.

Two sorts of asymmetric cryptosystems are used in the data communication area. A first type is used to *encrypt* a message to a given recipient and a second type is used to generate *electronic signatures*:

- For the purposes of *encryption*, the encoding key is made publicly accessible, while the decoding key becomes the secret key. In this way, any partner may encode messages and protect them from being read illegally, but only the key holder is able to decode and read them.

- In the case of *electronic signatures*, the converse is true; the decoding key is published, while the encoding key becomes the secret key. In this way, any partner may decode an encoded message, and knows afterwards that the message must come from the key holder since only the latter is able to encode messages with his private key. Thus, the encryption has the effect of an electronic signature.

Of the numerous asymmetric cryptosystems developed to date, it is mainly the *RSA* cryptosystem which is used (Rivest *et al.*, 1978). RSA is based on calculations in modular arithmetic, where certain operations, such as the extraction of nth roots, are only possible when the prime factor decomposition of the modulus is known. If this modulus is chosen to be the product of two sufficiently large prime numbers, subsequent decomposition of the modulus into its prime factors is only possible at excessive computational costs (several months or years computing time for 512-bit moduli). In addition, RSA has the advantage that a single public and private key may be used both for encryption and for electronic signatures. For this reason, we shall only speak of *public keys* and *private* or *secret keys* from now on. Section 11.4, contains a detailed discussion of the mechanism for publication of public keys and associated problems.

All asymmetric coding procedures have a severe disadvantage: they are computationally very expensive in comparison with symmetric procedures. Thus, in practice, fast symmetric coding systems are combined with slower asymmetric ones. The (possibly long) message is itself encoded using an efficient symmetric procedure. The encoding key for each message (called a *message key*), generated by a random key generator, is also transmitted to the message recipient in asymmetrically-encrypted form. In this process, the message key is encrypted with the recipient's public key and is thus only readable by the latter (Figure 11.4a).

The legitimate recipient, and only he, can recover the message key by decoding with his private key and thus he is able to decrypt the message itself (Figure 11.4b).

Another advantage of this method is apparent when a message is sent to several recipients simultaneously. In this case, the encoded message and the corresponding message key are the same for all recipients; only the

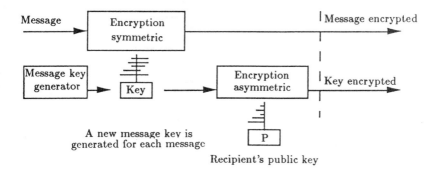

Figure 11.4a   Efficient encryption of a message.

message key itself must be encrypted separately for each recipient.

In a similar fashion, there are also efficient procedures for generating and verifying electronic signatures, which combine asymmetric encoding with efficiently-implementable checksum algorithms. Here a checksum is generated for the whole message content (*Manipulation Detecting Code, MDC*) and this is asymmetrically encrypted using the sender's private key (Figure 11.5a).

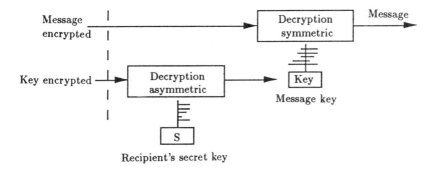

Figure 11.4b   Decryption of an efficiently-coded message.

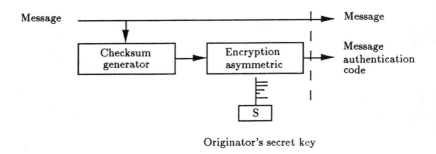

Figure 11.5a Efficient electronic signature.

On the one hand, the recipient can recalculate the checksum from the message content, while on the other hand, he can recover it by decoding the value transmitted by the sender using the sender's public key (Figure 11.5b). If these checksums agree, the recipient can be sure that the message comes from the given originator (the latter is the only one to possess the private key needed for the encoding); at the same time, he is able to check that the message was not illegally modified en route. This last point requires a 'good' checksum algorithm, in the sense that any alteration of the message content which leaves the checksum unchanged is necessarily associated with unrealistically high computational cost.

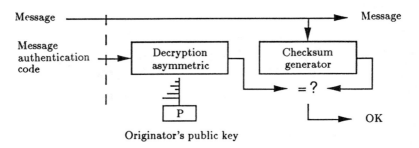

Figure 11.5b Checking an efficient electronic signature.

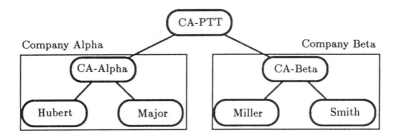

Figure 11.6   Example of the use of certificates.

11.4 Integrity of public keys

Central to every electronic message handling system are its users. In a secure message handling system based on asymmetric coding schemes, each user is assigned a user name together with a public and a private key. The public key is published (made available to all interested parties) together with the user name; the private key is only known to its key holder.

An interested partner can now authenticate the key holder through his ability to add his electronic signature to data elements. However, this only ensures that the partner corresponds to that key; authentication of the partner by name requires a mechanism to guarantee that names and public keys belong together. The problem is comparable to that of a personal identity card, in that a match between the partner and the photo on the identity card does not mean that the partner's name is actually that given on the identity card. The identity card might be forged or illegally produced. However, if the authenticity of the identity card can be verified using special features (special patterns, watermarks, stamps) and if the place at which the identity card was issued is deemed to be trustworthy, the authentication of the partner also includes the authentication of his name.

The idea of the identity card can be carried over to the electronic form. The corresponding 'identity cards' are called *certificates*. The structure and function of certificates is explained in the following paragraphs by means of an example (Figure 11.6). Alternatively, it is also possible to distribute pairs of names and keys to the partners via secure channels and store them with write protection. Pairs of names and keys which must be very widely distributed may be published in the mass media (for example, in a newspaper), but the publication procedure (typesetting, printing and distribution of a newspaper) must be monitored to prevent illegal modification of the name or of the public key.

In our example in Figure 11.6, we assume that Mr. Hubert and Mr. Major work for company Alpha, while Mr. Miller and Mr. Smith are employed by company Beta. The two firms work closely together and use secure electronic message handling for communication both internally and with each other. Company Alpha uses a central computer; Beta uses PCs interconnected over a local area network.

Case (a) Few subscribers

If there are few subscribers, the names and public keys of all possible communication partners may be stored in a table in the electronic message handling system. However, as explained above, it must be ensured that the names and public keys actually belong together. In practice, this means that the pairs of names and keys must be distributed via secure channels and stored in the systems with write protection.

In company Alpha, updating of these tables is the job of the (trusted) system administrator. In company Beta which uses a PC-based distributed message transfer system, a table must be held and updated on each PC, since according to the security policy in force in company Beta, the local area network which links the individual PCs is not considered to be secure enough.

For a large number of partners this procedure rapidly becomes impractical.

Case (b) Many subscribers in few organizations

In this case, an attempt is also made to distribute the public keys by electronic message transfer, while at the same time an electronic signature is used to protect the keys against alteration during distribution. The combination of names and public keys is electronically signed by a third party, the *Certificate Authority* (CA). Knowledge of the public key of the CA is in itself sufficient to test the authenticity of a certificate at any time.

By analogy with identity cards, the CA corresponds to the place of issue of the identity card, where all the partners covered are issued with identity cards including their names and addresses. In order to prevent forgery, the identity cards incorporate authentication features (special patterns, watermarks, stamps) which can only be generated by the place of issue itself. Whoever knows the authentication features used is able to authenticate the name of the partner from such an identity card.

In our example, Alpha and Beta could each operate a CA (called CA-Alpha and CA-Beta); the table of public keys now reduces to the keys for these two CAs. There are two possible ways of storing and requesting certificates: they may be stored by the subscriber involved who will send them on request to his communication partner by (insecure) message transfer, or they may be held in the directory (*X.500 directory service*, described in Chapter 12).

In practice, in addition to the name and the public key of the subscriber, a certificate also includes other entries such as the algorithm used for the signature, the name of the issuing CA and an expiry date. CCITT recommendation X.509 (88) (Authentication Framework) defines a certificate in ASN.1 as follows:

```
Certificate ::= SIGNED SEQUENCE {
    version              [0] INTEGER DEFAULT 0,
    serialNumber         INTEGER,
    signature            AlgorithmIdentifier,
    issuer               Name,
    validity             Validity,
    subject              Name,
    subjectPublicKeyInfo SubjectPublicKeyInfo }
```

Validity incorporates a period of validity, of dates between which the certificate is valid. SIGNED is a macro specified in CCITT X.509 (88), which lays down a standard method for the syntax of electronic signatures in ASN.1; the macros ENCRYPTED and SIGNATURE are also closely related:

```
ENCRYPTED MACRO ::=
  BEGIN
    TYPE  NOTATION ::= type (ToBeEncrypted)
    VALUE NOTATION ::= value (VALUE BITSTRING)
  END
```

ENCRYPTED expects any type of field as input (parameter ToBeEncrypted, without type specification); the encoded output is packed into an elementary field of type BITSTRING. The encoding itself is executed by first transferring the data to be encoded into ASN.1 transfer syntax and then encoding the resulting byte stream using some encoding algorithm:

```
SIGNED MACRO ::=
  BEGIN
    TYPE  NOTATION ::= type (ToBeSigned)
    VALUE NOTATION ::= value (VALUE)
      SEQUENCE {
      ToBeSigned,
      AlgorithmIdentifier,
      ENCRYPTED OCTETSTRING }
      -- checksum (MDC) of ToBeSigned encrypted with
      -- the senders private key
  END;
```

Again, the SIGNED macro expects any type of field as input (parameter ToBeSigned), from which it generates a sequence with three fields: the content to be protected by signature (ToBeSigned), statements about the algorithm used (AlgorithmIdentifier), and the signature itself. As far as the notation for the signature is concerned, ENCRYPTED indicates that a value is to be encrypted, namely the checksum (MDC) over the data field to be signed, which will be encrypted using the sender's private key. The checksum itself is of type OCTETSTRING.

The type AlgorithmIdentifier which provides information about the algorithm used and its parameters is defined by:

```
AlgorithmIdentifier ::= SEQUENCE {
   algorithm  OBJECT IDENTIFIER,
   parameters ANY DEFINED BY algorithm OPTIONAL }
```

The SIGNATURE macro is more or less identical with the SIGNED macro except that the data field to be signed is no longer included:

```
SIGNATURE MACRO ::=
  BEGIN
   TYPE NOTATION ::= type (OfSignature)
    VALUE NOTATION ::= value (VALUE)
     SEQUENCE {
      AlgorithmIdentifier,
      ENCRYPTED OCTETSTRING }
      -- checksum (MDC) of OfSignature encrypted with
      -- the senders private key
  END;
```

When using the SIGNED or the SIGNATURE macro it is advisable to include the algorithm identifier for the signature again within the data structure to be signed (in a redundant fashion). This complicates certain attacks against the signature in which attempts are made to replace the algorithm used by a different one.

Case (c) Very many subscribers, worldwide networks

The above solution with certificates and company-internal CAs also has its disadvantages. In the case of contacts with a large number of companies, the public key tables will become very large and the public key of every new CA must be requested over a secure channel.

The next logical step involves the introduction of higher-order CAs to protect the public keys of the CAs themselves and thus to simplify their distribution. This leads to a hierarchical structuring of CAs. In our example, we assume that the public telephone services (PTTs) have recognized the problem and have set up a higher-order CA, the CA-PTT, to issue certificates for company-specific CAs (see Figure 11.6). This noticeably simplifies the operation of the systems of Alpha and Beta, since the public key tables are reduced to a single entry, that of the CA-PTT.

At this point, it is appropriate to introduce the following notation (which largely conforms with X.509) for certificates and operations that may be used on them:

$User_p$ Public key belonging to a user.

$CA\langle\langle User\rangle\rangle$
> User's certificate issued by the CA. Every subscriber knowing the CA's public key may check the integrity of the public key contained in the certificate.

$CA_p * CA\langle\langle User\rangle\rangle$
> Operation which checks the integrity of the certificate and then extracts the public key of the user from the certificate.

Example Mr. Major verifies Mr. Smith's public key; to do this he must possess knowledge of the certificate CA-Beta$\langle\langle Smith\rangle\rangle$ and the public key CA-Beta$_p$:

$$Smith_p = CA\text{-}Beta_p * CA\text{-}Beta\langle\langle Smith\rangle\rangle$$

With the introduction of the CA-PTT, the public key of which is known to Mr. Hubert, in our example, he may now check Mr. Smith's public key according to the following formula (in two steps):

$$CA\text{-}Beta_p = CA\text{-}PTT_p * CA\text{-}PTT\langle\langle CA\text{-}Beta\rangle\rangle$$
$$Smith_p = CA\text{-}Beta_p * CA\text{-}Beta\langle\langle Smith\rangle\rangle$$

The sequence of certificates required to verify a given public key is called the *certification path*.

For certification paths we again extend our notation as follows:

$CA1\langle\langle CA2\rangle\rangle CA2\langle\langle User\rangle\rangle$
> Certification path in which CA1 certifies the public key of CA2; CA2 in turn certifies the user's public key.

$CA1_p * CA1\langle\langle CA2\rangle\rangle CA2\langle\langle User\rangle\rangle$
$= (CA1_p * CA1\langle\langle CA2\rangle\rangle) * CA2\langle\langle User\rangle\rangle$
> Operator to unpack a user's public key from a complete certification path. Note that the path is processed from left to right.

$CA \rightarrow User$
> Abbreviation for the certification path from a CA to a user, without detailed statements of the certificates used and the intermediate CAs.

In our example, we would have:

$$
\begin{aligned}
\text{CA-PTT} \to \text{Smith} \\
= \text{CA-PTT}\langle\langle\text{CA-Beta}\rangle\rangle \\
\text{CA-Beta}\langle\langle\text{Smith}\rangle\rangle
\end{aligned}
$$

The operation to determine a user's public key may now be generally described by

$$
\text{User}_p := \text{CA}_p * \text{CA} \to \text{User}
$$

In this method, one is tied to a hierarchical system; moreover, every system must know the public key of the highest CA in the hierarchy. Using another trick, the *reverse certificate*, it is possible to organize a secure open system of unlimited size, without knowing anything other than your own public key, and this even with non-hierarchically ordered CAs. In this case, users and hierarchically inferior CAs provide the CA assigned to them with a so-called *reverse certificate*. Even CAs that are not hierarchically related can provide each other with certificates, known as *cross certificates*. Now each user (for example, Mr. Major) only needs to know his own public key in order to be able to verify any other public keys according to the following scheme:

$$
\begin{aligned}
\text{Smith}_p := \text{Major}_p * \text{Major}\langle\langle\text{CA-Alpha}\rangle\rangle \\
\text{CA-Alpha}\langle\langle\text{CA-PTT}\rangle\rangle \\
\text{CA-PTT}\langle\langle\text{CA-Beta}\rangle\rangle \\
\text{CA-Beta}\langle\langle\text{Smith}\rangle\rangle
\end{aligned}
$$

The certification path now divides into two parts: a backwards path with reverse certificates (the first two lines in the above example) and a forwards path with normal certificates (lines three and four of the example). In the case of non-hierarchically organized CAs, the path may also involve cross certificates. In the following example, CA-Alpha provides CA-Beta with a cross certificate:

$$
\begin{aligned}
\text{Smith}_p := \text{Major}_p * \text{Major}\langle\langle\text{CA-Alpha}\rangle\rangle \\
\text{CA-Alpha}\langle\langle\text{CA-Beta}\rangle\rangle \\
\text{CA-Beta}\langle\langle\text{Smith}\rangle\rangle
\end{aligned}
$$

In abbreviated form (without the details of the certificates used), our example may be written as:

$$
\text{Smith}_p := \text{Major}_p * \text{Major} \to \text{Smith}
$$

This method has, in the meantime, been specified as the standard

method in CCITT recommendation X.509. In practice, all the methods
described above will be used, depending on the number of users and on the
system security requirements.

11.5 Security elements in X.400 (88)

Overview and classification

X.400 provides numerous mechanisms (*security elements of service*) for
defence against the various threats mentioned. These are specified in
recommendations X.400 (88) (Overview), X.402 (88) (Architecture) and
X.411 (88) (MTS). Essentially, there are two classes of security elements:
those which *protect connections* between systems and those which *protect
individual messages*. The *protection of the system* itself is purely a matter
for the operators of the system, and we cannot go into details here.

The standards use various terms for the security features, according
to the level of abstraction at which the system is being viewed:

- *Security elements of service* are those services provided by the MHS
  which have something to do with security.

- *Security services* is a term which comes from the 'OSI Reference
  Model: Security Framework' (ISO 7498-2). Amongst other things,
  this standard specifies a set of security services with which a
  communication system which is structured according to OSI may
  be made secure. Since X.400 adheres to this structure, these security
  services should be identifiable.

- *Security elements* are the security features provided by the various
  operations. Security elements are realized using corresponding
  security arguments.

- *Security arguments* are the security-specific fields provided for in the
  arguments and results of the various operations.

- In this chapter, the term *security feature* refers to any security-
  specific feature, without reference to any of the above levels of
  abstraction.

The end user is mainly interested in the security elements of services which
X.400 (88) offers at the individual message level. From the point of view
of the layer model, all security features are implemented within the MHS
(message transfer layer in X.400 (84), described in Chapter 2). These
security features use the X.400 (88) extension mechanism (EXTENSION)
mentioned in Chapter 9. To prevent an MTA or UA that does not support
the chosen security features from simply deleting the corresponding fields

or from attempting to handle cipher as plaintext, all fields associated with the security features are marked as CRITICAL. Hence, an MTA or UA that cannot process these fields will reject the message as 'undeliverable since optional service element not supported'. The same thing happens if an attempt is made to pass a secure message via an MTA with downgrading facilities into an X.400 (84) system (no security functionality).

Security elements to protect connections

Peer-entity authentication

Purpose   The partners of the connection can assert the authenticity of their opposing partners.

Realization   When the connection is opened and at regular intervals after that both partners exchange special data elements that enable both subscribers to satisfy themselves of the authenticity of their partner.

Strong authentication involves the X.509 two-way procedure using an asymmetric coding procedure. Here, electronically-signed data elements (tokens) containing the partner's address, a time stamp and a random number are exchanged and checked.

Security context

Purpose   In computer systems in which data is strictly separated according to its classification or sensitivity, this separation may also be applied to the connections and to the messages passing over them.

Realization   For each possible connection between systems, the sensitivity of messages to be transmitted over that connection is specified. In order to avoid possible confusion of messages of different sensitivities (and thus also, misclassification of a sensitive message in a wrong category), in case of problems, messages carried on each open connection all have the same sensitivity. Transmission of secret data in open form over an insecure line can be prevented by authorizing only 'unclassified' connections for this line. Whenever a connection is opened, the initiator specifies the level of classification of the messages to be transmitted (operation MTSBind, argument security-context).

Security elements to protect individual messages

Security arguments; the token

As previously mentioned, the message data fields needed for the security elements are supplied by the EXTENSION mechanism. Using the associated criticality mechanism, it is possible to ensure that messages from a target system that does not support the security element concerned are rejected, but that, on the other hand, the intermediate MTAs transport the message further, regardless of whether or not they themselves provide security elements. The security arguments per message include the following:

- originator certificate
- content-confidentiality-algorithm identifier
- message-origin-authentication check
- message-security label
- proof-of-submission request
- per message-recipient:
- message token
- content-integrity check
- proof-of-delivery request

Most of these fields have a simple structure; they are described in the appropriate subsection below. Only the *message token* field, of type *token*, requires an introductory explanation since it can provide many different security elements and has a correspondingly complex structure. Essentially, it contains the following information (the names correspond to the ASN.1 definition):

- recipient name
- time
- unencrypted token data field containing:
    — content-confidentiality-algorithm identifier
    — content-integrity check
    — message-security label
    — proof-of-delivery request
    — message-sequence number
- encrypted token data field, containing:
    — content-confidentiality key
    — content-integrity check
    — message-security label
    — content-integrity key
    — message-sequence number

The information in the 'token' is protected against manipulation using the sender's signature. The two token data fields may contain only a selection of the given fields, and fields may be omitted if they are empty. Some elements occur in both the unencrypted and the encrypted token data fields; in this case, it is possible to choose between the two token data fields according to whether or not confidentiality is required for the element.

The exact definition of the token in ASN.1 is very complicated and also uses a kind of extension mechanism (macros **TOKEN** and **TOKEN-DATA**). The only token type defined at present is the asymmetric token (based on asymmetric coding systems). However, the content of the two group fields (type TokenData in ASN.1) varies according to the use of the token. In addition to the *message token* just described, there is also a *bind token* for 'peer-entity authentication' as described above.

Message-origin authentication

Purpose   The recipient of a message may verify the origin of a message.

Realization   This is realized by electronic signature on the message. At the level of security elements, we distinguish between two groups of elements which may provide this functionality: *origin authentication* and *integrity check*. The elements of both groups are very similar to each other and may be used to guarantee the integrity as well as the origin of a message. However, the two groups of security elements differ considerably as soon as messages are encrypted for confidentiality. The services of the origin-authentication group operate on the encoded message content and enable all components involved in the message transmission (including MTAs) to determine the origin of the message. On the other hand, the security elements of the integrity-check group only operate on plaintext, and thus they may only be used from end-to-end (only where the message occurs in plaintext). The two groups also differ semantically: origin authentication proves only that the sender in question has sent the encrypted message, but does not necessarily know its content. Content integrity, on the other hand, can prove that the sender knows the message content.

Message-origin authentication uses the **EXTENSION** field 'message-origin-authentication check', which is basically a signature over the message content, message-content identifier and message-security label (see below).

Message-content integrity may optionally use either of the fields 'content-integrity check' or 'token'. Both of these are **EXTENSION** fields which may occur once per message recipient. The field 'content-integrity check' contains a signature covering the message content, both as an **EXTENSION** and within the token; within the token, the field may also be encrypted to protect it against attacks. Since the token is itself protected against manipulation by a signature, it is sufficient to use a checksum algorithm at this point (without using the sender's private key).

Other methods (such as protection of the message with a checksum algorithm) that require a secret key may also be used; the token even provides for a corresponding (encrypted) key field. The integrity of the message may also be guaranteed by encoding the message content using an appropriate procedure and a key agreed bilaterally beforehand, provided that the message itself contains sufficient redundancy for the integrity to be checked (which is again detrimental to secrecy).

Content integrity

Purpose   The recipient of a message is able to check whether the message has been altered during transmission.

Realization   This is realized by electronic signature, as previously explained under message-origin authentication.

Content confidentiality

Purpose   Only the legitimate recipient of the message is able to read the contents of the message.

Realization   This is realized, for example, by encrypting the message content using the recipient's public key. Since this encryption would be very time-consuming, a combination of asymmetric and symmetric encryption is used as in the subsection entitled 'Asymmetric (public key) cryptosystems'. The message itself is encrypted using a random message key and a symmetric coding procedure; the key itself is also given in asymmetrically encrypted form in the token's 'encrypted data' field.

Alternatively, the message may be encoded using a bilaterally-agreed procedure and key; the algorithm used and references to the key used are given in the 'content-confidentiality-algorithm identifier' EXTENSION field.

Message-security labelling

Purpose   This makes it possible to provide a message with a machine-readable classification. This is important for systems where this classification is used to control access rights and the separation of data into security classes.

Realization   This is realized by setting either the 'message-security label' EXTENSION field or the corresponding field in the token. In the token, it is also possible to protect the security label against (illegal) reading by implementing it in the encrypted part, in order that the classification of the message is not shown on the outside. Caution: outside the token, the field is only protected against manipulation if the 'proof of origin' security element (but not 'message integrity' which does not take account of the 'message-security label' field) is activated at the same time.

Message-sequence integrity

Purpose   This ensures that the sequence in which messages are sent is preserved on receipt and that messages are neither lost nor duplicated.

Realization   This involves the introduction of a message-sequence number in the message token and maintenance by the UA of a per sender/per recipient message-sequence register. The token protects the message-sequence number against illegal manipulation; it is also possible to encrypt the message-sequence number in order to keep it secret.

Proof of delivery

Purpose   This provides an electronic acknowledgement that attests to the fact that the recipient has received the message in readable form.

Realization   The recipient's UA signs the (decrypted) message electronically and sends the signature to the originator. An EXTENSION field (proof of delivery) is provided in the delivery report for this purpose; proof of delivery is requested using the message's 'proof-of-delivery request' EXTENSION field.

Proof of submission

Purpose   This provides an electronic confirmation that attests to the fact that the message actually has been sent (passed to an MTA).

Realization   The MTA neighbouring the UA signs the message electronically and sends the signature to the originator when requested using the message 'proof-of-submission request' EXTENSION field. The originator receives this signature in the 'proof of submission' field in the result of the message submission operation.

Non-repudiation of origin

Purpose   This is a stronger form of message authentication. The recipient of the message is able to verify the origin of the message, both to himself and to third parties.

Realization   This is realized by electronic signature. Only the sender should be able to generate the signature. Among other things, this requires an asymmetric encryption system. If the integrity were guaranteed by a symmetric encryption system and secret keys, the recipient could always forge the sender's signature.

Non-repudiation of delivery

Purpose   This is a stronger form of proof of delivery. The sender may also prove to third parties that his message has been correctly received.

Realization   This is realized by electronic signature of the (decrypted) message by the recipient using an appropriate asymmetric encryption system.

Non-repudiation of submission

Purpose   This is a stronger form of proof of submission, which again involves provability to third parties.

Realization   This is realized by electronic signature of the message by the MTA adjacent to the UA using a suitable asymmetric cipher system.

Message-flow confidentiality

Purpose   Even if enciphered messages are sent, an outsider might be able to draw conclusions about possible activities within one or more organizations based on the number and size of the messages sent (*statistical traffic analysis*). Additional measures may be taken to distort the results of such an analysis so that they are no longer meaningful.

Realization

- Deliberate routing of messages around relatively insecure connections.
- Introduction of empty messages (not recognizable as such).
- Messages sent to an intermediate recipient, who according to specific rules, forwards the message either to the end recipient or to another intermediate recipient.

11.6 Selected aspects of secure message transfer

Trusted components

A message transfer system contains numerous trusted components with specific tasks, the correct operation of which is crucial to the security of the system as a whole. A clear example of this is provided by CAs which, if they were to issue current certificates under false names or make known their private key, could jeopardize the electronic message transfer system as a whole. On closer inspection, it is apparent that nearly all components must be trusted in some respect:

Certification authority

- Checks the pairs of names and keys to be certified for authenticity and agreement with the official and/or organizational name of the key holder.
- Never certifies two different users with the same name.
- Recalls a certificate whenever there is reason to believe that the user's private key has been compromised or that the user is no longer authorized to use it.
- Keeps its own private key secret.
- Does not refuse its services without good reason.
- Checks all relevant conditions of authorization for users.

User

- Keeps his own private key secret.

Key generator

- Generates keys of high cryptographic quality.
- Keeps private keys secret.

MHS operator

- Provides the required availability.

MHS software

- Functions according to the requirements of X.400 (88) and the current 'security policy'.
- Keeps private keys secret.
- Actually applies the required security services to outgoing messages.

- Checks all incoming messages in full for consistency (valid signatures, etc.) and warns the user in the case of disagreement (for example, forged signature).

Since there are numerous trusted components, it follows that special measures are needed to guarantee this trustworthiness in practice. The next two paragraphs deal with this problem; the next paragraph discusses the need for a 'security policy', while the paragraph after that is concerned with the secure storage of private keys.

Security policy

The *security policy* within an organization prescribes the behaviour to be adopted against a danger to the organization or to its personnel. This may include fire safety precautions as well as measures against burglary or espionage. In companies that deal with sensitive (secret or important) messages, the classification and handling of these messages must also be controlled. Depending on the company, a security policy may impose more or less severe restrictions on the operation of the secure message transfer system. For example, a bank which uses a message transfer system to transmit payment instructions, may ban the use of the same system for other purposes such as the exchange of personal messages.

Every company has its own security policy, even if this just says 'no special measures required'.

X.400 (88) facilitates the imposition of a security policy even in the MHS area, in that traditional security elements, such as classification, are supported electronically and are left sufficiently open to be universally usable. Thus, the implementation of a security policy is primarily the task of the company organization and requires a 'user agent' suited to the company involved. The content and implementation of a security policy do not form part of the X.400 standards.

Typically, in the message transfer area the security policy controls such questions as:

- Possible classifications and their importance. For example, a 'highly confidential' message in the wrong hands may result in great damage to a company and thus should always be kept under lock and key.
- Permissible classifications of messages to and from a given user.
- Specification of the classification above which messages should be transmitted in cipher and of the procedure to be used. Here, a distinction may be made between company-internal and external originators and recipients.
- Specification of the classification of messages after they have been successfully encoded (and may no longer be read by third parties).

This freedom as far as security policies are concerned immediately leads to problems in the exchange of messages between companies with different security policies. In order that they are able to intercommunicate, the security policies of the organizations involved must first be checked for compatibility and altered if necessary. For example, two different companies must first define a common meaning of the term 'confidential' before they are able to exchange messages with this classification. This is particularly difficult if the term 'confidential' is already defined in different ways in the two companies.

Technologies for storing the private key

As shown in the previous paragraphs, the security of a system is crucially dependent on whether or not the end user is able to keep his private key secret. For RSA, such a key typically consists of two numbers of more than a hundred digits, which it is impossible for the user to keep in his head or to enter by hand at the terminal. Thus, storage in a non-volatile medium is essential. Various storage methods are available:

- Storage in a computer file; the operating system is responsible for the appropriate protection.

- Storage of the private key in the encoded state. The encoding key is a password which the user must enter whenever he logs into system or when the message transfer program is initiated. Here, prerequisites to secure functioning of the system include the selection of non-trivial passwords by the user, the protection of the password entry against (illegal) reading by the hardware used and by the operating system and a cryptographic system that is difficult to break.

- Storage of the private key in a personal storage module (for example, smart card) which the user must initially pass through a suitable module reader. A PIN code known only to the legitimate user must be entered to activate the storage module.

- Transfer of all asymmetric coding operations to a separate module outside the computer known as the *token* (not to be confused with the token data structure). When it is not in use, the token is either locked away or carried by the key holder. When in use, after activation (for example, by entry of a PIN code), the token is inserted in a mounting connected to the computer where it remains while it is being used. All crypto operations that require the private key are transferred from the main system to the token. Periodic mutual authentication of the user and the token may prevent an unauthorized process from using the token or the use of a forged token. The token itself is constructed in such a way that it is impossible to read the secret key from the token (for example, after theft). Older tokens usually have the same size and shape as a pocket calculator; new tokens, on the other hand (including keyboard and display), are the size and thickness of a credit card (*smart card*).

Of the above methods, the last provides the greatest security, firstly since the key holder always carries the token with him and secondly because the secret key is also protected against illegal attacks should the token fall into unauthorized hands. However, such tokens or *super smart cards* are not yet commonly used in practice.

11.7 Examples of the use of security mechanisms against threats

In this section we give some examples of typical threats and of how they may be countered by the security features described in Section 11.5

Eavesdropping, traffic analysis

Mr. Bad-Guy taps the data link between Alpha and Beta and eavesdrops (Figure 11.7).

If 'content confidentiality' is specified for all important messages, they are then encoded and cannot be read by Mr. Bad-Guy. However, using

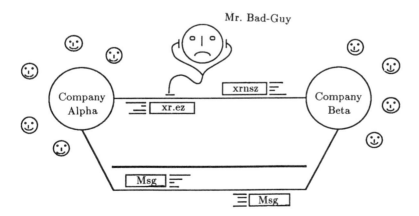

Figure 11.7   Traffic analysis – listening in to messages.

statistical traffic analysis, Mr. Bad-Guy may draw his own conclusions and, for example, decide that the sudden increase in the number of encoded messages is the start of a new joint project or even a takeover bid by Alpha for Beta.

These attacks may be countered by activation of the 'message-flow confidentiality service'. The actual message flow is hidden from the outside by diversion of messages over connections not monitored by Mr. Bad-Guy and by the introduction of encrypted empty messages.

Masquerade

We suppose that Alpha's central MTA may be reached over a public X.25 network. Mr. Bad-Guy attempts to dial in to Alpha's MTA over X.25 and to identify himself as MTA Beta, in order to introduce a forged message intended to disrupt the business relationship between Alpha and Beta (Figure 11.8).

Two obstacles may immediately be placed in the way of Mr. Bad-Guy's attempted attack or masquerade. Firstly, 'peer-entity authentication' can stop the penetration, since Mr. Bad-Guy does not know Alpha's secret key (which he needs) and cannot determine it by eavesdropping on the network. If the X.25 network is considered to be sufficiently trustworthy (this is usually the case for public networks) the spoof call can be detected at the X.25 level by checking the caller's address and rejected.

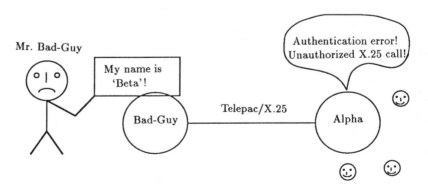

Figure 11.8   Masquerade at the MTA level.

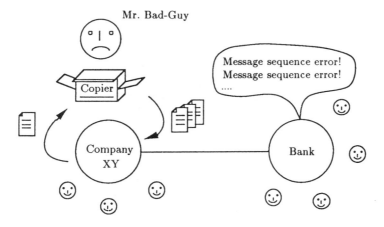

Figure 11.9   Duplication of messages.

Duplication of messages

Mr. Bad-Guy, a company employee, realizes that he has access to the system over which the payment instructions for wage payments are passed. Without further ado, he makes a hundred copies of the instruction for payment of his own wage (Figure 11.9; we assume that the firm makes ten thousand wage payments per month, so that this would not be apparent) and prepares to depart for a third-world country. However, his planned departure will not materialize since the payment instructions are secured using 'message-sequence integrity'.

11.8 Concluding remarks

Legal aspects of secure electronic message transfer

The extent to which contracts and other legal transactions may be executed over a secure electronic message transfer system depends on the legislation and legal practice of each country concerned. In Switzerland, for example, according to the law there is usually no fixed form of contract; on the other hand, the recognition of a relevant electronic record (with or without an electronic signature) as evidence or as a document is not yet legal practice.

As the law stands, a subscriber whose private key is compromised through no fault of his own and subsequently misused, is unprotected.

Current legal practice as far as electronic funds transfer and cash dispensers are concerned, for example, only protects a customer of a bank when the bank providing the service can be proved to have committed a gross error. Revision or at least clarification of the law in this area is urgently needed.

Knowledge of your partner is an important prerequisite to the conclusion of any contract. In electronic message transfer, however, many partners are too far away for easy clarification of matters such as their legal responsibility and whether or not they have reached the age of majority. A mechanism that allows one to request such fundamental information from a trustworthy source would be desirable and this is a possible task for an X.500 directory service. On the other hand, such a directory service would also have to consider personal-protection aspects and would, for example, only accept certain queries from specially authorized partners.

Political aspects of secure electronic message transfer

Secure electronic message transfer allows a subscriber to enter into contact with any other subscriber and to exchange messages without the risk of the messages being read by any other parties. Thus, the state (for example, the criminal prosecution authorities) loses a very controversial, but evidently successful, means of protecting its own interests. The opposition of various governments to security mechanisms in X.400 and their requests for restriction of the use of encryption mechanisms to 'established' companies must be viewed against this background.

Outlook

The 1988 version of the X.400 recommendations contains the preconditions for the realization of secure electronic message transfer systems. The numerous X.400-based systems available today are still based on X.400 (84) which does not provide for special security mechanisms. Many projects aimed at realizing secure electronic message transfer have been initiated both in universities and in the industrial domain. However, regrettably, this reflects the fact that the security features in X.400 (88) are too varied and sometimes too imprecisely defined to guarantee interoperation of systems from different manufacturers without further agreements. Thus, the specification of 'profiles' for security features in X.400 (88) is an urgent task. It will therefore be a few more years before secure systems are commercially available in large numbers.

12

X.500: a recommendation for directory services

Directory services may be viewed as an important aid to the simplification of message transfer. Moreover, their use is of general importance when directory services are viewed in the context of worldwide communication. Thus, this chapter abandons the framework of message transfer.

Section 12.1 gives a general overview and describes the recommendations for directory services. The other sections of this chapter describe the various ideas behind these recommendations.

Section 12.2 introduces the information model, and Section 12.3 describes the user's point of view.

Section 12.4 discusses aspects of the distribution of data across different computers.

Section 12.5 defines the embedding in the OSI model and gives a concrete description of the relationship to electronic message transfer.

Section 12.6 describes the use of directory services to realize the general security schemes first described in Chapter 11.

Lastly, Section 12.7 analyzes the recommendations from the point of view of the user and of the implementor and attempts to sketch forthcoming implementations.

12.1 Introduction

Features of directory services

Now, and increasingly in the future, communication systems are complicated structures, with a worldwide coverage, which consist of a large number of real objects. *Real objects* are the components of a communication system including people, organizations, computers, processes, file systems and electronic mailboxes. The information relating to a real object is called a *logical object* (or *object* for short) and its storage is called an *entry*. So that real objects in distributed applications may be unambiguously identified, they are given *names*. A real object may have several names. Since names are often used by human users, they must be *user friendly*. It should be possible to guess the name of a real object from known properties of that object. Moreover, names should have as long a period of validity as possible.

In order to generate communication relationships between real objects we need *addresses*. An address denotes the *position of a real object* with respect to the system architecture. Since the address of an object is determined by the specific realization of a communication system, it is often not suitable for use by human users. For example, the address of a user of the OSI network service is a 40-digit (decimal) number. Whenever there are changes to the network topology, it is possible that new addresses may have to be allocated to some of the real objects. Thus, addresses are not suitable for use as names, although they do identify real objects uniquely.

The main task of *directory services*, namely the assignment of a set of values to the name of a real object, derives directly from these introductory remarks. Such values include not only the address, but also all valuable information in the form of text, speech, images, etc. This definition gives rise to additional requirements on directory services. There immediately arises the question as to whether the information stored (the so-called *directory*) should be protected, with access permitted to authorized subscribers only.

The directory service includes operations to interrogate and alter the directory. *Retrieval operations* may be broadly divided into two classes. *White-pages queries* provide the information stored for one or more given names. *Yellow-pages queries* supply the names of objects that correspond to the criteria defined in the query. These terms come from telephony. The pages of 'normal' phone books, which contain the names of telephone subscribers together with their phone numbers, are usually white. In contrast, the 'yellow pages' include companies sorted according to their trade. The ordering criterion in this case is the company area of activity. Other directories are arranged according to streets and house numbers; these also amount to a yellow-pages service, where the postal address of the telephone subscriber is the ordering criterion.

Modification operations involve the insertion and removal of entries or their components. A further category of operations is needed to *manage* the directory.

Requirements on directory systems

A *directory system* is defined to be a set of real systems in the OSI sense (Section 1.2). The directory system manages the directory and provides the directory service. With the introduction of computer-supported communication services, directory services must also be available to computer applications. There are two clear reasons why directory systems are distributed. Firstly, modern communication systems are distributed applications which are used by a large number of public and private organizations, and secondly, the description of the real objects of such worldwide systems generates a very large amount of data.

Efficient distributed databases are still current topics of research, in other words, satisfactory solutions are not yet known. While directory systems may in some respects be viewed as databases, they permit simplifications that make them particularly interesting objects to study and also facilitate an efficient realization.

Directory systems have the following properties in common with distributed databases: the data is distributed and duplicated for fast access and high availability. In both cases, high expectations are placed on the availability. However, there are differences in the requirements for the consistency of the stored data: operations on distributed databases must guarantee the consistency of data; on the other hand, in the case of directory systems, such operations must only supply the data with a *high probability of correctness*. Errors can be tolerated, since in directory systems data retrieval is much more frequent than data modification and the retrieved data is used for subsequent operations (for example, to establish a connection to a communication partner with a requested address), when entries with errors will be identified. Directory systems have a *limited data consistency* whereby, after modifications, a directory system may be inconsistent for at most a given time interval.

Because of the distribution and large volume of data, directory systems must provide other tools that may be used to manage large data sets. These tools should also be able to manage remote data via standard protocols. They must provide methods for efficient automatic *data acquisition* and subsequent *maintenance* of the correctness of the data. One is often faced with the problem that data was acquired in existing database systems where it is now also being updated. Thus, the tools must be able to correctly update the directory regarding alterations in existing databases.

Directory systems have been around for a long time. Examples of systems currently in use include:

- *The Domain Name System* (Mockapetris, 1984) is a directory system for the so-called 'ARPA Internet', which is supported by the 'Defense Advanced Research Projects Agency' (DARPA) of the U.S. Department of Defense and which is a combination of various research networks (Quarterman and Hoskins, 1986).

- *Grapevine* (Birrel *et al.*, 1982) is a distributed system which was developed at the Xerox Palo Alto Research Centre and is now operated as a company-internal system by Xerox Corporation. Grapevine is primarily an electronic messaging system that guarantees secure message transfer and authenticates both senders and recipients of messages. Moreover, it has the functions of a directory service. The Grapevine environment consists of some 1500 computers on somewhat more than 50 local area networks, which are linked together in the 'Xerox Research Internet'.

- *The Clearinghouse* (Oppen and Dalal, 1983) is a directory system which was developed from the directory service components of Grapevine. Many of its concepts are a further development of ideas realized in the Grapevine Registration Service. The Clearinghouse was also developed by Xerox and is now productively used by 'Xerox Corporation'.

Overview of the X.500 recommendations

Directory services have been and remain the object of standardization: ISO working groups in cooperation with the IEC are currently discussing proposals for the international standard ISO 9594, which is divided into the eight parts ISO 9594-1 to ISO 9594-8 (Appendix B). At its plenary meeting at the end of 1988, CCITT released a recommendation for directory services designated by X.500 (Appendix B).

In the ISO context, the OSI directory service is specified as a collection of *Application Service Elements* (ASEs) and thus integrated into the standardization of the application layer (Section 1.3) which is presently being strongly driven forward.

The CCITT recommendations for directory services are, like the ISO standard, divided into parts. They include:

- An overview of the concepts and the model of a standardized directory service (in X.500).
- A description of the information model (in X.501, X.520 and X.521).
- The abstract specification of the services (in X.511).
- Aspects of the distribution of the directory service (in X.518).
- The description of the protocols to be used (in X.519).
- The description of the security aspects (in X.509).

Since the standardization of directory services must be seen in the context of OSI standardization, many additional references are required to more recent application layer standards (particularly those of the X.200 series – see Appendix B).

The remaining explanations and statements in this chapter are all taken to refer to the X.500 context. Thus, the qualifications, 'conforming to the standard', 'standardized', 'conforming to X.500' are omitted.

12.2 Information model

DIT

In order to envisage the functional description of the directory service, we must first know how the directory is structured. As noted below, the directory is a tree, known as the *Directory Information Tree* (DIT). Figure 12.1 shows an example of a DIT which we use in the following paragraphs to illustrate the various concepts.

Since the modelling of a real object depends on the context in which it is viewed, it may be represented by several (logical) objects. It is important here to distinguish between the actual entity of a communication system (real object) and its representation by the information relating to it (logical object). The parentheses around the adjective 'logical' indicate that,

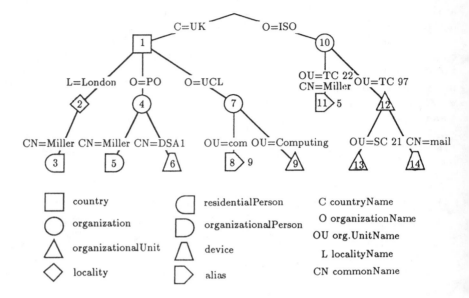

Figure 12.1   Fictitious example of a DIT.

in the following, the adjective 'logical' is dropped when the logical object is meant. For example, in Figure 12.1, Mr. Miller is represented by two different (logical) objects. Entry 3 contains the information relating to the object 'Mr. Miller as a private individual, resident in London' and entry 5 contains the information relating to 'Mr. Miller as an employee of the British Post Office (PO)'.

Objects

Each object has one or more *distinguished names* (*names* for short), which are used to identify it, and exactly one set of *object information*. The name serves as an identification within the DIT and the object information stores the relevant information. Both the name and the object information are sets of *attributes*. An attribute consists of an *attribute type* (*type*), which specifies amongst other things the name of the attribute, conditions for equality in the case of comparison, and the range of values and one or more *attribute values* (*values*). Figure 12.1 shows the attributes with abbreviated type identifications.

The names of the objects are hierarchically constructed from name components known as *Relative Distinguished Names* (RDNs) which themselves consist of one or more attributes. The qualification 'relative distinguished' means that the distinction is not global but relates to a single entry. Based on this structural principle, the directory has a tree structure where the nodes denote entries and the edges denote RDNs. The recommendations do not prescribe which attributes should be used for RDNs.

The root of the DIT is a fictitious entry with the empty name. A child entry inherits its name by the addition of its RDN to the name of the parent entry. It follows that the name of an object is simply the sequence of RDNs on the path from the root to the entry of the object. In Figure 12.1 both RDNs leading to the entries 3 and 5 are called {CN=Miller} and are thus not globally unique. For entries 2 and 4, on the other hand, they are unique. The RDN from entry 10 to entry 11 consists of two attributes: {OU=TC 22, CN=Miller}.

The name of the initial inclusion of an object is called the *main name*, others are called *alias names*. At the time of the initial inclusion a so-called *object entry* is stored with the object information under the main name. Whenever the same object is subsequently included under an alias name, an *alias entry* with a pointer to the object entry is stored. This pointer is just the main name of the object. In Figure 12.1, entry 11 is an alias entry for object entry 5 which belongs to the object 'Mr. Miller is an employee of the British Post Office (PO)'. Mr. Miller, who also has an executive position with ISO may now be addressed as 'Mr. Miller, Chairman of ISO Technical Committee TC 22' using alias entry 11. Thus, Mr. Miller has the three names:

- ({C=UK}, {L=London}, {CN=Miller}),
- ({C=UK}, {O=PO}, {CN=Miller}) and
- ({O=ISO}, {OU=TC 22, CN=Miller})

The first of these names is associated with the private individual and the last two refer to the business man.

Thus, alias names may also be used to access an object with several names. However, we stress that the information about this object is not copied and is only stored in one place. The X.500 recommendations thus, do not support *duplication of data* (Section 12.4).

Object classes

In order to structure the object entries in a uniform way, the objects are divided into *object classes*. For a given object entry, the object class

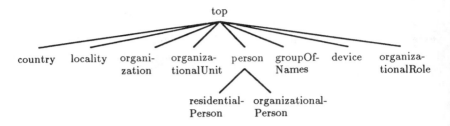

Figure 12.2   Object classes and their interrelationship.

determines the attributes that belong to the name, those that are mandatory, and those that may be optionally stored. In Figure 12.1, entries of the object classes 'country', 'organization', 'organizationalUnit', 'locality', 'organizationalPerson', 'residentialPerson', 'device' and 'alias' are stored.

A new object class may be derived from an existing one in the following way: all mandatory and optional attributes of the existing object class are inherited and it remains only to specify whether new attributes belong to the name and whether they are mandatory or optional. Figure 12.2 shows some pre-defined object classes and their interrelationship. An edge joining two object classes means that the lower object class is derived from the higher one.

This principle of attribute inheritance permits the step-by-step construction of complicated object classes from simpler ones. As Figure 12.2 shows, the object classes 'residentialPerson' and 'organizationalPerson' are derived from 'person'. Thus, attributes, such as, the forms of address, which are generally used to describe a person are stored in 'person' and specific attributes (such as, hobby or office name) are defined in 'residentialPerson' or 'organizationalPerson'.

DIT structure

The *DIT structure* is a directed graph (Figure 12.3). Its nodes are the object classes and its arrows link object classes which are allowed to have adjacent entries in the DIT. Two entries are adjacent if one is the child of the other. This adjacency relationship may have various meanings. In Figure 12.1, 2 lives in 1, 5 is employed by 4, 6 is owned by 4, 12 is part of 10, etc. The DIT structure determines the permitted shapes of the DIT. Figure 12.3 shows an extract of the DIT structure as proposed in Appendix B of X.521. The

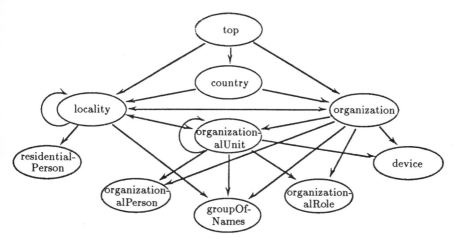

Figure 12.3   A possible DIT structure.

proposed DIT structure is only a proposal and not a recommendation since this appendix does not form part of the recommendations.

12.3 Services from the user's point of view

From the user's point of view, the directory system is an unstructured system which provides its services to the outside world in the form of *operations* via an *access point* (Figure 12.4). A user (whether a person or a process) uses these operations with the assistance of a *Directory User Agent* (DUA). The communication between the DUA and the directory system is connection-oriented. The operations *DirectoryBind* and *DirectoryUnbind* are used to establish and release the connection.

Classes of operations

The directory service operations themselves may be classified according to their properties. It is possible to distinguish between retrieval and modification operations, in addition, operations may relate to single entries or to groups of entries. These two independent characterizing features give rise to four *classes of operations* (*ports*). Since X.500 does not provide for operations to modify groups of entries, three ports remain. An access point

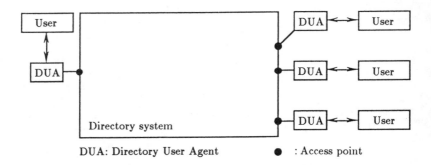

Figure 12.4 Access to the directory system.

to the directory system need not support all three ports. A DUA which is linked to a restricted access point may only provide a reduced service. Thus, DUA are configurable.

Table 12.1 shows the division into classes and the names of the three ports. The *readPort* contains operations to retrieve a single entry, the *searchPort* contains operations to retrieve a group of entries and the *modifyPort* contains operations to modify a single entry. The possibility that in the future further ports might be used to extend the functionality of directory services is left open. Operations of an additional port might cover the fourth class or permit management of the directory.

Operations

The following list describes the distribution of the operations across the three ports and gives examples to illustrate the use of the individual

Table 12.1 Characterization of the ports.

	Retrieval	*Modification*
Single entry	**readPort**	**modifyPort**
Group of entries	**searchPort**	

operations. These examples only make sense when the required information is actually stored in the directory; otherwise they result in an error response.

- The readPort contains the operations *Read, Compare* and *Abandon*. In Read and Compare, the required entry is identified using the name of the object sought.

  — Read returns the object information. The user may specify which attributes are relevant and should be indicated. For example, Read may be used to determine the electronic mail address of the object 'Mr. Miller is an employee of the British Post Office (PO)' of Figure 12.1.

  — Compare returns a Boolean value which indicates whether a given attribute value in an object entry agrees with the corresponding value in the directory. Among other things, Compare facilitates the mechanism for user authentication by password testing. Let us suppose that Mr. Miller has set up a mailbox on a computer which is represented by the entry 14 (Figure 12.1). When he wishes to read new incoming mail he identifies himself on this computer using his name and password. The computer may now use the Compare operation to check the password with the directory service, without knowing the password itself.

  — The Abandon operation also belongs to the readPort. This terminates readPort and searchPort operations if their results are no longer of interest. There is no means of interrupting operations of the modifyPort.

- The searchPort consists of the operations List and Search. The desired group of entries is a subtree of the DIT and is identified by the name of its root. The root entry is known as the base entry.

  — List lists all DIT entries that are hierarchically directly subordinate to the base entry. Thus, this operation may be used to generate a list of the children of an entry. Undesired entries may be filtered out. By repeated execution of this operation, it is possible to traverse and inspect the DIT. For example, a List with base entry 7 (Figure 12.1), restricted to organizationalUnits, returns all objects that are directly subordinate to UCL (University College, London) and belong to the object class 'organizationalUnit'. The result of this query based on the DIT of Figure 12.1 is entry 9 for the object 'Department of Computing'. Entry 8 is filtered out since it is of object class alias.

  — Search is not restricted to children, but searches the whole tree subordinate to the base entry. Undesired entries may also be filtered out in Search. This operation is suitable for yellow-pages queries. One possible Search operation on the DIT of Figure 12.1 is the search for all computers in the directory (object class 'device') in the United Kingdom. The base entry for this operation is entry 1 and its result is entry 6 for the DSA1 operated by the British Post Office.

• The modifyPort contains the operations *AddEntry, RemoveEntry, ModifyEntry* and *ModifyRDN*. The desired entry is identified by its name.

— AddEntry and RemoveEntry are used to insert or delete whole entries. They may only be applied to the leaf entries of the DIT, in other words, the object inserted or to be deleted must not be the parent of any other entry. If, for example, in Figure 12.1, the department in which Mr. Miller works (entry 5) were to be included in the DIT as a suborganization of the PO (entry 4), it could not be inserted directly between these two entries, but would have to be inserted as a leaf of entry 4 before moving entry 5 under the new entry. If entry 5 were not a leaf entry, the procedure would be even more complicated.

— ModifyEntry may be used to insert and delete whole attributes, to insert, delete and replace attribute values and to modify an alias entry.

— ModifyRDN may be used to modify the last component of the name of an entry. Here too, the entry must be a leaf entry of the DIT. This operation corresponds to a deletion followed by a reinsertion at the same parent entry under a different name. In our estimation, the ModifyRDN operation is unmotivated since it does not extend the functionality and involves an undesired shortening of the lifetime of names.

Parameters of operations and their information types

Every operation has a name and the three parameters *argument, result* and *error*. Argument is the input parameter that specifies the operation more precisely and also usually restricts it. Result and error are mutually exclusive output parameters, since they indicate a successful or unsuccessful termination of an operation. The structure of the three parameters is described by the so-called *information types*. The most important information types are *EntryInformation, ServiceControls, Filter* and *SecurityParameter*.

• EntryInformation contains the entries as they will be returned to the user in the result parameter.

- ServiceControls are used to specify the following criteria in queries: time limit, size limit, priority of the query, restriction to the local directory, etc. The ServiceControls also specify whether alias names should be dereferenced. Usually, the user is interested in the object information, therefore, dereferencing is performed automatically. In some cases, however, the alias entry is itself the target of an operation. For example, if the alias entry 11 in Figure 12.1 were to be deleted the dereferencing would have to be prevented, since otherwise entry 5 would be deleted.

- Filters may be used to *a priori* restrict the result sets in Search operations by associating additional conditions with the entries sought for. For example, in the above example of the Search operation a filter may also be used to specify that we are only interested in computers that are used for message transfer. Naturally, a prerequisite is that this information is stored in the directory.

- SecurityParameter has already been discussed in Chapter 11.

12.4 Aspects of the distributed architecture

Functional distribution

As mentioned in the introduction to this chapter, directory systems are distributed because they contain large amounts of data which is maintained by various institutions. Other reasons for distribution include the desire for high availability and location-independent functionality. The components of the directory system are called *Directory System Agents* (DSAs). They permit independent access from different places and together provide the desired service (Figure 12.5). As explained below, each DSA stores and manages only a part of the directory. In order to respond to user queries that refer to information stored on another DSA, DSAs must be interconnected. Only in this way can a DSA decompose a user request into subtasks and charge other DSAs with their processing.

A DSA provides services both to DUAs and to DSAs. Thus, a DSA offers the operations that it offers to DUAs in an analogous form to other DSAs. The operations analogous to Bind and Unbind to establish and release connections between DSAs are known as DSABind and DSAUnbind. The operations between the DSAs are jointly known as distributed ports. For example, a searchPort offers the operations List and Search to a DUA, while a distributedsearchPort offers the operations

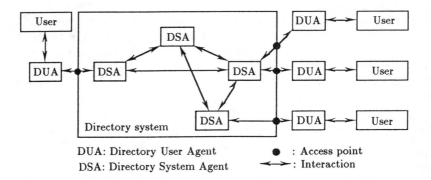

DUA: Directory User Agent   ●   : Access point
DSA: Directory System Agent   ◄——► : Interaction

Figure 12.5   Components of the directory system.

DistributedList and DistributedSearch to other DSAs. In order to handle problems associated with the distribution, the distributed-port operations require several additional information types as input parameters. The analogous operations differ only syntactically and not semantically.

Important additional information types include *Originator, OperationProgress* and *TraceInformation*:

- Originator provides further information about the originator of an operation, in order that the partial results obtained may be correctly returned.

- DSAs that are entrusted with subtasks of operations may use OperationProgress to inform themselves about subtasks which have already been completed.

- TraceInformation specifies the path of a user request within the directory system and thus detects processing loops or inconsistencies in the DIT.

Data distribution

While the directory-service user is not interested in the distribution of data, from the point of view of the directory system, questions arise as to how to partition the directory, how to distribute these partitions to the DSAs and how to manage the information about the distribution.

Partitioning the DIT into contexts

A *context* (*naming context*) is a subtree of the DIT not necessarily extending to the leaf nodes. The name of the root entry of this subtree is defined to be the *prefix* (*context prefix*). Contexts may be used to form a hierarchical partitioning of the DIT, in other words to cover it completely without overlapping (Figure 12.6). A context is managed by exactly one DSA, although a DSA may manage several contexts. The context with the empty prefix is called the *root context*; its hierarchically directly subordinate contexts are *first-level contexts* (FL contexts) and the DSAs which store these are called *first-level DSAs* (FL DSAs). Figure 12.6 shows four contexts (a, b, c and d) distributed across three DSAs (A, B and C). The prefixes are ({C=UK}) for a, ({C=UK}, {O=PO}) for b, ({C=UK}, {O=UCL}) for c and ({O=ISO}) for context d; a and d are FL contexts and A and C are FL DSAs. Although the recommendations do not support duplication of data, parts of the DIT may be redundantly stored by bilateral arrangement. In this respect, X.500 takes two precautions. Firstly, tasks may specify whether their responses may use copies, and secondly, responses state whether they are based on copies or originals.

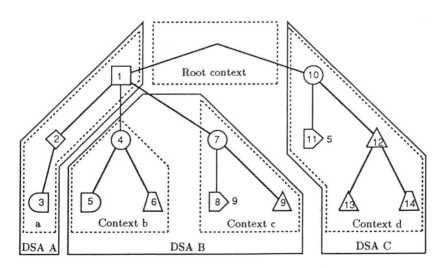

Figure 12.6 Hypothetical decomposition of the DIT of Figure 12.1.

References for context distribution

Information about the distribution of contexts is expressed in terms of *references*. A reference belongs to a context which it brings into a hierarchical relationship with another context. There are five types of references:

- *Subordinate references* are used for directly subordinate contexts whose RDN is known. They consist of this RDN together with the name and the presentation address of the DSA which stores this context. In Figure 12.6, contexts b and c are subordinate to context a. Since context a knows the RDN leading to b and c (Figure 12.1: {O=PO} and {O=UCL}) it has the two subordinate references [1, {O=PO}, DSA B, ⟨Address B⟩] and [1, {O=UCL}, DSA B, ⟨Address B⟩]. The number 1 means that the reference is attached to entry 1.

- *Non-specific subordinate references* consist of the name and the presentation address of the DSA that stores a directly subordinate context for which the RDN is unknown. If in Figure 12.6, a does not know the RDN for entry 7, it will have to store a non-specific subordinate reference to the context c in the form [1, DSA B, ⟨Address B⟩].

- *Superior references* contain the name and the presentation address of the DSA that stores a superior context. FL contexts and the root context have no superior references. The contexts b and c in Figure 12.6 have the superior reference [DSA A, ⟨Address A⟩].

- *Cross references* are used for the purposes of optimization. They are composed of the prefix of a context which is not directly subordinate or superior, together with the name and presentation address of the DSA on which this context is stored. Context d in Figure 12.6 may store a cross reference to context b, so as to enable it to access this information directly without having to go via context a. The reference has the form [({C=UK},{O=PO}), DSA B, ⟨Address B⟩].

- *Internal references* are used to find the entries within a context and consist of the RDN of these entries together with a pointer to the local database. The latter is outside the recommendations. For every entry there is exactly one internal reference. For the RDN to be sufficient to identify an entry, the local structure of the DIT within the context must be known. The storage of this information lies outside of X.500. The internal reference to entry 3 in Figure 12.6 is [2, {CN=Miller}, ⟨Address 3⟩]. The number 2 indicates that entry 3 is the child of entry 2. Their representation is not prescribed by the recommendations.

The directory system must be organized in such a way that every DUA has access to any entry (via its connected DSAs). Thus, each DSA must be able to use the references of its contexts to determine the DSA on which an entry is stored. A reference to a sought-for context need not necessarily be explicit, but may be constructed using a *reference path*. To guarantee that a path will always be found, a DSA must know at least one superior reference and all subordinate references (including non-specific subordinate references). In addition, in order to increase its efficiency, a DSA may store any number of cross references.

Thus, there is always a path which may lead via the root context. The root context has a special role to play here, since it is not stored in a single DSA but is duplicated on every FL DSA; therefore, every FL context knows every other FL context via the subordinate references of the root context. The information about FL contexts is thus redundantly stored. This approach is based on the assumption that a worldwide system will have a small number of FL DSAs (for example, one per country), which together provide an efficient data throughput, high reliability and a flexible distributed authority in the management of the whole directory.

Operational distribution

A user request can often not be handled locally, since the related information is distributed over several DSAs. The user request is therefore not a single indivisible operation but contains several processing phases. In these cases, according to the locally stored references, other DSAs must be included to forward subrequests. The various reference types give rise to three modes of DSA interaction.

Modes of DSA interaction

We distinguish the three modes of DSA interaction, *chaining, multicasting* and *referral* (Figure 12.7). The numbers in the figure indicate the order of events:

- A DSA uses chaining when it is able to determine conclusively from its subordinate, superior and cross references which DSA should be used to process subtasks.

- Multicasting is used when a DSA cannot determine conclusively from its non-specific subordinate references which DSA has the data needed to process subtasks, or when it knows beforehand that several DSAs are involved.

- A referral is always a response to a request in chaining mode or multicasting mode which could not be processed or which could only be incompletely processed. The response then contains a reference

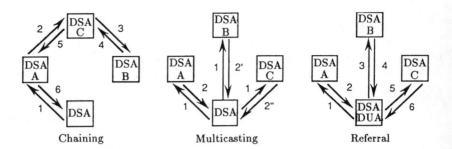

Figure 12.7   Modes of DSA interaction.

to another DSA which must again be tasked either in chaining mode
or in multicasting mode. Interestingly, in the referral mode, a DUA
may also undertake the coordination.

The choice of the interaction mode is generally left to the DSA. However,
the user may forbid chaining so that a DSA tasked in this way must answer
with a referral or an error message.

Phases in the processing of a user request

The processing of a user request may be chronologically subdivided into
three phases, *name resolution, evaluation* and *result merging.* If several
DSAs are involved in an operation, these three phases are executed in every
DSA and operation progress and trace information are adjusted accordingly:

- *Name resolution* uses internal references to determine from the name
  of the entry whether the entry is stored locally. If this is the case, the
  name resolution terminates and the task may enter the next phase,
  otherwise the other references are used to search for the DSA which
  manages the entry.
- *Evaluation* is called once the name resolution has found an internal
  reference. It executes the operation itself. Since in the List and Search
  operations the desired entries may be stored on different DSAs, in
  certain circumstances several other DSAs may be involved in the
  evaluation phase.

- Once the results of the evaluation are available these are combined into an overall result by *result merging*. This result is then sent back to the originator.

An example of the execution of an operation is given by the DIT with the hypothetical decomposition given in Figure 12.6. Let us suppose that a user is connected by a DUA to a first-level DSA in Australia and that he wishes to use the List operation in chaining mode to see those objects which are stored directly subordinate to the entry {C=UK}. The Australian DSA first initiates a name resolution and searches in vain for internal references to the RDN {C=UK}. However, since as a first-level DSA it knows the root context, it finds a specific subordinate reference to DSA A and transfers the operation (action 1 in Figure 12.7) there. During name resolution, DSA A finds an internal reference (entry 1 in Figure 12.6). During the evaluation phase, DSA A looks for all children of entry 1 stored locally, and as a first subresult finds entry 2 with RDN {L=London}. However, he also has two subordinate references to DSA B (Figure 12.6). Thus, DSA A sets up a connection to DSA B and transfers the operation (action 2 in Figure 12.7) with the added information types OperationProgress and TraceInformation. DSA B finds the two local entries 4 and 7 (name resolution), evaluates the required information (evaluation), collects a subresult (result merging) and returns this to DSA A (action 5 in Figure 12.7; actions 3 and 4 have no counterparts in this example). DSA A now starts its result merging phase. It merges the two subresults together and returns them to the DSA in Australia (action 6 in Figure 12.7). The operation terminates with the delivery of the result to the DUA.

12.5 Embedding in the OSI model

Section 12.3 discussed services offered to the user by the directory system via a DUA. If the DUA of the user and the DSA which represents the directory system are located in different real open systems (Section 1.2), their communication is defined by the *Directory Access Protocol* (DAP). Section 12.4 described those aspects which are important for the forwarding of subtasks via DSAs. When two communicating DSAs are located in different real open systems their communication is defined by the *Directory System Protocol* (DSP).

In the OSI sense, DUAs and DSAs are application processes and their OSI-related parts are application entities (Section 1.2). Figure 12.8a shows the communication between a DUA and a DSA which is defined by the DAP. Figure 12.8b shows the analogous situation of the communication of two DSAs which is defined by the DSP.

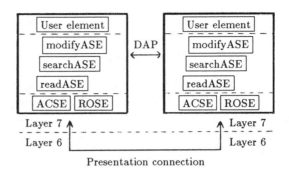

Figure 12.8a Embedding in the OSI reference model: DAP.

The DUA and DSA application entities may be coarsely subdivided into three subsets, *user element, directory-specific application service elements* and *general application service elements*. An ASE consists of a set of functions that facilitates a certain OSI-conforming interoperation of the connected application entities (Section 1.3).

The user element is the interface between the OSI environment and the environment of the real system. Here, the directory service operations are available to the user.

The directory-specific ASEs reflect the division into ports and are named accordingly. For the DAP, they are known as *readASE, searchASE* and *modifyASE*, while for the DSP they are *distributedReadASE, distributedSearchASE* and *distributedModifyASE*. Since the directory-specific ASEs map their total functionality onto the services of the general ASEs, the DAP and the DSP form a set of syntactic and semantic definitions of this mapping.

General ASEs provide supporting services for very different applications. The directory service agents use two such, the *Association Control Service Element* (ACSE) and the *Remote Operations Service Element* (ROSE). The general ASEs have already been described in some detail in Section 1.3.

Relationship to X.400

MHSs are expected to be the first and most important users of directory services. Only X.400 (88) provides the prerequisite that the directory service

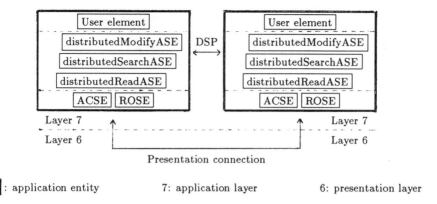

Figure 12.8b   Embedding in the OSI reference model: DSP.

should be usable directly or indirectly, in that it redefines the term *O/R name*. As explained in Section 2.5, an O/R name in X.400 (84) denotes an address, for which we use the term *O/R address*. In X.400 (88), an O/R name may now contain either an O/R address or a directory name or both. Directory names in the X.500 sense are distinguished names. Based on the new definition of O/R names, there are several ways in which an MHS may use the directory service:

- *User-friendly names.* The originators and the recipients of messages may be denoted by user-friendly names. If an O/R name consists of a name alone, this must be supplemented with the corresponding address using the directory service. The division of the O/R name into a name and an address component is sensible since the first component is used by the user and the second by the message transfer system (MTS). According to the X.400 recommendations, it is possible to use names for communication between a user agent (UA) and a message store (MS), an MS and a message transfer agent (MTA) and between a UA and an MTA, but not for communication between MTAs. This means that the UA of the originator, its MS or the first MTA of the MTS must search for and use the corresponding address in the directory.

- *Distribution lists* (DL). A group of recipients may be combined on a DL. This has an O/R address and also a name, if it is managed by the directory service. If the name of a distribution list occurs in the recipient field of a message, this must be expanded with the corresponding O/R addresses by the first MTA and replaced by the O/R addresses of the DL members by the MTA responsible for the DL (*expansion point*). Both actions are executed using the directory service. The O/R addresses obtained may again denote distribution lists. Thus, a special O/R address may be embedded several times or the O/R address of the original distribution list may re-occur. For this reason, all *notifications* and *interpersonal message receipts* are sent back to the MTA responsible and not directly to the message originator. It is then the task of this MTA to forward these to the originator or to the administrator of the distribution list.

- *Functionality of the MHS components* (Chapter 9). The services supported by a UA, an MS or an MTA may be stored in its directory entry. If details of the functionality of a component are requested directly via the directory service, no *probe message* need be sent and the load on the MTS is lightened.

- *Mutual authentication.* Before the communication itself, the MHS components mutually authenticate each other. More details of this service may be found in Chapter 11 and in Section 12.6.

- *Interactive use.* The X.400 user may consult the directory service directly to find recipients and their O/R addresses. If he has the name, he may determine the corresponding O/R address using the Read operation. If he has only part of the name or other information he must use the Search operation.

Figure 12.9 shows the functional model of the relationship between X.500 and X.400. It is clear that the use of a directory system is a local concern of individual MHS components; therefore, it has no effect on the MHS protocols and does not force the supplier or manager of another component to integrate these services. The model does not require a global directory system. Every component that wishes to gain from a directory system must possess a local DUA, since there are no protocols between X.500 and X.400 components. In Figure 12.9, the X.400 components that make use of the directory service are emphasized.

Various component configurations may be deduced from the functional model. If a DUA is located in a UA system, it forms a type of intelligent terminal, that in addition to message transfer, permits interactive use of the directory system. If a DUA is integrated in an MS system, the number of DUAs is reduced, since typically an MS serves several UAs. Incorrect messages may be intercepted before they are delivered to the MTS. As a final variant, the DUA may be located in an MTA system. This has the disadvantage that the messages to be processed have already been transmitted. However, one advantage in this case would

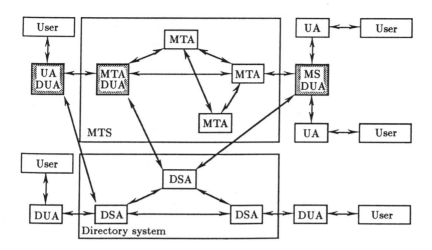

Figure 12.9   Functional model of the relationship between X.500 and X.400.

be the fact that the DUA may be used simultaneously to evaluate names and distribution lists. An effective implementation would probably combine several of the components shown in Figure 12.9 into a single system, so that, for example, a DSA and an MTA would be coupled with a DUA and located in the same system.

12.6 Security

Chapter 11 raised the problem of security using the example of message handling and proposed generally valid solutions which may be implemented using directory services. In this section, we consider the topic of security, this time from the point of view of the directory service.

For directory services we may distinguish two security-related types of tasks. Firstly, communication between a user and the directory system must be secured and secondly, the security service may provide mechanisms to help secure the exchange of information between arbitrary partners in a communication system:

- In *communication with the directory system*, the user and the directory system must mutually authenticate each other so that, on the one hand, the user is certain that he is actually connected to the desired service provider and on the other hand, the directory system is able to control access rights to the directory and provide the account for the facilities used. In addition, duplication, misdirection and amendment of information while it is being exchanged must be prevented.

- For *the exchange of information between arbitrary subscribers* to a communication system, the same security requirements apply, which we may summarize by the terms *subscriber authentication* and *information authentication*. For this purpose, the directory system may store passwords, certificates, etc., and may provide the operations with security parameters.

The second type of task is more general since the directory system itself may be viewed as a subscriber to the communication system. The security scheme defined in X.500 supports this general case. It distinguishes between two different levels of security. *Simple authentication* only permits subscriber authentication. It is based on passwords which are stored in the directory. The subscribers authenticate each other by unencoded transmission of their names and passwords. Thus, simple authentication should be restricted to local communication. Only *strong authentication* supports the protection of the transmitted information in addition to subscriber authentication. This technique was described in detail in Chapter 11.

12.7 Outlook

In this chapter, we have shown that an X.500 directory system is a complex distributed system; conforming implementations will therefore be correspondingly expensive. However, it must be stressed that X.500 only incorporates a minimum of the desired concepts and functions. Broadly speaking it involves:

- A definition of a structure for a hierarchical name space, which allows the various naming authorities freedom as far as the specific layout is concerned.
- Guidelines for a sensible layout of this name space.
- A specification of retrieval, search and simple modification operations.
- Instructions for interoperation of DSAs, operated by different organizations.

In response to the question as to which desirable functions are not defined in X.500, it is helpful to look at the history of these recommendations. We see that from 1984 to 1986 earlier versions were discussed, which in addition to the functions of the current version, also had the following features:

- The name space did not have a tree structure but was of the form of an acyclic graph. Thus, objects (even without the alias mechanism) could have several names. The term *distinguished name* is in fact a relict from these proposals and was earlier used to indicate one of several possible names.

- The concept of *descriptive names* was used in an attempt to use any stored information to name an object. A descriptive name for a hypothetical fellow citizen (given as a set of attributes) might be: {*Number of pets=3, Hobby=Sailing, Profession=Electrician*}. The question arises as to whether this expression is actually a name at all, in other words whether it designates precisely one object. Efficient distributed algorithms capable of answering this question are still the object of research.

  The attraction of descriptive names is that they eliminate the difference between white-pages and yellow-pages queries.

- Support for duplicated data using *shadowing*. A DSA could request part of the data of another DSA for the purposes of local storage and rapid access. At the same time, it would oblige the supplier of the information to inform it of possible changes.

- Alterations were not restricted to the removal or generation of leaf nodes; in this case it was possible to remove any node from the graph and to include any new node. Note that here the expression DIT would be out of place since the directory does not have a tree structure.

- A scheme to allocate access rights to entries, based on the so-called *access control lists*.

The earlier versions were rejected largely because of their complexity. Not only were there good reasons to doubt that such standards could be implemented, but there were also difficulties in finding a correct definition of the semantics of complicated operations (for example, the removal of a node in a graph). Here, one of the main problems was to guarantee the consistency of the graph. However, it is to be expected that, with experience of the development of the first products and of the use of pilot systems, some of the old ideas will again surface and will be discussed during a revision of the recommendations. Above all we expect that extensions will be necessary in respect of access control and directory management.

The authors are aware of a small number of projects aimed at developing software conforming to X.500. The first prototypes were shown at the Hannover Fair (CeBIT '89). Thus, we expect that a number of commercial X.500 implementations will be available to interested users towards the end of 1991. However, we would not expect the availability of an implementation to lead on its own to a correctly functioning worldwide directory; the main problems lie in the organizational area, in other words, in the interplay between the users and individual DSAs.

Early experience in this area will be provided by pilot projects in universities, both in Europe and in the USA. In addition, there are plans to hold so-called *multivendor shows* (as with the introduction of X.400) at important fairs, where X.500 prototypes or products from various manufacturers will be jointly used to form a directory system.

These activities will yield valuable knowledge about the testing of implementations for their conformance to the standards. It is expected that, as for X.400, test suites will be developed and standardized for X.500 (Chapter 13).

Despite its restrictions, discussed above, X.500 will doubtless become an important and indispensable link between different OSI applications.

13

Conformance testing of X.400 implementations

'This product conforms to the recommendations of the X.400 (84)
series and to the NBS, COS, U.S.GOSIP, TOP 3.0, CEPT and
CEN/CENELEC profiles ...'
Product announcement

13.1 Introduction

For several years now, computer manufacturers and software houses have
offered implementations of the CCITT X.400 (84) recommendations. At
so-called *multivendor demonstrations* at major fairs (for example, CeBIT
in Hannover), all members of the public interested in e-mail have been
shown that it is possible to exchange electronic mail between different
computers and independently-developed implementations according to the
X.400 (84) recommendations. Despite the international standardization of
communication protocols and services, this is not self-evident.

As is clear from the previous chapters, the recommendations of
the X.400 series define a complex, hierarchically-structured system, the
implementation of which is not straightforward. Because of its complexity,
a formal verification of the software is not practically possible. Testing
is the only method of discovering and eliminating errors in the software.
Moreover, as experience with other large software projects shows, it cannot
be assumed that implementations leaving the development department of
the manufacturer or the software house to be marketed as a product are
error-free.

Further problems arise when possibly-incompatible implementations
are interconnected into a worldwide message handling service. The number
of different functions, the multiplicity of possible options, the alternative
choices of underlying services and protocols and the differences in the basic
communication services do not actually make it easier for an implementor
to implement the recommendations correctly. It necessarily follows from the
spectrum of options outlined above that implementations may differ from
each other to such an extent that an exchange of messages is impossible. The
reality, in the form of implementations of communication services, seldom
agrees with the ideal of the OSI world; an exchange of messages is only
possible on paper.

These problems have also been recognized by ISO. For several years,
experts have been developing a methodology for testing communication
protocols and services. This methodology involves the definition of the
test environment and of test cases, the implementation of tests on a real
system, the execution of tests and the certification of implementations of
OSI standards. All these activities are termed *conformance testing*. The

ISO standard 'OSI Conformance Testing Methodology and Framework' ISO 9646 is divided into six parts: Part 1: General Concepts, Part 2: Abstract Test Suite Specification, Part 3: The Tree and Tabular Combined Notation (TTCN), Part 4: Test Realization, Part 5: Requirements on Test Laboratories and Clients for the Conformance Assessment Process, and Part 6: Test Laboratory Operations.

In conjunction with the recommendations of the X.400 (84) series, CCITT has also recognized that the OSI reference model can only find general acceptance if it is shown that the protocols defined for the OSI applications are implementable. In particular, for message handling systems, this means that the protocols and services defined in the recommendations X.410 (84), X.411 (84) and X.420 (84) can be implemented and that the implementations should be able to exchange messages. In CCITT, a group has been formed that is exclusively devoted to the conformance testing of X.400 implementations. The results of the work of this group are given in the recommendation X.403 (88) 'Message Handling Systems Conformance Testing'. Comparison of this document with the corresponding ISO document shows that an intensive exchange of ideas has taken place. Thus, in this section we use the conformance testing of X.400 implementations to describe the general principles for the testing of communication protocols.

For some time we have been used to the certification of technical products by independent organizations such as the Technischer Überwachungsverein (TÜV) in Germany. We may expect the same thing in the future for OSI products. The product announcement quoted above is a step in this direction. 'Conforms to' means that the product complies with the technical specification (in this context, this amounts to the recommendations of the X.400 (84) series and the profiles discussed in Chapter 5). However, the announcement does not tell us who (which organizations or institutions) has verified the conformance to the recommendations and profiles. In many European countries and in the USA, *test laboratories* have been built to provide interested parties with the infrastructure for conformance testing of implementations of OSI standards. These test laboratories are authorized to certify that an implementation conforms to the OSI standard.

As discussed in Section 2.3 (Management domains), the ADMDs guarantee immediate wide-area connectivity between arbitrary subscribers to the message handling system. In order to provide a reliable service, the administrator of an ADMD (usually the national PTT company) may require that X.400 implementations of all connected PRMDs should be tested. In Switzerland, the PTT operates a test laboratory (known as OSI-LAB) to verify the conformance of an implementation.

Conformance testing does not involve bilateral testing of each implementation against each other. Instead, the test laboratory represents the partner entity for the protocol implementation to be tested. Messages are exchanged between the test laboratory and the implementation and *vice versa.* The messages to be exchanged and the conditions that must be met by this exchange are defined by *test cases.* The test cases are collected together into a *test suite* for an OSI standard. Like an OSI standard, test suites are formally agreed by the appropriate committees; afterwards, they are referred to as *conformance test suite standards.*

In software engineering, great attention is paid to the testing of programs and program systems. In comparison with this, conformance testing is a very young discipline. The term conformance was first introduced in the 1988 edition of the CCITT recommendations (Blue Book) for all OSI standards (including X.400 (84) and (88)). For example, in the service and protocol specifications X.419 (88) (Text Communication – Protocol Specification) and X.420 (88) (Text Communication – Interpersonal Messaging System) the requirements on an implementation in respect of conformance are explicitly defined. It is an almost paradoxical fact that the testing of implementations of the X.400 (84) series is defined in the recommendation X.403 (88).

We note that conformance testing only includes limited tests of robustness (how does the implementation behave if incorrect data is sent or incorrect actions are initiated?) and does not involve performance testing at all. Neither is conformance testing a proof of the correctness of an implementation, since testing can only show the presence of errors. However, conformance testing does increase the probability that implementations of an OSI standard are actually able to communicate with one another and exchange messages. The international standardization of conformance testing is leading to the possibility of mutual recognition of test results and an exchange of test cases. In this sense, conformance testing is a considerable step towards 'open systems'.

In the next section, we introduce the terminology of conformance testing. The aim of the section is to indicate the requirements that must be satisfied by an implementation before it can be classified as a *conforming implementation.*

13.2 Conformance testing: terminology

The term conformance testing involves two separate groups of activities. Firstly, conformance testing covers all 'intellectual' activities associated with the definition of tests (study of the OSI standards and profiles and definition of test cases, standardization of the test cases). Secondly, conformance testing involves the 'manual' activity of

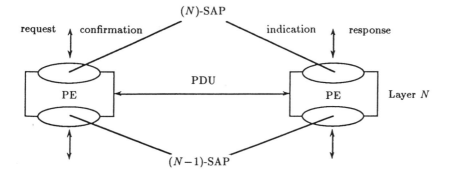

Figure 13.1   Elements of a specification of protocols and services.

testing an implementation (*Implementation Under Test* (IUT)), which comprises the selection of test cases, the installation of the test cases on a real system, the execution of the tests and the analysis of the test results.

The product announcement at the beginning of this chapter reads:

'This product conforms to the recommendations of the X.400 (84) series ...'.

This statement implies the question as to the requirements that an implementation must fulfil in order to be designated as 'conforming to ...'. These requirements are called *conformance requirements* and are derived from the OSI standard and from profiles. A *conforming implementation* complies with all the conformance requirements.

An OSI standard uses an (N)-protocol (Section 1.2) to define how two (N)-peer entities (PEs) provide the (N)-service using the underlying $(N-1)$-service and the (N)-PDUs exchanged between them. $(N+1)$-entities access the (N)-service by calling service primitives (request, indication, response or confirmation). The (N)-protocol defines the time sequence of events, the formats of the service primitives (the parameter types and the parameters) and the format of the PDUs exchanged between the peer entities (see also Section 1.2 and Figure 13.1).

The (N)-service is subdivided into service classes and services (in the sense of functions). For message handling systems, service classes were introduced in the recommendation X.400 (84), both for the MTS and for the interpersonal messaging service (IPM service). In Chapter 2, we introduced all the X.400 (84) services by name. At this point it remains to repeat the division into service classes. These are as follows:

- MTS – Basic, submission and delivery, conversion, query and status and inform.

- IPM – Basic, submission and delivery and conversion (see MTS), cooperating IPM UA action, cooperating IPM UA information conveying, query (see MTS), status and inform (MT service elements).

The service class 'status and inform' requires some explanation since it has not been previously introduced. The services assigned to this class are 'alternate recipient assignment' and 'hold for delivery'. The first of these services may be used to deliver incoming messages to a UA that does not have all the recipient attributes specified in the messages. This, for example, enables a company to process messages on behalf of subscribers who are not directly attached to a message handling system. 'Hold for delivery' enables a UA to instruct its MTA to delay sending acknowledgements.

Recommendation X.401 (84) expands this division into service classes by distinguishing between basic and optional services. All optional service elements are assigned the attribute *essential* or *additional*. Services classified as *essential* are supported by the administrations (ADMDs in the sense of Section 2.4). Additional services may be made available by the administrations for national use and also internationally on the basis of bilateral agreements. The classification of services given in Chapter 5 is more refined, where semantic differences are negligible.

The optional services of the IPMS may be set on a per message basis. The classification of services in X.401 distinguishes between whether a message is sent or received. If the ADMD supports an optional service, then a user may generate and send a message with the service. On the recipient's side this means that the service is passed on to the UA which then makes it available to the recipient. For optional MTS services, the classification of services does not distinguish between send and receive sides, since in the MTL, all systems involved in message transfer must be able to send and receive all kinds of messages.

The classification in Table 13.1 applies to the 'importance indication' service introduced in Chapters 2 and 5. The classification of the services of the IPM, MT and RTS layers is adopted by recommendation X.403 (88) to define the conformance requirements for implementations of X.400 (84). X.403 (88) specifies that an implementation conforms to the recommendations if and only if it satisfies the conformance requirements listed below.

- IPM and MT services
  - — All basic services must be correctly implemented.
  - — All essential optional services must be correctly implemented and the division according to sender and recipient must be taken into account.
  - — All additional optional services supported by the implementation must be correctly implemented.
  - — All the conditions and limitations given in the profile 'X.400-series Implementor's Guide Version 5' (CCITT, 1986) must be adhered to.
- RTS service
  - — The RTS service defined in X.410 (84) must be correctly implemented.
  - — All the conditions and limitations given in the profile 'X.400-series Implementor's Guide Version 5' (CCITT, 1986) must be adhered to.

Whether an implementation correctly implements the services defined in the recommendations will be checked by conformance testing.

It is clear from the above list that an implementation can only be successfully tested if those responsible for the conformance testing have access to all important information relevant to an implementation. In particular, this information includes a list of all services and options implemented. This list may be used to check the conformance requirements and to select the test cases needed to check an implementation (Section 13.6). So-called *Protocol Implementation Conformance Statements* (PICSs) are used to ascertain this information. Recommendation X.403 (88) defines a so-called PICS proforma for the IPMS, the MTS and the RTS, to be filled in by the implementors prior to the testing of an implementation. The PICS proforma for the IPMS is shown in Table 13.2. A distinction is made between a PICS proforma for the service elements and a PICS proforma for the protocol elements.

In addition to the definition of the conformance requirements on an implementation as described in great detail in this section, they can

Table 13.1 'Importance indication' service element (from X.401 (84)).

IPM optional user facilities	Origination by UA	Reception by UA
... Importance Indication	Additional	Essential

Table 13.2   PICS proforma for the IPMS.

Service	Origination STD	IMP	Reception STD	IMP	STD: standard
...					(X.400 recommendation)
Importance indication	O		M		IMP: implementation
...					M: mandatory / O: optional

UAPDU	Origination STATUS STD	IMP	CONST IMP	Reception STATUS STD	IMP	CONST IMP	CONST STD
...							
subject	M			M			256
importance	O			M			
...							

STATUS IMP contains an indication as to whether the protocol element is supported.
CONST IMP contains an indication as to whether the restrictions defined in the column CONST STD are adhered to.

be defined in a different way in a standard or a recommendation. In general, we distinguish between the following forms (ISO 9646):

- The OSI standard distinguishes between *mandatory, conditional* and *optional* services, as in the above example. Conditional services are those to which the OSI standard has attached conditions. An implementation must support these services if, and only if, the given conditions are applied.

- The OSI standard explicitly defines allowed and forbidden behaviour of an implementation.

- The OSI standard defines *static* and *dynamic conformance requirements*.

    — *Static conformance requirements.* These define minimal requirements on an implementation to guarantee interworking with other implementations. The static conformance requirements refer to all the services that an implementation should correctly support and define the dependencies on the underlying services (protocol stack). They may be very general (for example, the grouping of services and options into protocol classes) or very detailed (for example, the specification of values or ranges of values for protocol parameters and timers).

— *Dynamic conformance requirements.* The dynamic conformance requirements define the behaviour of an implementation in different phases during the communication with other entities. Thus, these also define the permitted temporal behaviour of an implementation which may be observed at the interfaces. ISO 9646 uses the term *maximal behaviour* for this.

The conformance requirements may be used to define when an implementation conforms to the OSI standard.

Conforming implementation   A protocol implementation conforms to the OSI standard if the (static and dynamic) conformance requirements according to the PICS are correctly implemented.

Table 13.3 gives an overview of the protocol entities considered in the X.400 (84) recommendations and includes the definitions of the service classes and the PICS. In addition, the table identifies the test events to be specified (ASPs) and the test documents for the IPMS, MTS and RTS.

Table 13.3   Test objects and the relevant documents (Lange, 1988).

Layer	Entity	Proto-col	Classifi-cation of the service tests	Test results	Test documents	PICS
Local user functions						
UAL	UAE	P2	X.400 user services	ASP	CTSM.1	X.403 Appendix B
MTL	MTAE	P1	X.400 user services	ASP from X.411	CTSM.2	X.403 Appendix C
RTS		X.410	ASP from X.410	ASP from X.410	CTSM.3	X.403 Appendix D
Presentation layer (no services are called)						
Session layer						

In the next section we consider one aspect of conformance testing, namely the test methods, in more detail. First, we show how a test system architecture may be derived from the general model of a layer of the OSI reference model (Figure 13.1). Then we investigate the influence of the test system architecture on the test specification. The section ends with an evaluation of the test methods described.

13.3 Abstract test methods

It is easy to derive a general model for a test system from the structure of an (N)-layer outlined in Figure 13.1. The model shown in Figure 13.2 is obtained by viewing one of the protocol entities as the IUT and representing the partner entity by the tester. In this configuration, the tester is able to observe the IUT via the given service access points (SAPs; *Points of Control and Observation* (PCOs), in the terminology of ISO 9646), and to interact with it by calling *Abstract Service Primitives* (ASPs) at the SAP. In the context shown here, and in general when the word 'abstract' is used, abstract means an implementation-independent definition of a service primitive; implementation independent in the sweeping sense that a direct realization in the form described is not intended. In what follows, we use only the terms introduced in ISO 9646 and X.403 (88) (for example, ASP and PCO).

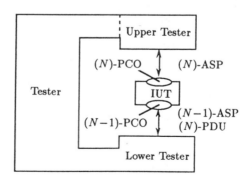

Figure 13.2 Configuration of tester and IUT.

The internal structure of the IUT remains hidden to the tester. For conformance testing only the observable behaviour of the IUT defined in the (N)-protocol is important. In software engineering, such testing is known as *black-box* testing. In the configuration of Figure 13.2, the tester is able to stimulate the IUT by calling service primitives ((N)-ASPs or $(N-1)$-ASPs) and to analyze the $(N-1)$-ASPs and (N)-ASPs generated by the IUT. The (N)-PDU is coded as an $(N-1)$-SDU.

In the terminology of conformance testing, the part of the tester that controls the interface above the IUT and initiates and monitors actions there is called the *Upper Tester* (UT), while that part of the tester consisting of the tester in the narrower sense (Section 13.5), including the control of the IUT from below, is called the *Lower Tester* (LT) or just the *tester*. Usually, the UT is not part of the tester. This is implied in Figure 13.2. From this division of the responsibilities between UT and LT it necessarily follows that special procedures to coordinate the actions of the UT and the LT (*test coordination procedures*) must be agreed and specified in the test suite.

In general, it cannot be assumed that an IUT is directly observable via its interfaces to layer N+1 and layer N−1. Thus, ISO 9646 distinguishes the following abstract test methods according to the interfaces over which the UT and the LT control the IUT. The test methods directly affect the way in which the tests are defined, as will become apparent from the following discussion of the test methods.

- *Local test method.* The abstract test suite is specified using the observable and controllable (N)-ASPs, (N)-PDUs and $(N-1)$-ASPs. The test method requires access to the interfaces above and below the IUT together with a mapping from the (N)- and $(N-1)$-ASPs to their counterparts in the *System Under Test* (SUT). (The IUT is to be regarded as part of the SUT.) The test coordination procedure is defined in the test suite, but no assumptions about a possible realization are made (Figure 13.2). Possible access to the (N)-PCO by the UT and to the $(N-1)$-PCO by the LT is assumed and should be supported by the SUT. The UT and the LT coordinate their actions according to the defined test coordination procedure.

- *Distributed test method.* The abstract test suite is specified using the observable and controllable (N)-ASPs, (N)-PDUs and $(N-1)$-ASPs, which are initiated on the tester's side (Figure 13.3). Access to the interface above the IUT and a mapping of the (N)-ASPs onto their counterparts in the SUT are required. The test coordination procedure is defined in the test suite, but no assumptions are made about a possible realization. Possible access to the (N)-PCO by the UT is assumed and should be supported by the SUT. The LT should be able to initiate and receive the possible $(N-1)$-ASPs on the side of the tester. The UT and the LT coordinate their actions according to the defined test coordination procedure.

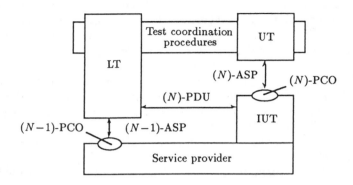

Figure 13.3 Distributed test method.

- *Coordinated test method.* The abstract test suite is specified using the observable and controllable (N)-ASPs, (N)-PDUs and $(N-1)$-ASPs, which are initiated on the tester's side (Figure 13.4). Access to the interface above the IUT and a mapping of the (N)-ASPs onto their counterparts in the SUT are required. The test coordination procedure is defined in the test suite in the form of a *test management protocol.* Possible access to the (N)-PCO by the UT is assumed and should be supported by the SUT. The UT should implement the test management protocol and be able to initiate and receive the stimuli of the SUT defined in the test suite.

- *Remote test method.* The abstract test suite is specified using the $(N-1)$-ASPs observable and controllable by the tester together with the received (N)-PDUs (Figure 13.5). The (N)-PCO on the SUT side is not used. The (N)-PDUs generated by the SUT are received at the $(N-1)$-PCO of the tester. The test coordination procedure is defined in the test suite, but no assumptions about a possible realization are made. The SUT should be able to execute some of the functions of the UT. The LT should be able to initiate and receive the possible $(N-1)$-ASPs on its side. The definition of tests of the form 'IUT as sender' (Section 13.4) is made indirectly, that is, the test cases specify exactly what the tester should receive at the $(N-1)$-PCO.

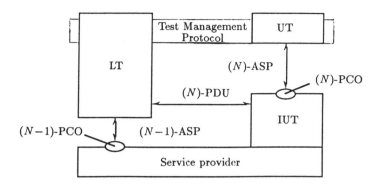

Figure 13.4   Coordinated test method.

These test methods may be subdivided into groups of *local tests* and *external tests* (distributed, coordinated and remote tests) and are applicable to the testing of '*single-layer IUTs*' and '*multi-layer IUTs*'. Single-layer IUTs are those which include exactly one layer of the OSI reference model. Multi-layer IUTs are those which include protocol implementations from several adjacent layers. *Embedded IUTs* are those which are embedded in an implementation of several layers.

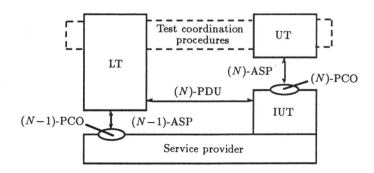

Figure 13.5   Remote test method.

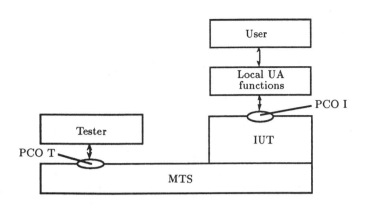

Figure 13.6   Remote single-layer testing of X.400 (84).

In ISO 9646 the test methods and IUT and SUT configurations described here are referred to in shorthand as follows:

Single-layer IUT (S),   multi-layer IUT (M) and embedded IUT (E).

Local (L),   distributed (D),   coordinated (C) and remote (R) testing.

Thus, for example, DS denotes distributed, single-layer testing. The test methods L, D, C and R may be arbitrarily combined with S, M and E.

In CTSM.1 (CCITT, 1988) and X.403 (88) the test method R is defined for the UAL. This results in the configuration of tester and IUT shown in Figure 13.6.

The PCO T (tester) and in particular, the PCO I (IUT) also define a control of the IUT via the UT. In X.403 (88) it is noted that the PCO I only serves to define the test cases. On the IUT side, no special precautions (for example, the explicit introduction of an interface to the UAL) need to be taken in order to exercise control over the IUT as specified in the test suite. Instead it is assumed that the local UA functions are sufficient to achieve the desired control over the IUT.

Which of the abstract test methods described here are used in practice? From the above discussion, it is clear that the method of 'remote testing' has found a place in test suite standardization. This method may be used to test any implementation of an OSI standard, since it makes no assumptions about provisions to enable an IUT to support the testing (for example, for access at the interfaces to the IUT). All other methods, in particular local testing, assume that the IUT can be *directly* controlled at one or both service interfaces (for example, in the form of procedure calls to initiate and receive service primitives). This cannot be assumed in the general case. The advantage of this method lies in the fact that, in testing, side effects (for example, caused by the underlying service provider) may be excluded. Otherwise local testing may be used to detect a fault in the IUT unambiguously. In other test methods a fault in the IUT might also have been traced back to irremovable uncontrollable side effects. Remote testing is the only method that can always be used.

13.4 Abstract test suite

The intellectual work itself, which is structured over several phases, begins with the definition of the *abstract test suite*. The conformance requirements that an implementation must satisfy (where 'must' refers to mandatory services and all implemented options) are derived, based on the relevant OSI standard and the profiles. This activity results in the division of the test suite into *test groups*. As a rule, the test groups refer to the services defined in the OSI standard. Next, the *test cases* are specified, where every test case in a test group covers a selected property of the service. In the 'Test Strategies' subsection (below), criteria are introduced that specify the properties selected for testing in more detail. ISO 9646 Part 3 introduces the *Tree and Tabular Combined Notation* (TTCN) for the specification of tests. Finally, all cross references between the test cases and to PICS and *Protocol Implementation Extra Information for Testing* (PIXIT) are recorded. Like an OSI standard, an abstract test suite is subject to the corresponding CCITT or ISO standardization process.

  In the next paragraph we introduce the structure of a test suite. We describe the structure of the test suites for the recommendations of the X.400 (84) series, based on the general specifications in ISO 9646. At this point, we mention one particular feature. In Section 1.4 (The presentation layer) we introduced the ASN.1 language. A predecessor of this language exists in X.409 (84). Since X.400 (84) is the first application of this description language, special account of this is also taken in the conformance testing. In a large number of all test cases for the protocols P1 and P2, properties of X.409 are tested with a view to obtaining information about the ability of an IUT to encode and decode PDUs defined in X.409. To round off the paragraph we introduce the test suites relevant to X.400 (84). Particular attention is paid to the TTCN test notation.

Structure of the test suites for IPMS, MTS and RTS

A test suite is defined to be the collection of all test cases for an OSI protocol. It has a hierarchical structure (Figure 13.7). The test suite

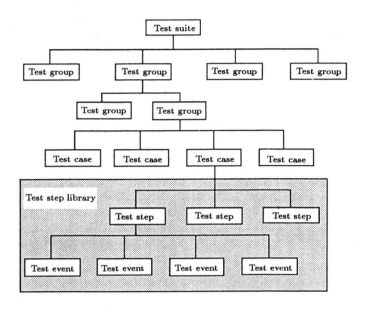

Figure 13.7   Structure of a test suite.

is subdivided into test groups. Each test group may be subdivided into further test groups. Finally, a test group is subdivided into individual test cases. Each test case is composed of sequences of *test events*. The test events define elementary actions. The hierarchical structure of a test suite defines a type of modularization. The collection of test events into so-called *test steps* provides another method of constructing test suites in a modular fashion. Modularization improves the readability and maintainability of the test suite.

In recommendation X.403 (88) the following subdivision of a test suite into test groups is specified for the IPMS, MTS and RTS test suites:

- One test group per service element and option defined in the OSI standard.

- Separate test groups for IUT as sender and recipient.

- Separate test groups for valid and invalid protocol behaviour.

Although we noted in the introduction to this chapter that conformance testing does not involve testing the robustness of an implementation, the test cases in the 'invalid protocol behaviour' test group include tests of this type. They are used to check whether an implementation reacts to errors in a 'well-behaved' way.

At the next highest level of the hierarchical structure test groups may, according to their nature, be collected into other test groups. For the IPMS and the MTS, recommendation X.403 (88) distinguishes between the following test groups:

- *Initial tests.* These test cases are used to begin the conformance testing of an X.400 implementation. They are few in number. These tests may be used to determine whether an IUT correctly supports the mandatory services. It is then clear that an IUT is largely working correctly. The initial tests are followed by tests from all other groups. Only when all tests have been executed is it possible to make specific statements about the ability or inability of an IUT to support given services and protocol elements.

- *X.409 tests.* Tests of this group may be used to check whether an IUT is able to encode and decode PDUs (more precisely, X.409 PDUs) correctly (more precisely, according to the X.409 encoding rules).

- *Protocol element tests.* This group contains test cases for every P2 and P1 protocol element. Since the protocol elements may be traced back to services (Section 2.5), protocol element tests may also be realized via tests of the corresponding services.

- *Service element tests.* Service element tests may be used to check the capabilities of an IUT via the services it supports. The definition of the test cases takes into account the fact that individual services may be tested in isolation from all others and in combination with other services. The initial tests make use of the possibility of testing combinations of services, for example, in the test suite for P2 a handful of initial tests are defined in which nearly all the services of the IPMS or the MTS are referenced.

The discussion of the service element tests has shown that a strict division of the test groups at this level is impossible. Protocol elements are tested by tests of the service elements; X.409 tests are partially mapped onto tests of the service elements. Indeed, tests are only defined to check particular characteristics of X.409 that cannot be checked otherwise. Here we include, for example, tests that check whether an IUT is able to process 'Octet Strings' with different length codings (short form, long form, indefinite form) correctly. Figure 13.8 illustrates the interdependence of test groups.

The RTS supports the generation, maintenance and deletion of associations between MTAEs and the transmission of PDUs. The most

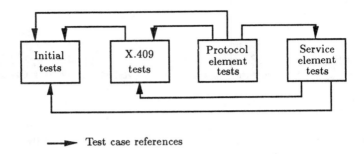

Test case references

Figure 13.8   IPMS and MTS test groups and their relationship.

important tests for the RTS may be derived from this brief description of the services. In detail these tests comprise:

- Tests involving the generation and negotiation of association parameters (dialogue mode, possession of authorization labels).
- Tests for the proper deletion of associations.
- Tests for data transfer. These tests should determine whether the association parameters negotiated during connection set-up are correctly handled.
- Tests to check the recovery of interrupted associations.
- X.409 tests. These relate to the encoding and decoding of session-layer service data units.

The allocation of test cases to test groups for the 'importance indication' service shown in Figure 13.9 follows from the above arguments. Clearly these test cases belong to the group of service element tests.

Why the test group for invalid behaviour should consist of the test cases 'negative importance' and 'undefined positive importance' is not immediately clear. The next subsection (test strategies) is devoted to this problem.

Test strategies

For reasons of cost and time, implementations cannot be completely tested. Thus, a restriction on the number of test cases is unavoidable. Nonetheless, in order to give substance to the claim that conformance testing identifies almost all non-conforming implementations, it is vital to make the test cases

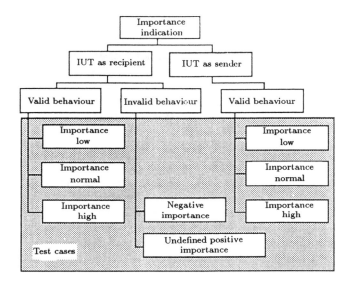

Figure 13.9   Test groups and test cases for 'importance indication'.

as efficient as possible. Here, efficiency means that every test case has a single well-defined *test purpose*. Thus, the number of test cases is *a priori* not greatly reduced and careful definition of the test purpose of each test case enables those conducting the tests to detect IUT errors without ambiguity.

In the introduction to this chapter we noted that *ad hoc* methods of defining test cases for conformance testing are inadequate. Instead, test cases must be defined according to a generally-accepted test strategy. This will ensure that all aspects of a protocol that are viewed as major are tested and guarantees an optimal test coverage (insofar as that is possible).

X.403 (88) (and naturally also ISO 9646) even provides considerable support when discussing test strategies. It specifies that the number of tests should be minimized, taking into account the following criteria:

- Valid behaviour
    - If a protocol element is defined to have a small number of values then test cases should be specified for each value. For the 'importance' protocol element this means that a test case should be defined for each of the values 'low', 'normal' and 'high'.
    - If a range of values is defined for the protocol element,

tests should be developed that cover the boundary cases and some general cases. In Chapter 5, we showed that length restrictions are specified for some protocol elements. These length restrictions may now be interpreted as defining the upper limit of a range of values. Thus, it is possible to define minimum and maximum values. For example, every 'subject' of a communication is restricted to a maximum of 128 characters (Table 5.5). Clearly a minimal value of a 'subject' is just one character and a maximal value of a 'subject' is 128 characters. Generally-valid cases then lie somewhere in between.

— If no restrictions are imposed on the range of values of a protocol element, tests should specify general cases and should also consider unusual cases ('exotic'). This problem arises, for example, in message addressing. Any number of people may be named as possible recipients. However, the definition of test cases should be restricted to a few cases that check whether the different address formats were understood by an IUT.

• Invalid behaviour

— The number of possible tests should be reduced to a few typical errors. In the case of 'importance', negative and undefined-positive 'importance' are the representative errors. Negative 'importance' is an error because only positive values have been specified for coding 'importance' and undefined-positive 'importance' is an error because this represents a correctly coded value with an undefined meaning.

The use of these criteria to select tests implies that the expected test coverage is large. The number of test cases may be further reduced, as far as possible, using the symmetry between 'IUT as sender' and 'IUT as recipient'. This is also reflected in Figure 13.9 (Test cases for 'importance indication').

In this and the previous paragraphs we have described the theory of conformance testing for X.400 implementations. Conformance testing is a very formalized process. In a finite period of time, it should be determined whether or not an IUT is an implementation conforming to the X.400 recommendations. This should not depend on which tester is used to test the IUT. Thus, the same test suite should be installed on all possible testers. In Section 13.5 we explain how test cases may be implemented on a tester and which utilities may be used. Since there is a strict division of labour between those who define a test suite and those who operate a test system, we need a notation that provides a formal description of test cases and test suites. Such a notation is described in the next subsection. One advantage of a formal description of a test suite is shown by the fact that such a description may be processed by machines. Thus, it is possible to discover and correct obvious errors such as are always made when programs are written.

Tree and tabular combined notation (TTCN) – an example of a test notation

The *Tree and Tabular Combined Notation* (TTCN) is defined in Part 3 of ISO standard 9646. This is also a component of CCITT recommendation X.403 (88). In addition to the above advantage of checking the contents of a test suite described in TTCN, this formal notation permits the development of tools to support the design and implementation of test suites. For this reason and since TTCN is increasing in importance, we provide a detailed introduction. This is given using the test suite for the IPMS (CCITT, 1988).

Like a block-structured programming language, TTCN divides a test suite into a *declarations part* (test suite overview, declarations part and constraints part) and a *dynamic part*. These are described consecutively below:

- *Test suite overview.* This part describes the test suite ('Message Handling Systems Conformance Testing Specification Manual X.403/CTSM.1 for Interpersonal Messaging Systems X.420 (1984)'). In CTSM.1 there follows a list of all test cases and (correspondingly) of their allocation to one of the groups of initial tests, X.409 tests or protocol element and service element tests. This list is in the form of a table (Table 13.4). All cross-references between the test groups are specified.

  The designators are freely chosen. The description describes the purpose of the test case. Entries in the column headed 'References' are pointers from each test case to another test group (the initial tests).

  As a rule the test suite overview also defines the PICSs that are important for this test suite (the PICSs in Table 13.3).

Table 13.4   Tests for services.

Designator	Description	References
...	...	...
301.2.1.1	IPMessage without O/R name	001.2.1.1
301.2.1.2	IPMessage with O/R name	001.2.1.2

Table 13.5   SUBMIT.request – service primitives.

SUBMIT.request		
Name	*Range of values or type*	*Type*
Recipient O/R	SEQUENCE OF P1.ORName	M
Originator O/R	P1.ORName	M
Content	P2.UAPDU	M
Content type	P1.ContentType	M
Encoded information types	P1.EncodedInformationTypes	C
NDN suppress	SEQUENCE OF BOOLEAN	C
Priority	P1.Priority	M
Deferred-delivery time	SEQUENCE OF P1.Time	C
Delivery notice	SEQUENCE OF BOOLEAN	C
Conversion prohibited	BOOLEAN	C
Disclose recipients	BOOLEAN	M
Alternative recipients allowed	BOOLEAN	C
Content return	BOOLEAN	C
UA content ID	P1.UAContentID	C
Explicit conversion	SEQUENCE OF P1.ExplicitConversion	C

- *Declarations part.* This part contains the declaration of all test suite parameters, all PCOs, all ASPs used and all timers. The test suite parameters are used to initialize the test suite. Parameters (for example, for recipient addresses) may be used to make the description of the test cases independent of the actual IUT. These declarations are also tabulated so as to increase the readability of a TTCN test suite. Table 13.5 is an example of this for the ASP SUBMIT.request.

  The service primitive SUBMIT.request is defined in X.411 (84). The same document also contains the definitions of all the parameters, their descriptions and their classifications as mandatory (M) or conditional (C). The CTSM.1 test suite has extended these definitions by adding the range of values and the type of parameter. The declarations part of a test suite also includes the definition of the configuration of the tester and IUT (and thence a specification of the abstract test methods). In Figures 13.10 and 13.11 this is shown for the IPMS and the MTS. Figure 13.11 is given here in order to show that complicated test scenarios are sometimes conceivable and indeed necessary. Since the MTS is concerned with the sending of messages, it must also be possible to test this. This leads to the configuration consisting of an IUT (MTAE) and two testers shown

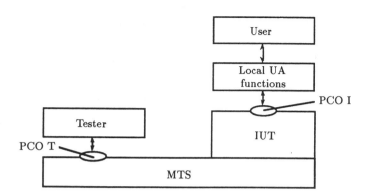

Figure 13.10 Abstract test methods for the IPMS.

in Figure 13.11, where the IUT provides for the relaying of communications between the testers.

- *Dynamic part.* This is the centrepiece of a test suite. All test cases are specified in this part. The collection of the test cases into test groups is preserved. The form of TTCN in Table 13.6 is defined

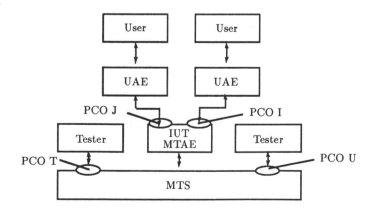

Figure 13.11 Abstract test methods for the MTS.

Table 13.6 Test case in TTCN from CTSM.1.

Behaviour description	Label	Constraints reference	Result	Line
Dynamic behaviour				
Defaults: LIB_otherwise[I], LIB_unexpected[T], LIB_subconfirmation				
T!SUBREQ		Subreq		(1)
I!Start T/I-Tmr				(2)
I?REC		Rec	pass	(3)
I?TIMEOUT T/I-Tmr			fail	(4)

to describe the test cases. Each line of the table (lines (1)–(4)) describes a test event. The test events define the PCO (T or I) at which the ASP (SUBMIT.request, start of a timer or RECeive) should take place. In addition, an entry in the column headed 'Constraints reference' defines the current data values for the ASP which should be used when the ASP is called. Here these data values are only referenced by an identifier ('Subreq'). This is a reference to the constraints part. Each test event may be assigned a result value ('pass' or 'fail'), where a test case is successful if the sequence of test events ends with the result 'pass'. For the test cases shown in Table 13.6 this means that the IUT with the test event 'REC' receives the message sent from the tester and that the data values in the constraint reference 'Rec' agree with the values actually received. Then, according to the definition of the test case, the IUT has executed this test case successfully.

Apart from sequences and alternatives (test events with the same level of indentation – for example, SUBREQ and Start), TTCN has far fewer control structures than usual in programming languages. The TTCN control structures include 'goto'. In the column 'Label', a label may be declared for a test event, to which later test events may point. Then dynamic control will be transferred to the test event (or alternative) marked by the label.

When describing a test case, in order not to lose sight of what is important, it is possible to refer to test steps that define a control behaviour for all conceivable exceptions (all test steps must be named in the 'Defaults' line). Test events from these test steps are always used when in individual cases there is no specification as to how to handle an event.

The test case in Table 13.6 defines a framework for the case in which the tester wishes to transmit to the IUT IPMs. In order to generate other test cases from this, it is on the whole only necessary to alter the entries in the column headed 'Constraints reference'.

- *Constraints part.* This part of a TTCN test suite defines the current data values which will be used in the test events of the dynamic part. This includes all IPM ASPs, all base PDUs and test PDUs and library modules.

    Table 13.5 shows an example of an IPM ASP. Base PDUs define complete P2 PDUs. These base PDUs may be used to derive test PDUs. This is done by replacing parts of a base PDU. Table 13.7 gives an example of this. The ASN.1 notation is used to define PDUs.

    BASE_PDU defines a P2 communication which consists of a head and a body. In order to generate a test PDU which can be sent from the tester to the IUT if the 'importance' is set to 'low', only the head of the base PDU needs to be replaced. The test PDU defined in this way could, for example, in the test case of Table 13.6, be bound into the subreq constraints reference.

    The procedure outlined above is not however applicable when the IUT sends PDUs to the tester. As a rule, an IUT will not allow direct control to be exercised over the generated PDUs. The values for some protocol elements will certainly be generated automatically by the UAE (for example, the `IPMessageID`). In all cases in which an IUT sends to the tester, the constraints part describes only those parts of a PDU relevant to the test case. This may, for example, occur as shown by PDU_2 in Table 13.7.

The CTSM.1 test suite consists of approximately 250 test cases. In the next section, amongst other things, we discuss how such a test suite can be implemented on a test system.

13.5 Implementation of conformance tests

The implementation of conformance tests certainly involves something more than simply the implementation of the test cases of a test suite. This is a crucial point. The implementation of conformance tests also includes the provision of test tools (*means of testing*), which consist of hardware and software. The hardware is the machine including all communication equipment on which the software of the test tools is held. This includes: editors, test drivers and programs for communication and evaluation. Some components of this software will be dealt with in more detail. Evaluation programs are needed to analyze the conformance log recorded by the test tools. All information and results relevant to the execution of a test are recorded in a conformance log.

Table 13.7 Base and test PDUs (Lange, 1988).

Description	Value or reference	Comments

BASE_PDU
SEQUENCE {
  Heading
  Body}
	
	[BASE_PDU_Heading]
	[Base_PDU_Body]	

BASE_PDU_Heading SET {IPMessageID}	 [{L_IPMessageID_1}]	
BASE_PDU_Body SEQUENCE OF { Body}	 [{L_Bodypart_1}]	

TEST_PDU
BASE_PDU
REPLACE
  BASE_PDU_HEADING
BY
  SET {IPMessageID,
  importance INTEGER}
	
	[L_IPMessageID_1]
	[0]
		
		low

L_Bodypart_1 CHOICE {IA5Text}	 [{L_IA5Text_1}]	

L_IA5Text_1
SEQUENCE { SET {
  repertoire INTEGER}
  IA5String
	
	[{5}]
	['4D657373616765'H]
		
		{ia5}

PDU_2 Partial definition: Components of interest PDU_2_Heading importance INTEGER	 [2]	 high

The communication software represents a substantial part of the real tester. By *real tester*, we mean that part of the test tools which contains the implementation of the LT including the definition of the UT and the test coordination procedure.

As already noted, the main task of the test tools is to support an implementation of the test cases (the abstract test suite). The MHTS/400 (*Message Handling Test System/400*) installed on the OSI-LAB of the Swiss PTT (Danet GmbH, 1987) mainly uses an ASN.1 editor for this. This editor may be used to edit the ASPs, the PDUs and the base and test PDUs

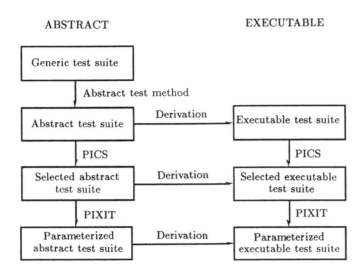

ABSTRACT   EXECUTABLE

Figure 13.12   Derivation of the PETS from an ATS.

defined in the declarations and constraints part and the library modules. An ASN.1 compiler allows the user to check the syntactic correctness of his PDUs. In the X.400 case this is restricted to the P2 and P1 PDUs.

As soon as the test suite (also termed abstract test suite in the context discussed here) is implemented in the test system, it can be prepared to test an IUT. In ISO 9646 this procedure is known as *derivation*. In the derivation of an *Executable Test Suite* (ETS) from an abstract test suite (Figure 13.12), implementation details of the test system and the IUT are used (for example, assumptions about the time behaviour of the real tester and the IUT). Specially-developed tools may be used for this process. (On the MHTS/400 this is almost exclusively done by hand, but predefined script files may be revised.) An executable test suite consists solely of executable test cases. Each executable test case is structurally (in respect of test sequences and assignment of verdicts) identical to an abstract test case in the abstract test suite.

The PICS (Table 13.2) defines which options are supported by the IUT. Test cases to test an IUT are *selected* from an abstract or an executable test suite and these are used to test the functions implemented by the IUT. The result of this step is called a *Selected Abstract Test Suite* (SATS) or a *Selected Executable Test Suite* (SETS) (Figure 13.12). *Parameterization* follows according to the IUT's PIXIT. The PIXIT contains important information for testing IUTs, which selection of the test cases may restrict further. Thus, the standard supports the *Parameterized Abstract Test Suite* (PATS) and the *Parameterized Executable Test Suite* (PETS). Figure 13.12 shows the derivation of the PETS from an ATS.

An IUT is tested by a parameterized executable test suite. The derivation of the executable test suite from the abstract test suite need not necessarily follow the above steps. Individual steps may be interchanged. The possible transitions from an abstract test suite to a parameterized executable test suite are shown in Figure 13.12. The term 'generic test suite' is applied to a complete implementation-independent description of a test suite that is independent of a particular abstract test method.

Now the testing of an IUT may begin. As one might imagine, testing involves the consecutive execution of all test cases of a PETS. Since conformance testing is a formal procedure that results in the IUT being issued with a certificate equivalent to a seal of approval, an organizational framework must be defined for this procedure. This is described in Section 13.6.

13.6 Conformance testing and certification

Installation of the test suite on a test system and derivation of the PETS complete the preparations for testing an IUT. This is now followed by execution of the conformance tests.

Execution of the conformance tests is divided into test preparation, execution of the tests in the narrower sense and generation of the test report. An overview of the procedure is given in Figure 13.13.

Conformance testing involves the representative of the test laboratory (*test laboratory manager*) and a person from the company that manufactured the X.400 system who is responsible for the IUT (*client test manager*). ISO 9646 Part 5 (Requirements on Test Laboratories and Clients for the Conformance Assessment Process) and X.403 (88) specify that the test laboratory and the client test manager also have to come to an agreement on the abstract test methods, the abstract test suite and the conditions under which the tests are carried out. As a general rule, whenever problems arise during the test phase itself, the test laboratory and the client test manager may agree to repeat all or part of the process or even break off the testing.

In Figure 13.13, rectangles denote activities, symbols with rounded corners denote documents and arrows denote the information flow and the relationships between activities and documents.

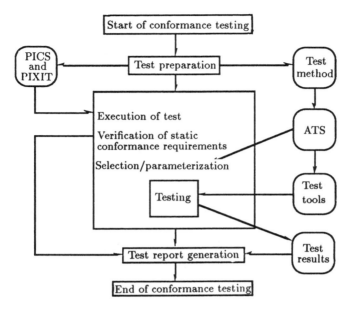

Figure 13.13   Conformance testing – process.

- *Test preparation.* The test laboratory and the client test manager agree on the organization and sequence of the tests. They then check the PICS and PIXIT. This involves checking the completeness of the contents of the PICS and PIXIT and their formal agreement with the format defined in the relevant OSI standard. In addition, the IUT is analyzed and the test methods are chosen as a function of the capabilities of the IUT (accessible PCOs) and the test systems (availability of abstract test suites). Under certain circumstances, according to the agreement reached about the test method, the IUT must be prepared for testing.

- *Execution of the tests.* In a first phase, the static conformance requirements are checked using the PICS and PIXIT prepared by the client test manager. The check is followed by the selection of the test cases and the parameterization of the test suite. Finally, testing begins with the basic interconnection tests, the capability tests and the behaviour tests.

- *Test report.* On completion of the tests, the test report is generated. This states whether the IUT conforms to the OSI standard. The report is known as the *System Conformance Test Report* (SCTR) or the *Protocol Conformance Test Report* (PCTR) and contains information about the IUT and the test laboratory, a list of all abstract test cases for which executable test cases were generated and the result of applying the test cases to the IUT (pass, fail or inconclusive).

13.7 Summary and outlook

This chapter has provided an overview of the conformance testing of X.400 implementations. The discussion of CTSM.1 (CCITT, 1988) is based on work by Beyschlag (Beyschlag and Pitteloud, 1988) and Lange (Lange, 1988).

On the general topic of conformance testing, the work of D.Rayner (Rayner, 1987) provides a valuable introduction.

Conformance testing appears to be increasing in importance. For some time, numerous private organizations and companies (mainly in the USA) have shown great commitment to conformance testing. As the example of the OSI-LAB shows, this commitment almost always results in the development of software to run on existing hardware. However, other approaches have been followed. Some companies have developed special systems for conformance testing. These are software configurable so that any protocol may be tested.

One major problem in conformance testing is the definition of the abstract test suite. Some projects in universities and private and publicly supported research institutes have investigated ways in which test suites may be automatically generated from a protocol definition. One solution to this problem requires that the protocols should be formally described in a computer-processable form. In 1988 the formal description techniques Estelle (ISO 9074) and LOTOS (ISO 8807) were standardized by ISO. At present, OSI standards are almost all specified informally. However, methods have already been developed to generate test cases from a formal specification. Since these methods restrict the form of the protocol specification and the nature of the implementation, it is not possible to speak of a breakthrough.

Work on ISO standard 9646 is continuing. It is planned that ISO 9646 should become an international standard in 1991.

Closing remarks

Today, many common data communication applications, possibly with the exception of telex or facsimile, only connect subscribers within a company or a closed subscriber user group. The reason for this is that putting a communication service into operation requires complicated bilateral or multilateral arrangements concerning the protocols and equipment to be used, particularly if the potential partners operate data processing installations produced by different manufacturers. Moreover, some of those responsible for computing or communication services fear (wrongly, as we showed in Chapters 3 and 11) that linking their installation into a network over which they do not have complete control represents a security risk.

One of our objectives was to show how existing barriers between independent organizations may be overcome using X.400.

The implementation of X.400 systems does not require high-performance infrastructures, such as, networks with high transmission rates. While we may view MHS as a new application, it will be some years before the use of electronic mail becomes as commonplace as is use of the telephone today.

We are convinced that X.400 will become a successful standard, in other words, that it will be widely implemented and will lead to an improvement in the ability of thousands and millions of people to communicate with one another.

PART IV

Appendices

A

Definitions of P1 and P2 in ASN.1

CCITT Red Book, Vol. VIII, Fasc. VIII.7, Geneva, 1985, 150ff

Formal definitions of the PDU formats of P1

P1 DEFINITIONS ::=

BEGIN
-- *P1 makes use of types defined in the following module*
-- *T73: Recommendation T.73*

a) Formal definition of an MPDU

MPDU ::=
      CHOICE {
      [0] IMPLICIT UserMPDU, ServiceMPDU }

ServiceMPDU ::=
      CHOICE {
      [1] IMPLICIT DeliveryReportMPDU,
      [2] IMPLICIT ProbeMPDU }

b) Formal definition of a UserMPDU

UserMPDU ::=
SEQUENCE { UMPDUEnvelope, UMPDUContent }
UMPDUEnvelope ::=
      SET {
      MPDUIdentifier,
      originator ORName,
      original EncodedInformationTypes OPTIONAL,
      ContentType,
      UAContentID OPTIONAL,
      Priority DEFAULT normal,
      PerMessageFlag DEFAULT {},
      deferredDelivery [0] IMPLICIT Time OPTIONAL,

```
        [1] IMPLICIT SEQUENCE OF
            PerDomainBilateralInfo OPTIONAL,
        [2] IMPLICIT SEQUENCE OF
            RecipientInfo, TraceInformation }
```

UMPDUContent ::= OCTETSTRING

-- *time*
Time ::= UTCTIME

-- *various envelope information*
MPDUIdentifier ::= [APPLICATION 4]
```
        IMPLICIT SEQUENCE {
        GlobalDomainIdentifier, IA5String }
```

ContentType ::= [APPLICATION 6]
```
        IMPLICIT INTEGER { p2(2) }
```

UAContentID ::= [APPLICATION 10]
```
        IMPLICIT PrintableString
```

Priority ::= [APPLICATION 7]
```
        IMPLICIT INTEGER {
        normal(0), nonUrgent(1), urgent(2) }
```

PerMessageFlag ::= [APPLICATION 8]
```
        IMPLICIT BITSTRING {
        discloseRecipients(0),
        conversionProhibited(1),
        alternateRecipientAllowed(2),
        contentReturnRequest(3) }
```

-- *per-domain bilateral information*
PerDomainBilateralInfo ::=
```
        SEQUENCE {
        CountryName,
        AdministrationDomainName,
        BilateralInfo }
```

BilateralInfo ::= ANY

-- *recipient information*
RecipientInfo ::=
```
        SET {
        recipient ORName,
        [0] IMPLICIT ExtensionIdentifier,
        [1] IMPLICIT PerRecipientFlag,
        [2] IMPLICIT ExplicitConversion OPTIONAL }
```

ExtensionIdentifier ::= INTEGER

PerRecipientFlag ::= BITSTRING

ExplicitConversion ::=
       INTEGER {ia5TextTeletex(0), teletexTelex(1) }

-- *trace information*
TraceInformation ::= [APPLICATION 9]
       IMPLICIT SEQUENCE OF
       SEQUENCE {
           GlobalDomainIdentifier,
           DomainSuppliedInfo }

DomainSuppliedInfo ::=
       SET {
       arrival [0] IMPLICIT Time,
       deferred [1] IMPLICIT Time OPTIONAL,
       action [2] IMPLICIT INTEGER { relayed(0),
           rerouted(1) },
       converted EncodedInformationTypes OPTIONAL,
       previous GlobalDomainIdentifier OPTIONAL }

-- *global domain identifier*
GlobalDomainIdentifier ::= [APPLICATION 3]
       IMPLICIT SEQUENCE {
       CountryName,
       AdministrationDomainName,
       PrivateDomainIdentifier OPTIONAL }

CountryName ::= [APPLICATION 1]
       CHOICE {
       NumericString,
       PrintableString }

AdministrationDomainName ::= [APPLICATION 2]
       CHOICE {
       NumericString,
       PrintableString }

PrivateDomainIdentifier ::=
    CHOICE {
    NumericString,
    PrintableString }

-- O/R name
ORName ::= [APPLICATION 0]
    IMPLICIT SEQUENCE {
    StandardAttributeList,
    DomainDefinedAttributeList OPTIONAL }

StandardAttributeList ::=
    SEQUENCE {
    CountryName OPTIONAL,
    AdministrationDomainName OPTIONAL,
    [0] IMPLICIT X121Address OPTIONAL,
    [1] IMPLICIT TerminalID OPTIONAL,
    [2] PrivateDomainName OPTIONAL,
    [3] IMPLICIT OrganizationName OPTIONAL,
    [4] IMPLICIT UniqueUAIdentifier OPTIONAL,
    [5] IMPLICIT PersonalName OPTIONAL,
    [6] IMPLICIT SEQUENCE OF OrganizationalUnit
        OPTIONAL }

DomainDefinedAttributeList ::=
    SEQUENCE OF DomainDefinedAttribute

DomainDefinedAttribute ::=
    SEQUENCE {
    type PrintableString,
    value PrintableString }

X121Address ::= NumericString

TerminalID ::= PrintableString

OrganizationName ::= PrintableString

UniqueUAIdentifier ::= NumericString

PersonalName ::=
    SET {
    surName [0] IMPLICIT PrintableString,
    givenName [1] IMPLICIT PrintableString
    OPTIONAL,
    initials [2] IMPLICIT PrintableString
    OPTIONAL,

```
    generationQualifier [3] IMPLICIT
    PrintableString OPTIONAL }
```

OrganizationalUnit ::= PrintableString

PrivateDomainName ::=
```
    CHOICE {
    NumericString,
    PrintableString }
```

-- *encoded information types*
EncodedInformationTypes ::= [APPLICATION 5]
```
    IMPLICIT SET {
    [0] IMPLICIT BITSTRING {
        undefined(0), tLX(1), ia5Text(2),
        g3Fax(3), tIF0(4), tTX(5), videotex(6),
        voice(7), sFD(8), tlF1(9) },
    [1] IMPLICIT G3NonBasicParams OPTIONAL,
    [2] IMPLICIT TeletexNonBasicParams OPTIONAL,
    [3] IMPLICIT PresentationCapabilities
        OPTIONAL
```
-- *other non-basic parameters are for further study*
```
}
```

G3NonBasicParams ::=
```
BITSTRING {
    twoDimensional (8),
    fineResolution(9),
    unlimitedLength(20),
    b4Length(21),
    a3Width(22),
    b4Width(23),
    uncompressed(30) }
```

TeletexNonBasicParams ::=
```
    SET {
    graphicCharacterSets [0] IMPLICIT T61String
    OPTIONAL,
    controlCharacterSets [1] IMPLICIT T61String
    OPTIONAL,
    pageFormats [2] IMPLICIT OCTETSTRING
    OPTIONAL,
    miscTerminalCapabilities [3] IMPLICIT
    T61String OPTIONAL,
    privateUse [4] IMPLICIT OCTETSTRING
    OPTIONAL }
```

```
PresentationCapabilities ::=
T73.PresentationCapabilities
```

c) Formal definition of a delivery report

```
DeliveryReportMPDU ::=
      SEQUENCE {
      DeliveryReportEnvelope,
      DeliveryReportContent }

DeliveryReportEnvelope ::=
      SET {
      report MPDUIdentifier,
      originator ORName,
      TraceInformation }

DeliveryReportContent ::=
      SET {
      original MPDUIdentifier,
      intermediate Traceinformation OPTIONAL,
      UAContentId OPTIONAL,
      [0] IMPLICIT SEQUENCE OF
          ReportedRecipientInfo, returned
      [1] IMPLICIT UMPDUContent OPTIONAL,
          billingInformation
      [2] ANY OPTIONAL }

ReportedRecipientInfo ::=
      SET {
      recipient [0] IMPLICIT ORName,
      [1] IMPLICIT ExtensionIdentifier,
      [2] IMPLICIT PerRecipientFlag,
      [3] IMPLICIT LastTraceInformation,
          intendedRecipient,
      [4] IMPLICIT ORName OPTIONAL,
      [5] IMPLICIT SupplementaryInformation
          OPTIONAL}


-- last trace information
LastTraceInformation ::=
      SET {
      arrival [0] IMPLICIT Time,
      converted EncodedInformationTypes OPTIONAL,
      [1] Report }
```

```
Report ::=        CHOICE {
    [0] IMPLICIT DeliveredInfo,
    [1] IMPLICIT NonDeliveredInfo }

DeliveredInfo ::=
    SET {
    delivery [0] IMPLICIT Time,
    typeOfUA [1] IMPLICIT INTEGER {
        public(0), private(1) } DEFAULT public }

NonDeliveredInfo ::=
    SET {
    [0] IMPLICIT ReasonCode,
    [1] IMPLICIT DiagnosticCode OPTIONAL }

ReasonCode ::=
    INTEGER {
    transferFailure(0),
    unableToTransfer(1),
    conversionNotPerformed(2) }

DiagnosticCode ::=
    INTEGER {
    unrecognizedORName(0),
    ambiguousORName(1),
    mtaCongestion(2),
    loopDetected(3),
    uaUnavailable (4),
    maximumTimeExpired (5),
    encodedInformationTypesUnsupported (6),
    contentTooLong(7),
    conversionImpractical(8),
    conversionProhibited(9),
    implicitConversionNotRegistered(10),
    invalidParameters(11) }

-- supplementary information
SupplementaryInformation ::=
    PrintableString
-- length limited and for further study
```

d) Formal definition of a probe MPDU

```
ProbeMPDU ::= ProbeEnvelope

ProbeEnvelope ::=
```

```
        SET {
      probe MPDUIdentifier,
      originator ORName,
      ContentType,
      UAContentID OPTIONAL,
      original EncodedInformationTypes OPTIONAL,
      TraceInformation,
      PerMessageFlag DEFAULT {},
      contentLength [0] IMPLICIT INTEGER OPTIONAL,
      [1] IMPLICIT SEQUENCE OF
          PerDomainBilateralInfo OPTIONAL,
      [2] IMPLICIT SEQUENCE OF RecipientInfo }
```

END -- *of P1 definitions*

CCITT Red Book, Vol. VIII, Fasc. VIII.7, Geneva, 1985, 192ff

Formal definitions of the PDU formats of P2

```
P2 DEFINITIONS ::=

BEGIN
-- P2 makes use of types defined in the following modules:
-- P1: X.411, §3.4
-- P3: X.411, §4.3
-- SFD: this Recommendation, §5
-- T73: T.73, §5


UAPDU ::=
      CHOICE {
      [0] IMPLICIT IM-UAPDU,
      [1] IMPLICIT SR-UAPDU }

-- IP message UAPDU
IM-UAPDU ::=
      SEQUENCE { Heading, Body }

-- heading
Heading ::=
      SET {
      IPMessageID,
      originator [0] IMPLICIT ORDescriptor
          OPTIONAL,
      authorizingUsers [1] IMPLICIT SEQUENCE OF
          ORDescriptor OPTIONAL,
```

```
-- only if not the originator
primaryRecipients [2] SEQUENCE OF Recipient
    OPTIONAL,
copyRecipients [3] IMPLICIT SEQUENCE OF
    Recipient OPTIONAL,
blindCopyRecipients [4] IMPLICIT SEQUENCE OF
    Recipient OPTIONAL,
inReplyTo [5] IMPLICIT IPMessageID OPTIONAL,
-- omitted if not in reply to a previous message
obsoletes [6] IMPLICIT SEQUENCE OF
    IPMessageID OPTIONAL,
crossReferences [7] IMPLICIT SEQUENCE OF
    IPMessageID OPTIONAL,
subject [8] CHOICE { T61String } OPTIONAL,
expiryDate [9] IMPLICIT Time OPTIONAL,
-- if omitted, expiry date is never
replyBy[10] IMPLICIT Time OPTIONAL,
replyToUsers [11] IMPLICIT SEQUENCE OF
    ORDescriptor OPTIONAL,
-- each O/R descriptor must contain an O/R name
importance [12] IMPLICIT INTEGER { low(0),
    normal(1), high(2) } DEFAULT normal,
sensitivity [13] IMPLICIT INTEGER {
    personal(1), private(2),
    companyConfidential(3) } OPTIONAL,
autoforwarded [14] IMPLICIT BOOLEAN DEFAULT
    FALSE
-- indicates that the forwarded message
-- body part(s) were autoforwarded
}
```

IPMessageID ::= [APPLICATION 11]

IMPLICIT SET {
```
    ORName Optional,
    PrintableString }
```

ORNAME ::= P1.ORNAME

ORDescriptor ::=
```
    SET {
    -- at least one of the first two members must be present
    ORName OPTIONAL,
    freeformName [0] IMPLICIT T61String OPTIONAL,
    telephoneNumber [1] IMPLICIT PrintableString
        OPTIONAL }
```

```
Recipient ::=
      SET {
      [0] IMPLICIT ORDescriptor,
      reportRequest [1] IMPLICIT BITSTRING {
      receiptNotification(0),
      nonReceiptNotification(1),
      returnIPMessage(2) } DEFAULT {},
      -- if requested, the O/R descriptor must contain
      -- an O/R name
      replyRequest [2] IMPLICIT BOOLEAN DEFAULT
         FALSE
      -- if true, the O/R descriptor must contain an O/R name
      }

-- body
Body ::= SEQUENCE OF BodyPart

BodyPart ::=
      CHOICE {
      [0]   IMPLICIT IA5Text,
      [1]   IMPLICIT TLX,
      [2]   IMPLICIT Voice,
      [3]   IMPLICIT G3Fax,
      [4]   IMPLICIT TIF0,
      [5]   IMPLICIT TTX,
      [6]   IMPLICIT Videotex,
      [7]   NationallyDefined,
      [8]   IMPLICIT Encrypted,
      [9]   IMPLICIT ForwardedIPMessage,
      [10] IMPLICIT SFD,
      [11] IMPLICIT TIF1 }

-- body part types
IA5Text ::=
      SEQUENCE {
      SET {
            repertoire [0] IMPLICIT INTEGER {
            ia5(5),ita2(2) }
            DEFAULT ia5
            -- additional members of this set
            --are a possible future extension
      },
      IA5String }

TLX ::= -- for further study
-- Author's remark: In X.400 (84) no type is defined for TLX,
-- thus the construct is syntactically incorrect.
```

```
Voice ::=
     SEQUENCE {
     SET, -- members are for further study
     BITSTRING }

G3Fax ::=
     SEQUENCE {
     SET {
             numberOfPages [0] IMPLICIT INTEGER
                OPTIONAL,
             [1] IMPLICIT P1.G3NonBasicParams
                OPTIONAL
     },
     SEQUENCE OF BITSTRING }

TIF0 ::= T73Document

T73Document ::=
     SEQUENCE OF T73.ProtocolElement

TTX ::=
     SEQUENCE {
     SET {
             numberOfPages
             [0] IMPLICIT INTEGER OPTIONAL,
                telexCompatible
             [1] IMPLICIT BOOLEAN
                DEFAULT FALSE,
             [2] IMPLICIT P1.TeletexNonBasicParams
                OPTIONAL },
     SEQUENCE OF T61String }

Videotex ::=
     SEQUENCE {
     SET, -- members are for further study
       VideotexString }

NationallyDefined ::= ANY

Encrypted ::=
     SEQUENCE {
     SET, -- members are for further study
     BITSTRING }

ForwardedIPMessage ::=
     SEQUENCE {
     SET {
```

```
            delivery
            [0] IMPLICIT Time OPTIONAL,
            [1] IMPLICIT DeliveryInformation
                OPTIONAL
      },
      IM-UAPDU }
```

DeliveryInformation ::= P3.DeliverEnvelope
-- *This merely reuses a data type definition does not imply*
-- *that the information was ever carried in P3*

SFD ::= SFD.Document
-- *note that SFD and T73 document use the same space of*
-- *application-wide tags which is different from that*
-- *used for other MHS protocols*

TIF1 ::= T73Document

-- *IPM status report UAPDU*
SR-UAPDU ::=
```
      SET {
      [0] CHOICE {
          nonReceipt [0] IMPLICIT
          NonReceiptInformation,
          receipt [1] IMPLICIT ReceiptInformation
          },
      reported IPMessageID,
      actualRecipient [1] IMPLICIT ORDescriptor
          OPTIONAL,
      intendedRecipient [2] IMPLICIT ORDescriptor
          OPTIONAL,
      -- only present if not actual recipient
      -- the O/R descriptor must contain an O/R name
      converted P1.EncodedInformationTypes OPTIONAL
      }
```

NonReceiptInformation ::=
```
      SET {
      reason [0] IMPLICIT INTEGER {
      uaeInitiatedDiscard(0), autoForwarded(1)
      },
      nonReceiptQualifier [1] IMPLICIT INTEGER {
      expired(0), obsoleted(1),
      subscriptionTerminated(2) } OPTIONAL,
      comments [2] IMPLICIT PrintableString
          OPTIONAL,
```

--on auto-forward
`returned [3] IMPLICIT IM-UAPDU OPTIONAL }`

ReceiptInformation ::=
`    SET {`
`receipt [0] IMPLICIT Time,`
`typeOfReceipt [1] IMPLICIT INTEGER {`
`explicit(0), automatic(1) } DEFAULT explicit,`
`[2] IMPLICIT P1.SupplementaryInformation`
`OPTIONAL }`

END *-- of P2 definitions*

B

List of OSI standards

The following tables give an overview of a large number of relevant OSI standards (status 1 March 1992). Many of these documents are at the stage of a draft, for example, draft proposal (DP) or draft international standard (DIS) and have not yet been formally released as international standards (IS). Since the list of documents that are still being worked on is of considerable interest, we have also included proposals and working papers in the overview.

As mentioned at the beginning of the book, this overview is reprinted from the quarterly specialist journal 'Computer Communication Review' (CCR) of the ACM Special Interest Group on Data Communications (SIGCOMM) (SIGCOMM, 1991). According to the author and the publisher, it is planned to keep the overview up to date and to publish it every three to six months in CCR.

How to order standard documents

CCITT documents

CCITT recommendations may be ordered from:

International Telecommunication Union
Place des Nations
CH-1211 Geneva 20
Switzerland

The CCITT red and blue books each consist of a number of volumes (fascicles). The following volumes of the red and blue books are relevant to X.400:

X.400 (84) CCITT Recommendations X.400 – X.430
Data Communication Networks; Message Handling Systems
CCITT Red Book, Vol. VIII, Fasc. VIII.7, ITU, Geneva, 1985.

X.400 (88) CCITT Recommendations X.400 – X.420
Data Communication Networks; Message Handling Systems
CCITT Blue Book, Vol. VIII, Fasc. VIII.7, ITU, Geneva, 1989.

ISO documents

ISO international standards may be ordered from the relevant national standardization organization (for example, the American National Standards Institute (ANSI) in the USA or the British Standards Institution (BSI) in the UK).

DP and DIS documents are harder to obtain since they are mostly distributed as internal working papers to the members of the working group involved in the standardization process.

UN/EDIFACT documents

The latest versions of the UN/EDIFACT documents may be obtained in electronic form (MS-DOS diskette 5.25 in., 360 Kbyte) under the names UNTDID and UNTDED from:

United Nations
UN Economic Commission for Europe
Trade Division
Palais des Nations
CH-1211 Geneva
Switzerland

Overview of the X.400 (84) CCITT recommendations

CCITT Recommendation	Title
X.400	MHS: System Model – Service Elements
X.401	MHS: Basic Service Elements and Optional User Facilities
X.408	MHS: Encoded Information Type Conversion Rules
X.409	MHS: Presentation Transfer Syntax and Notation
X.410	MHS: Remote Operations and Reliable Transfer Server
X.411	MHS: Message Transfer Layer
X.420	MHS: Interpersonal Messaging User Agent Layer
X.430	MHS: Access Protocol for Teletex Terminals

Some relevant CCITT recommendations in the T series

CCITT Recommendation	Title
T.50	International Alphabet No. 5
T.61	Character repertoire and coded character sets for the international Teletex service
T.73	Document interchange protocol for the telematic services

Status of OSI (and related standards). 1/3/92[1]

Reference model of Open Systems Interconnection: ISO 7498, CCITT Recommendation X.200

ISO CD 7498-1	ISO 7498-2	ISO 7498-3	ISO 7498-4
Basic Reference Model *[second edition, incorporating Addendum 1 and commentaries; ballot closes 20.3.92]*	Security Architecture *[final text 19.7.88]*	Naming and Addressing *[published 1.3.89]*	Management Framework *[published 15.11.89]*

ISO 7498-1/Add.1	ISO 7498-1/PDAM2
Addendum 1: Connectionless Data Transmission *[published 15.7.87; will be superseded by ISO 7498-1 second edition]*	Amendment 2: Multipeer Data Transmission *[suspended 1.7.87]*

---

[1] Dates are in the format day/month/year.

Layer-independent standards

ISO TR 8509 CCITT X.210	OSI Service Conventions *[published 1.9.87]*
ISO DTR 10730	Tutorial on Naming and Addressing *[ballot closed 6.12.91]*
ISO DIS 10731	Conventions for the Definition of OSI Services *[ballot closed 26.1.92]*

Formal description techniques

ISO 8807	LOTOS – A Formal Description Technique Based on the Temporal Ordering of Observational Behaviour *[published 15.2.89]*
ISO 8807/PDAM1	Amendment 1: Graphical Representation (G-LOTOS)
ISO 9074	ESTELLE – A Formal Description Technique Based on an Extended State Transition Model *[published 15.7.89]*
ISO 9074/DAM1	Amendment 1: ESTELLE Tutorial *[ballot closed 1.11.91]*
ISO 9496	CCITT High-Level Language (CHILL) *[published 1.8.89]*
ISO TR 10167	Guidelines for the Application of Estelle, LOTOS, and SDL *[published 15.12.91]*

Conformance testing

ISO 9646-1	OSI Conformance Testing Methodology and Framework, Part 1: General Concepts *[awaiting publication]*
ISO 9646-1/PDAM1	Amendment 1: Protocol Profile Testing and Methodology *[awaiting PDAM ballot]*
ISO 9646-1/PDAM2	Amendment 2: Multi-party Testing *[awaiting PDAM ballot]*
ISO 9646-2	Part 2: Abstract Test Suite Specification *[awaiting publication]*
ISO 9646-2/PDAM1	Amendment 1: Protocol Profile Testing and Methodology *[awaiting PDAM ballot]*
ISO 9646-2/PDAM2	Amendment 2: Multi-party Testing *[awaiting PDAM ballot]*
ISO 9646-3	Part 3: Tree and Tabular Combined Notation *[awaiting publication]*
ISO 9646-3/PDAM1	Amendment 1: TTCN Extensions *[awaiting PDAM ballot]*
ISO 9646-4	Part 4: Test Realization *[published 15.7.91]*
ISO 9646-4/PDAM1	Amendment 1: Protocol Profile Testing and Methodology *[awaiting PDAM ballot]*

ISO 9646-4/ PDAM2	Amendment 2: Multi-party Testing *[awaiting PDAM ballot]*
ISO 9646-5	Part 5: Requirements on Test Laboratories and Their Clients for the Conformance Assessment Process *[awaiting publication]*
ISO 9646-5/ PDAM1	Amendment 1: Protocol Profile Testing and Methodology *[awaiting PDAM ballot]*
ISO 9646-5/ PDAM2	Amendment 2: Multi-party Testing *[awaiting PDAM ballot]*
ISO CD 9646-6	Part 6: Test Laboratory Operations *[awaiting CD ballot]*
ISO CD 9646-7	Part 7: Implementation Conformance Specification *[new work item]*

Registration authorities

ISO 9834-1 CCITT X.660	Procedures for Specific OSI Registration Authorities, Part 1: General Procedures *[awaiting publication]*
ISO DIS 9834-2	Part 2: Registration Procedures for OSI Document Types *[ballot closed 8.5.91]*
ISO 9834-3	Part 3: Procedures for the Assignment of Object Identifier Component Values for Joint ISO–CCITT Use *[published 27.9.90]*
ISO 9834-4	Part 4: Registration of VTE-Profiles *[published 1991]*
ISO 9834-5	Part 5: Registration of VT Control Object Definitions *[published 1991]*
ISO DIS 9834-6	Part 6: Registration of Application Process Titles and Application Entity Titles *[ballot closed 13.3.91]*

Abstract syntax notation

ISO 8824 CCITT X.208	Specification of Abstract Syntax Notation 1 (ASN.1) *[published 15.12.90; includes Addendum 1, ASN.1 Extensions]*
ISO 8824/PDAM2	Amendment 2 *[ballot closed 29.10.91]*
ISO CD 8824-2	Part 2: Information Object Specification *[awaiting CD ballot]*
ISO CD 8824-3	Part 3: Constraint Specification *[awaiting CD ballot]*
ISO CD 8824-4	Part 4: Parameterisation of ASN.1 Specifications *[awaiting CD ballot]*
ISO 8825 CCITT X.209	Specification of Basic Encoding Rules for Abstract Syntax Notation 1 (ASN.1) *[published 15.12.90; includes Addendum 1, ASN.1 Extensions]*
ISO 8825/PDAM2	Amendment 2 *[ballot closed 29.10.91]*

| ISO CD 8825-2 | Part 2: Packed Encoding Rules *[awaiting CD ballot]* |
| ISO CD 8825-3 | Part 3: Distinguished Encoding Rules *[awaiting CD ballot]* |

Security

ISO 9796	Security Techniques – Digital Signature Scheme Giving Message Recovery *[published 15.9.91]*
ISO 9798-1	Security Techniques – Entity Authentication Mechanisms, Part 1: General Model *[published 15.9.91]*
ISO CD 9798-2	Security Techniques – Entity Authentication Mechanisms, Part 2: Entity Authentication using Symmetric Techniques
ISO CD 9798-3	Security Techniques – Entity Authentication Mechanisms, Part 3: Entity Authentication using Public Key Algorithms
ISO 9979	Data Cryptographic Techniques – Procedures for the Registration of Cryptographic Algorithms *[published 1991]*
ISO CD 10181-1	Security Frameworks Part 1: Overview
ISO DIS 10181-2	Part 2: Authentication *[ballot closed 15.12.91]*
ISO CD 10181-3	Part 3: Access Control *[second CD ballot closed 18.10.91]*
ISO CD 10181-4	Part 4: Non-repudiation *[working draft]*
ISO CD 10181-5	Part 5: Confidentiality *[working draft]*
ISO CD 10181-6	Part 6: Integrity *[working draft]*
ISO CD 10181-7	Part 7: Security Audit *[ballot closed 10.12.91]*
ISO CD 10745	Upper Layers Security Model *[awaiting CD ballot]*
CCITT X.800	Security Architecture for OSI for CCITT Applications

Multi-layer Standards (Profiles)

ISO TR 10000-1	Framework and Taxonomy of International Standardized Profiles, Part 1: Framework *[published 15.5.90]*
ISO TR 10000-2	Part 2: Taxonomy of Profiles *[published 1.6.90]*
ISO ISP 10607-1	International Standardized Profile AFTnn – File Transfer, Access and Management, Part 1: Specification of ACSE, Presentation, and Session protocols for the use of FTAM *[published 1990]*
ISO ISP 10607-2	Part 2: Definition of Document Types, Constraint Sets, and Syntaxes *[published 1990]*
ISO ISP 10607-2/ Am.1	Amendment 1: Additional Definitions *[published 1991]*
ISO ISP 10607-3	Part 3: AFT11 – Simple File Transfer Service (unstructured) *[published 1990]*

ISO ISP 10607-4	Part 4: AFT12 – Positional File Transfer Service (flat) *[published 1991]*
ISO ISP 10607-5	Part 5: AFT22 – Positional File Access Service (flat) *[published 1991]*
ISO ISP 10607-6	Part 6: AFT3 – File Management Service *[published 1991]*
ISO PDISP 10608-1	International Standardized Profile TA – Connection-mode Transport Service over Connectionless Network Service, Part 1; General Overview and Subnetwork-independent Requirements *[ballot closed 12.1.91]*
ISO PDISP 10608-2	Part 2: TA51 Profile Including Subnetwork-dependent Requirements for CSMA/CD LANs *[ballot closed 12.1.91]*
ISO PDISP 10608-5	Part 5: TA1111/TA1121 Profiles Including Subnetwork-dependent Requirements for X.25 Packet Switched Data Networks Using Switched Virtual Circuits *[ballot closed 12.1.91]*
ISO DISP 10609-1	International Standardized Profiles TB, TC, TD and TE – Connection-mode Transport Service over Connection-mode Network Service, Part 1: Subnetwork-type Independent Requirements for Group TB *[ballot closed 12.1.91]*
ISO DISP 10609-2	Part 2: Subnetwork-type Independent Requirements for Group TC *[ballot closed 12.1.91]*
ISO DISP 10609-3	Part 3: Subnetwork-type Independent Requirements for Group TD *[ballot closed 12.1.91]*
ISO DISP 10609-4	Part 4: Subnetwork-type Independent Requirements for Group TE *[ballot closed 12.1.91]*
ISO DISP 10609-5	Part 5: Definition of Profile TB 1111/TB 1121 *[ballot closed 12.1.91]*
ISO DISP 10609-6	Part 6: Definition of Profile TC 1111/TC 1121 *[ballot closed 12.1.91]*
ISO DISP 10609-7	Part 7: Definition of Profile TD 1111/TD 1121 *[ballot closed 12.1.91]*
ISO DISP 10609-8	Part 8: Definition of Profile TE 1111/TE 1121 *[ballot closed 12.1.91]*
ISO DISP 10609-9	Part 9: Subnetwork-type Dependent Requirements for Network Layer, Data Link Layer and Physical Layer Concerning Permanent Access to a Packet Switched Data Network Using Virtual Call *[ballot closed 12.1.91]*
ISO DISP 10610-1	International Standardized Profile FOD26 – Office Document Format – Simple Document Structure – Character Content Only, Part 1: Document Application Profile *[ballot closes 29.3.92]*

ISO DISP 11181-1	International Standardized Profile FOD26 – Office Document Format – Enhanced Document Structure – Character, Raster Graphics, and Geometric Graphics Content Architectures, Part 1: Document Application Profile *[ballot closes 29.3.92]*
ISO DISP 11182-1	International Standardized Profile FOD36 – Office Document Format – Extended Document Structure, Part 1: Document Application Profile *[ballot closes 29.3.92]*
ISO DISP 11183-1	International Standardized Profiles AOMnn – Management Communication Protocols, Part 1: Specification of ACSE, Presentation and Session Protocols for Use by ROSE and CMISE *[ballot closes 29.3.92]*
ISO DISP 11183-2	International Standardized Profiles AOMnn – Management Communication Protocols, Part 2: AOM12, Enhanced Management Communications *[ballot closes 29.3.92]*
ISO DISP 11183-3	International Standardized Profiles AOMnn – Management Communication Protocols, Part 3: AOM11, Basic Management Communications *[ballot closes 29.3.92]*

Application Layer Standards

ISO 9545 CCITT X.207	Application Layer Structure *[published 15.12.89]*
ISO 9545/DAM1	Amendment 1: Extended Application Layer Structures *[ballot closes 24.4.92]*

Association control (ACSE)

ISO 8649 CCITT X.217	Service Definition for the Association Control Service Element *[published 15.12.88]*
ISO 8649/Am.1	Amendment 1: Peer-entity Authentication during Association Establishment *[published 1990]*
ISO 8649/Am.2	Amendment 2: Connectionless ACSE Service *[published 1.9.91]*
ISO 8650 CCITT X.227	Protocol Specification for the Association Control Service Element *[published 15.12.88]*
ISO 8650/Am.1	Amendment 1: Peer-entity Authentication during Association Establishment *[published 1990]*
ISO DIS 8650-2	Part 2: PICS Proforma *[awaiting DIS ballot]*
ISO 10035	Connectionless ACSE Protocol Specification *[published 15.7.91]*

| ISO 10169-1 | Conformance Test Suite for the ACSE Protocol, Part 1: Test Suite Structure and Test Purposes *[published 15.12.91]* |

Security

ISO CD xxxxx-1	Generic Upper Layer Security, Part 1: Model *[working draft; CD expected mid-1992]*
ISO CD xxxxx-2	Part 2: Service Definition *[working draft; CD expected mid-1992]*
ISO CD xxxxx-3	Part 3: Protocol Specification *[working draft; CD expected mid-1992]*
ISO CD xxxxx-4	Part 4: PICS Proforma *[working draft]*
ISO CD xxxxx-5	Part 5: Generic Transfer Syntax, Encoding Procedures and Syntax Notation *[working draft]*

Commitment, concurrency, and recovery (CCR)

ISO 9804 CCITT X.861	Service Definition for the Commitment, Concurrency, and Recovery Service Element *[published 1990]*
ISO 9804/PDAM1	Amendment 1: Service Enhancements
ISO 9804/DAM2	Amendment 2: Support for Session Mapping Changes *[ballot closed 19.1.92]*
ISO 9805 CCITT X.871	Protocol Specification for the Commitment, Concurrency, and Recovery Service Element *[published 1990]*
ISO 9805/PDAM1	Amendment 1: Service Enhancements
ISO 9805/DAM2	Amendment 2: Support for Session Mapping Changes *[ballot closed 19.1.92]*
ISO CD 9805-2	Part 2: PICS Proforma *[awaiting second CD ballot]*

Reliable transfer (RTS)

| ISO 9066-1
CCITT X.218 | Reliable Transfer, Part 1: Model and Service Definition *[published 15.11.89]* |
| ISO 9066-2
CCITT X.228 | Part 2: Protocol Specification *[published 15.11.89]* |

Remote operations (ROS)

| ISO 9072-1
CCITT X.219 | Remote Operations, Part 1: Model, Notation, and Service Definition *[published 15.11.89]* |

ISO 9072-2	Part 2: Protocol Specification *[published 15.11.89]*
CCITT X.229	

Remote Procedure Call (RPC)

ISO CD 11578-1	Remote Procedure Call Specification, Part 1: Model *[ballot closes 20.3.92]*
ISO CD 11578-2	Part 2: Service Definition *[ballot closes 20.3.92]*
ISO CD 11578-3	Part 3: Protocol Specification *[ballot closes 20.3.92]*
ISO CD 11578-4	Part 4: Interface Definition Notation *[ballot closes 20.3.92]*
ISO CD 11578-5	Part 5: PICS Proforma *[working draft]*

Management

ISO 9595	Common Management Information Service (CMIS)
CCITT X.710	Definition *[published 16.7.90]*
ISO 9595/DAM1	Amendment 1: Cancel/Get
ISO 9595/DAM2	Amendment 2: Add, Remove, and SetToDefault
ISO 9595/PDAM3	Amendment 3: Support for Allomorphism
ISO 9595/DAM4	Amendment 4: Access Control *[ballot closed 19.1.92]*
ISO 9596	Common Management Information Protocol (CMIP)
CCITT X.711	Specification *[second edition published 1.6.91]*
ISO 9596/DAM1	Amendment 1: Cancel/Get
ISO 9596/DAM2	Amendment 2: Add, Remove, and SetToDefault
ISO 9596/PDAM3	Amendment 3: Support for Allomorphism
ISO DIS 9596-2	Part 2: PICS Proforma *[ballot closed 1.1.92]*
ISO 10040 CCITT X.701	Systems Management Overview *[awaiting publication]*
ISO DIS 10164-1 CCITT X.730	Systems Management, Part 1: Object Management Function *[ballot closed 13.3.91]*
ISO DIS 10164-2 CCITT X.731	Part 2: State Management Function *[ballot closed 13.3.91]*
ISO DIS 10164-3 CCITT X.732	Part 3: Attributes for Representing Relationships *[ballot closed 13.3.91]*
ISO DIS 10164-4 CCITT X.733	Part 4: Alarm Reporting Function *[ballot closed 13.3.91]*
ISO DIS 10164-5 CCITT X.734	Part 5: Event Report Management Function *[ballot closed 13.3.91]*
ISO DIS 10164-6 CCITT X.735	Part 6: Log Control Function *[ballot closed 13.3.91]*

ISO DIS 10164-7 CCITT X.736	Part 7: Security Alarm Reporting Function *[ballot closed 13.3.91]*
ISO DIS 10164-8 CCITT X.740	Part 8: Security Audit Trail Function *[ballot closed 1.1.92]*
ISO CD 10164-9 CCITT X.741	Part 9: Objects and Attributes for Access Control
ISO CD 10164-10 CCITT X.742	Part 10: Accounting Meter Function
ISO CD 10164-11 CCITT X.739	Part 11: Workload Monitoring Function *[ballot closed 4.10.91]*
ISO CD 10164-12 CCITT X.745	Part 12: Test Management Function *[awaiting CD ballot]*
ISO CD 10164-13 CCITT X.738	Part 13: Measurement Summarization Function *[awaiting CD ballot]*
ISO CD 10164-*sm* CCITT X.744	Part *sm*: Software Management Function *[working draft]*
ISO CD 10164-*tc* CCITT X.737	Part *tc*: Confidence and Diagnostic Test Classes *[working draft]*
ISO CD 10164-*ti* CCITT X.743	Part *ti*: Time Management Function *[working draft]*
ISO DIS 10165-1 CCITT X.720	Structure of Management Information, Part 1: Management Information Model *[ballot closed 13.3.91]*
ISO DIS 10165-2 CCITT X.721	Part 2: Definition of Management Information, (replaces original parts 2 and 3) *[ballot closed 13.3.91]*
ISO DIS 10165-4 CCITT X.722	Part 4: Guidelines for the Definition of Managed Objects *[ballot closed 13.3.91]*
ISO CD 10165-5	Part 5: Generic Management Information *[ballot closed 15.12.91]*
ISO CD 10165-6	Part 6: Requirements and Guidelines for Management Information Conformance Statement Proformas *[awaiting CD ballot]*

File transfer, access, and management (FTAM)

ISO 8571-1	File Transfer, Access and Management (FTAM), Part 1: General Introduction *[published 1.10.88]*
ISO 8571-1/Am.1	Amendment 1: Filestore Management *[awaiting publication]*
ISO 8571-1/DAM2	Amendment 2: Overlapped Access *[ballot closed 27.10.91]*
ISO 8571-1/ PDAM3	Amendment 3: Service Enhancement *[ballot closed; awaiting DAM or second PDAM ballot]*
ISO 8571-2	Part 2: The Virtual Filestore Definition *[published 1.10.88]*

ISO 8571-2/Am.1	Amendment 1: Filestore Management [awaiting publication]
ISO 8571-2/DAM2	Amendment 2: Overlapped Access [ballot closed 27.10.91]
ISO 8571-2/ PDAM3	Amendment 3: Service Enhancement [ballot closed; awaiting DAM or second PDAM ballot]
ISO 8571-3	Part 3: The File Service Definition [published 1.10.88]
ISO 8571-3/Am.1	Amendment 1: Filestore Management [awaiting publication]
ISO 8571-3/DAM2	Amendment 2: Overlapped Access [ballot closed 27.10.91]
ISO 8571-3/ PDAM3	Amendment 3: Service Enhancement [ballot closed; awaiting DAM or second PDAM ballot]
ISO 8571-4	Part 4: The File Protocol Specification [published 1.10.88]
ISO 8571-4/Am.1	Amendment 1: Filestore Management [awaiting publication]
ISO 8571-4/DAM2	Amendment 2: Overlapped Access [ballot closed 27.10.91]
ISO 8571-4/ PDAM3	Amendment 3: Service Enhancement [ballot closed; awaiting DAM or second PDAM ballot]
ISO 8571-5	Part 5: PICS Proforma [published 1990]
ISO 8571-5/ PDAM1	Amendment 1: Filestore Management and Overlapped Access [working draft]
ISO DIS 10170-1	Conformance Test Suite for the FTAM Protocol, Part 1: Test Suite Structure and Test Purposes [ballot closed 8.5.91]

Virtual terminal (VT)

ISO 9040	Virtual Terminal Service – Basic Class [published 1990; includes Addendum 1, Extended Facility Set]
ISO 9040/Am.2	Amendment 2: Additional Functional Units [awaiting publication]
ISO 9041	Virtual Terminal Protocol – Basic Class [published 1990; includes Addendum 1, Extended Facility Set]
ISO 9041/Am.2	Amendment 2: Additional Functional Units [awaiting publication]
ISO DIS 9041-2	Part 2: PICS Proforma [ballot closed 25.10.91]
ISO DIS 10184-1	Terminal Management, Part 1: Model [awaiting DIS ballot]
ISO CD 10184-2	Part 2: Service Definition [working draft]
ISO CD 10184-3	Part 3: Protocol Specification [working draft]
ISO DIS 10739-1	Conformance Test Suite for Virtual Terminal, Part 1: Test Suite Structure and Test Purposes [awaiting DIS ballot]

Job transfer and manipulation (JTM)

ISO 8831	JTM Concepts and Services *[published 1.7.89]*
ISO 8832	Specification of the Basic Class Protocol for JTM *[published 1.7.89]*
ISO 8832/DAM1	Amendment 1: Full Class Protocol for Job Transfer and Manipulation *[ballot closed 11.4.91]*

The directory

ISO DIS 9594-1 CCITT X.500	The Directory, Part 1: Overview of Concepts, Models, and Services *[published 1990]*
ISO 9594-1/ PDAM1	Amendment 1: Replication, Schema, and Access Control *[second PDAM ballot closes 5.9.92]*
ISO DIS 9594-2 CCITT X.501	Part 2: Information Framework *[published 1990]*
ISO 9594-2/ PDAM1	Amendment 1: Access Control *[fourth PDAM ballot closes 5.9.92]*
ISO 9594-2/ PDAM2	Amendment 2: Schema Extensions *[second PDAM ballot closes 5.9.92]*
ISO 9594-2/ PDAM3	Amendment 3: Replication *[third PDAM ballot closes 5.9.92]*
ISO DIS 9594-3 CCITT X.511	Part 3: Access and System Services Definition *[published 1990]*
ISO 9594-3/ PDAM1	Amendment 1: Access Control *[fourth PDAM ballot closes 5.9.92]*
ISO 9594-3/ PDAM2	Amendment 2: Replication, Schema, and Enhanced Search *[third PDAM ballot closes 5.9.92]*
ISO DIS 9594-4 CCITT X.518	Part 4: Procedures for Distributed Operation *[published 1990]*
ISO 9594-4/ PDAM1	Amendment 1: Access Control *[fourth PDAM ballot closes 5.9.92]*
ISO 9594-4/ PDAM2	Amendment 2: Replication, Schema, and Enhanced Search *[third PDAM ballot closes 5.9.92]*
ISO DIS 9594-5 CCITT X.519	Part 5: Access and System Protocols Specification *[published 1990]*
ISO 9594-5/ PDAM1	Amendment 1: Replication *[ballot closes 5.9.92]*
ISO DIS 9594-6 CCITT X.520	Part 6: Selected Attribute Types *[published 1990]*
ISO 9594-6/ PDAM1	Amendment 1: Schema Extensions *[third PDAM ballot closes 5.9.92]*

ISO DIS 9594-7 CCITT X.521	Part 7: Selected Object Classes *[published 1990]*
ISO 9594-7/ PDAM1	Amendment 1: Schema Extensions *[third PDAM ballot closes 5.9.92]*
ISO DIS 9594-8 CCITT X.509	Part 8: Authentication Framework *[published 1990]*
ISO 9594-8/ PDAM1	Amendment 1: Access Control *[third PDAM ballot closes 5.9.92]*
ISO DIS 9594-9	Part 9: Replication and Knowledge Management *[ballot closes 5.9.92]*

Message handling (MHS)

ISO DIS 10021-1 CCITT X.400	Message Oriented Text Interchange System (MOTIS) [Message Handling], Part 1: System and Service Overview *[published 1990]*
ISO DIS 10021-2 CCITT X.402	Part 2: Overall Architecture *[published 1990]*
CCITT X.403	Message Handling: Conformance Testing *[final text in preparation]*
ISO DIS 10021-3 CCITT X.407	Part 3: Abstract Service Definition Conventions *[published 1990]*
CCITT X.408	Message Handling: Encoded Information Type Conversion Rules *[final text in preparation]*
ISO DIS 10021-4 CCITT X.411	Part 4: Message Transfer System – Abstract Service Definition and Procedures *[published 1990]*
ISO DIS 10021-5 CCITT X.413	Part 5: Message Store – Abstract Service Definition *[ballot closed 30.12.88]*
ISO DIS 10021-6 CCITT X.419	Part 6: Protocol Specifications *[published 1990]*
ISO DIS 10021-7 CCITT X.420	Part 7: Interpersonal Messaging System *[published 1990]*
ISO CD 10021-11	Part 11: MTS Routing *[ballot closed 27.5.91]*
CCITT X.435	MHS Application for EDI Messaging

Office document architecture (ODA) and interchange format (ODIF)
Document transfer, access, and manipulation (DTAM)

CCITT T.400	Document Transfer, Access, and Manipulation (DTAM) – General Introduction
ISO 8613-1 CCITT T.411	Text and Office Systems – Office Document Architecture and Interchange Format, Part 1: Introduction and General Principles *[published 1.9.89]*

ISO 8613-1/DAM1	Amendment 1: Document Application Profile Proforma and Notation *[ballot closed 1.7.90]*
ISO 8613-1/DAM2	Amendment 2: Conformance Testing Methodology
ISO 8613-2 CCITT T.412	Part 2: Document Structures *[published 1.9.89]*
ISO 8613-4 CCITT T.414	Part 4: Document Profile *[published 1.9.89]*
ISO 8613-4/ PDAM1	Amendment 1: Additive Extensions for Filing and Retrieval Attributes
ISO 8613-4/ PDAM2	Amendment 2: Document Application Profile Proforma and Notation *[ballot closed 15.9.89]*
ISO 8613-5 CCITT T.415	Part 5: Document Interchange Format *[published 1.9.89]*
ISO 8613-6 CCITT T.416	Part 6: Character Content Architectures *[published 1.9.89]*
ISO 8613-7 CCITT T.417	Part 7: Raster Graphics Content Architectures *[published 1.9.89]*
ISO 8613-7/DAM1	Amendment 1: Tiled Raster Graphics Content Architectures
ISO 8613-8 CCITT T.418	Part 8: Geometric Graphics Content Architectures *[published 1.9.89]*
ISO CD 8613-9	Part 9: Audio Content Architectures *[new work item]*
ISO CD 8613-10	Part 10: Formal Specifications
ISO 8613-10/DAM1	Amendment 1: Formal Specification of the Document Profile *[published 1991]*
ISO 8613-10/DAM2	Amendment 2: Formal Specification of the Raster Graphics Content Architectures *[ballot closed 11.4.91]*
ISO 8613-10/DAM3	Amendment 3: Annex C – Formal Specification of the Character Content Architectures *[ballot closes 12.6.92]*
ISO CD 10033	Text and Office Systems – Office Document Interchange, Flexible Disks *[ballot closed 19.9.88]*
ISO DIS 10175-1	Text and Office Systems – Document Printing Application, Part 1: Abstract Service Definition and Procedures *[ballot closes 5.5.92]*
ISO DIS 10175-2	Text and Office Systems – Document Printing Application, Part 2: Protocol Specification *[ballot closes 5.5.92]*
CCITT T.419	Document Transfer, Access, and Manipulation (DTAM) – Composite Graphics Content Architectures
CCITT T.431	Document Transfer, Access, and Manipulation (DTAM) – Introduction and General Principles
CCITT T.432	Document Transfer, Access, and Manipulation (DTAM) – Service Definition
CCITT T.433	Document Transfer, Access, and Manipulation (DTAM) – Protocol Specification

| CCITT T.441 | Document Transfer, Access, and Manipulation (DTAM) – Operational Structure |

Remote database access (RDA)

| ISO DIS 9579-1 | Remote Database Access, Part 1: General Model, Services, and Protocol *[ballot closes 3.4.92]* |
| ISO DIS 9579-2 | Part 2: SQL Specialization *[ballot closes 3.4.92]* |

Transaction processing (TP)

ISO DIS 10026-1	Distributed Transaction Processing, Part 1: Model *[second DIS ballot closed 15.11.91]*
ISO DIS 10026-2	Part 2: Service Definition *[second DIS ballot closed 15.11.91]*
ISO DIS 10026-3	Part 3: Transaction Processing Protocol Specification *[ballot closed 22.9.90]*
ISO CD 10026-4	Part 4: PICS Proforma *[ballot closed, awaiting DIS or third CD ballot]*
ISO CD 10026-5	Part 5: Application Context Proforma *[awaiting DIS ballot]*
ISO CD 10026-6	Part 6: Unstructured Data Transfer *[ballot closed; awaiting DIS or second CD ballot]*
CCITT X.850	Distributed Transaction Processing Model for OSI for CCITT Applications
CCITT X.860	Distributed Transaction Processing Service Definition for OSI for CCITT Applications
CCITT X.870	Distributed Transaction Processing Protocol for OSI for CCITT Applications

Computer graphics metafile (CGM)

ISO 8632-1	Metafile for the Storage and Transfer of Picture Description Information, Part 1: Functional Specification *[published 1.8.87]*
ISO 8632-1/Am.1	Amendment 1: Audit Trail Metafile *[published 1990]*
ISO 8632-1/ PDAM2	Amendment 2: 3D Static Picture Capture Metafile
ISO 8632-1/DAM3	Amendment 3 *[ballot closed 3.7.91]*
ISO 8632-2	Part 2: Character Encoding *[published 1.8.87]*
ISO 8632-2/Am.1	Amendment 1: Audit Trail Metafile *[published 1990]*
ISO 8632-2/DAM3	Amendment 3 *[ballot closed 3.7.91]*

ISO 8632-3	Part 3: Binary Encoding *[published 1.8.87]*
ISO 8632-3/Am.1	Amendment 1: Audit Trail Metafile *[published 1990]*
ISO 8632-3/DAM3	Amendment 3 *[ballot closed 3.7.91]*
ISO 8632-4	Part 4: Clear Text Encoding *[published 1.8.87]*
ISO 8632-4/Am.1	Amendment 1: Audit Trail Metafile *[published 1990]*
ISO 8632-4/DAM3	Amendment 3 *[ballot closed 3.7.91]*

Graphical kernel system (GKS)

ISO 7942	Graphical Kernel System Functional Description *[published 1985]*
ISO 7942/Am.1	Amendment 1: Audit Trail Metafile *[published 1991]*
ISO 8651-1	GKS Language Bindings, Part 1: FORTRAN *[published 11.10.88]*
ISO 8651-2	Part 2: Pascal *[published 11.10.88]*
ISO 8651-3	Part 3: Ada *[published 11.10.88]*
ISO 8651-4	Part 4: C *[published 1991]*
ISO 8805	Graphical Kernel System for Three Dimensions (GKS-3D) Functional Description *[published 11.10.88]*
ISO 8806-4	Graphical Kernel System for Three Dimensions (GKS-3D) Language Bindings, Part 4: C *[published 1991]*
ISO TR 9973	Registration of Graphical Items *[published 11.10.88]*

Programmer's hierarchical interactive graphics interface (PHIGS)

ISO 9592-1	Programmer's Hierarchical Interactive Graphics Interface, Part 1: Functional Description *[published 21.5.89]*
ISO 9592-1/DAM1	Amendment 1: PHIGS Plus Support *[ballot closed 25.10.91]*
ISO 9592-2	Part 2: Archive File Format *[published 21.5.89]*
ISO 9592-2/DAM1	Amendment 1: PHIGS Plus Support *[ballot closed 25.10.91]*
ISO 9592-3	Part 3: Clear-text Encoding for Archive File *[published 21.5.89]*
ISO 9592-3/DAM1	Amendment 1: PHIGS Plus Support *[ballot closed 25.10.91]*
ISO DIS 9592-4	Part 4: PHIGS Plus *[ballot closed 2.11.91]*
ISO 9593-1	PHIGS Language Bindings, Part 1: FORTRAN *[published 22.8.90]*
ISO DIS 9593-2	Part 2: Pascal *[awaiting DIS ballot]*

ISO 9593-3	Part 3: ADA *[published 16.7.90]*
ISO 9593-4	Part 4: C *[published 1991]*

Graphical device interfaces

ISO DIS 9636-1	Interfacing Techniques for Dialogues with Graphical Devices – Functional Specification, Part 1: Overview, Profiles, and Conformance *[ballot closed 8.9.90]*
ISO DIS 9636-2	Part 2: Control *[ballot closed 8.9.90]*
ISO DIS 9636-3	Part 3: Output *[ballot closed 8.9.90]*
ISO DIS 9636-4	Part 4: Segments *[ballot closed 8.9.90]*
ISO DIS 9636-5	Part 5: Input and Echoing *[ballot closed 8.9.90]*
ISO DIS 9636-6	Part 6: Raster *[ballot closed 8.9.90]*

Fonts, text composition, and page layout

ISO 8879	Standard Generalized Markup Language *[published 15.10.86]*
ISO 8879/Am.1	Amendment 1 *[published 1.7.88]*
ISO 9069	SGML Document Interchange Format (SDIF) *[published 15.9.88]*
ISO 9070	Registration Procedures for Public Text Owner Identifiers *[published 1.2.90]*
ISO 9541-1	Font and Character Information Interchange, Part 1: Architecture *[published 15.9.91]*
ISO 9541-2	Part 2: Interchange Format *[published 15.9.91]*
ISO DIS 9541-3	Part 3: Glyph Shape Representations *[ballot closed 20.10.91]*
ISO TR 9573	Techniques for Using SGML *[published 1.12.88]*
ISO DIS 10036	Procedure for Registration of Glyph and Glyph Collection Identifiers *[ballot closed 17.11.90]*
ISO TR 10037	Guidelines for SGML Syntax-Directed Editing Systems *[awaiting publication]*
ISO CD 10179	Document Style Semantics and Specification Language (DSSSL) *[awaiting CD ballot]*
ISO CD 10180	Standard Page Description Language *[awaiting CD ballot]*

Manufacturing message service (MMS)

| ISO DIS 9506-1 | Industrial Automation Systems – Systems Integration and Communications – Manufacturing Message Specification, Part 1: Service Definition *[ballot closed 14.8.88]* |
| ISO DIS 9506-2 | Part 2: Protocol Specification *[ballot closed 14.8.88]* |

Distributed office applications (DOA)

| ISO DIS 10031-1 | Distributed Office Applications, Part 1: General Model *[ballot closed 12.10.89]* |
| ISO DIS 10031-2 | Part 2: Referenced Data Transfer *[ballot closed 12.10.89]* |

Electronic data interchange (EDI)

| ISO 9735 | EDIFACT Syntax Rules *[published 1.7.88]* |

Banking information interchange

| ISO CD 9955 | Methodology and Guidelines for the Development of Application Protocols for Banking Information Interchange |

Library applications

ISO 10160	Documentation – Interlibrary Loan Service Definition *[awaiting publication]*
ISO 10161	Documentation – Interlibrary Loan Protocol Specification *[awaiting publication]*
ISO 10162	Documentation – Application Service for Information Systems – Bibliographic Search, Retrieval and Update Service *[awaiting publication]*
ISO 10163	Documentation – Application Protocol for Information Systems – Bibliographic Search, Retrieval, and Update Protocol *[awaiting publication]*

Document filing and retrieval

| ISO 10166-1 | Document Filing and Retrieval, Part 1: Abstract Service Definition and Procedures *[published 1991]* |
| ISO 10166-2 | Part 2: Protocol Specification *[published 1991]* |

Presentation Layer Standards

ISO 8822 CCITT X.216	Connection Oriented Presentation Service Definition *[published 15.8.88]*
ISO 8822/Am.1	Amendment 1: Connectionless-mode Presentation Service *[published 15.9.91]*
ISO 8822/PDAM2	Amendment 2: Support of Session Symmetric Synchronization Service
ISO 8822/PDAM3	Amendment 3: Unlimited User Data
ISO 8822/PDAM4	Amendment 4: Procedures for Registration of Abstract Syntaxes
ISO 8822/DAM5	Amendment 5: Incorporation of Additional Synchronization Functionality *[ballot closed 19.1.92]*
ISO 8823 CCITT X.226	Connection Oriented Presentation Protocol Specification *[published 15.8.88]*
ISO 8823/PDAM2	Amendment 2: Support of Session Symmetric Synchronization Service
ISO 8823/PDAM3	Amendment 3: Unlimited User Data
ISO 8823/PDAM4	Amendment 4: Procedures for Registration of Transfer Syntaxes
ISO 8823/DAM5	Amendment 5: Incorporation of Additional Synchronization Functionality *[ballot closed 19.1.92]*
ISO DIS 8823-2	Part 2: PICS Proforma *[awaiting DIS ballot – synchronized with Session PICS]*
ISO 9576	Connectionless Presentation Protocol Specification *[published 15.7.91]*
ISO DIS 9576-2	Part 2: PICS Proforma *[ballot closed 4.11.91]*
ISO DIS 10729-1	Conformance Test Suite for the Presentation Layer, Part 1: Test Suite Structure and Test Purposes for the Presentation Protocol *[ballot closed 27.12.91]*
ISO CD 10729-2	Part 2: Test Suite for ASN.1 Encodings *[awaiting CD ballot]*
ISO CD 10729-3	Part 3: Embedded Abstract Test Suite for CO Presentation Profile *[working draft]*

Session Layer Standards

ISO 8326 CCITT X.215	Basic Connection Oriented Session Service Definition *[published 15.8.87]*
ISO 8326/Add.1	Addendum 1: Session Symmetric Synchronization *[final text 1.12.88]*
ISO 8326/Add.2	Addendum 2: Incorporation of Unlimited User Data *[final text 27.6.88]*

ISO 8326/Am.3	Amendment 3: Connectionless Session Service *[awaiting publication]*
ISO 8326/DAM4	Amendment 4: Incorporation of Additional Synchronization Functionality *[ballot closes 19.1.92]*
ISO 8327 CCITT X.225	Basic Connection Oriented Session Protocol Specification *[published 15.8.87]*
ISO 8327/Add.1	Addendum 1: Session Symmetric Synchronization *[final text 1.12.88]*
ISO 8327/Add.2	Addendum 2: Incorporation of Unlimited User Data *[final text 27.6.88]*
ISO 8327/DAM3	Amendment 3: Incorporation of Additional Synchronization Functionality *[ballot closed 19.1.92]*
ISO CD 8327-2	Part 2: PICS Proforma *[awaiting second CD ballot]*
ISO 9548	Connectionless Session Protocol *[published 1989]*
ISO CD 9548-2	Part 2: PICS Proforma *[ballot closed 13.9.91]*
ISO TR 9571	LOTOS Description of the Session Service *[published 1.11.89]*
ISO TR 9572	LOTOS Description of the Session Protocol *[published 1.11.89]*
ISO 10168-1	Conformance Test Suite for the Session Protocol, Part 1: Test Suite Structure and Test Purposes *[awaiting publication]*
ISO CD 10168-2	Part 2: Generic Test Suite *[working draft]*
ISO CD 10168-3	Part 3: Abstract Test Suite for CS Method *[working draft]*
ISO DIS 10168-4	Part 4: Test Management Protocol Specification *[ballot closed 7.9.91]*

Transport Layer Standards

ISO 8072 CCITT X.214	Transport Service Definition *[published 15.6.86]*
ISO 8072/Add.1	Addendum 1: Connectionless-mode Transmission *[published 15.6.86]*
ISO 8073 CCITT X.224	Connection Oriented Transport Protocol Specification *[second edition published 15.12.88; DIS ballot on consolidated text closes 5.6.92]*
ISO 8073/Add.1	Addendum 1: Network Connection Management Subprotocol (NCMS) *[published 1.12.88]*
ISO 8073/Add.2	Addendum 2: Class 4 Operation over Connectionless Network Service *[published 15.9.89]*
ISO 8073/Am.3	Amendment 3: Protocol Implementation Conformance Statement Proforma *[awaiting publication]*

ISO 8073/DAM4	Amendment 4: Transport Protocol Enhancements *[awaiting DAM ballot]*
ISO 8602	Protocol for Providing the Connectionless-mode Transport Service *[published 15.12.87]*
ISO DTR 10023	LOTOS Description of ISO 8072 *[awaiting second DTR ballot]*
ISO DTR 10024	LOTOS Description of ISO 8073 *[awaiting DTR ballot]*
ISO DIS 11570	Transport Protocol Identification Mechanism *[ballot closes 26.6.92]*

Conformance testing

ISO DIS 10025-1	Transport Protocol Conformance Testing, Part 1: General Principles
ISO CD 10025-2	Part 2: Test Suite Structure and Test Purposes
ISO DIS 10025-3	Part 3: Transport Test Management Protocol Specification *[ballot closes 30.7.92]*

Management

ISO DIS 10737-1	Elements of Management Information Related to OSI Transport Layer Standards, Part 1: Transport Protocol Management Specification *[ballot closes 12.6.92]*

Security

ISO DIS 10736	Transport Layer Security Protocol *[ballot closes 5.5.92]*
ISO 10736/PDAM1	Amendment 1: Security Association Establishment *[ballot closes 5.5.92]*

Network Layer Standards

ISO 8348 CCITT X.213	Network Service Definition *[published 15.4.87; DIS ballot on consolidated text for second edition closes 12.6.92]*
ISO 8348/Add.1	Addendum 1: Connectionless-mode Transmission *[published 15.4.87]*
ISO 8348/Add.2	Addendum 2: Network Layer Addressing *[published 1.6.88]*
ISO 8348/Add.3	Addendum 3: Additional Features of the Network Service *[published 15.10.88]*
ISO 8348/DAM4	Amendment 4: Removal of the Preferred Decimal Encoding of the NSAP Address *[ballot closes 17.4.92]*

ISO 8348/PDAM5	Amendment 5: Allocation of a New AFI Value and IDI Format for the NSAP Address *[working draft]*
ISO 8648	Internal Organization of the Network Layer *[published 15.2.88]*
ISO 8880-1	Protocol Combinations to Provide and Support the OSI Network Service, Part 1: General Principles *[published 15.12.90]*
ISO 8880-2	Part 2: Provision and Support of the Connection-mode Network Service *[published 15.12.90]*
ISO 8880-2/DAM1	Amendment 1: Addition of the ISDN Environment *[ballot closed 27.10.91]*
ISO 8880-2/DAM2	Amendment 2: Addition of the PSTN and CSDN Environments *[ballot closes 28.5.92]*
ISO 8880-3	Part 3: Provision and Support of the Connectionless Network Service *[published 15.12.90]*
ISO TR 9577	Protocol Identification in the Network Layer *[published 15.11.90]*
ISO TR 10172	Network/Transport Protocol Interworking Specification *[published 15.9.91]*
dpANS X3.216	American National Standard – Structure of the Domain-Specific Part (DSP) of the OSI Network Service Access Point (NSAP) Address *[ANSI public review period ended 15.2.92]*

Internetwork protocol

ISO 8473	Protocol for Providing the Connectionless-mode Network Service (Internetwork Protocol) *[published 15.12.88]*
ISO 8473/Add.3	Addendum 3: Provision of the Underlying Service Assumed by ISO 8473 over Subnetworks which Provide the OSI Data Link Service *[published 1.9.89]*
ISO 8473/PDAM4	Amendment 4: PICS Proforma *[ballot closed 7.1.92]*
ISO 8473/PDAM5	Amendment 5: Provision of the Underlying Service for Operation over ISDN Circuit-switched B-channels *[ballot closed 26.12.91]*

X.25 packet level protocol

ISO 8208	X.25 Packet Layer Protocol for Data Terminal Equipment *[second edition published 15.3.90]*
ISO 8208/Am.1	Amendment 1: Alternative Logical Channel Identifier Assignment *[published 1.6.91]*
ISO 8208/Am.3	Amendment 3: Static Conformance Requirements *[published 1.6.91]*

ISO 8878 CCITT X.223	Use of X.25 to Provide the Connection-oriented Network Service *[published 1.9.87]*
ISO 8878/Add.1	Addendum 1: Priority *[published 15.6.90]*
ISO 8878/Add.2	Addendum 2: Use of an X.25 PVC to Provide the OSI CONS *[published 15.6.90]*
ISO 8878/Am.3	Amendment 3: Conformance *[published 1.6.91]*
ISO DIS 8878-2	Part 2: PICS Proforma *[ballot closes 28.5.92]*
ISO 8881	Use of the X.25 Packet Level Protocol in Local Area Networks *[published 1.12.89]*
ISO 8882-1	X.25 DTE Conformance Testing, Part 1: General Principles *[awaiting publication]*
ISO 8882-3	Part 3: Packet Level Conformance Suite *[published 1.12.91]*
ISO 8882-3/ PDAM1	Amendment 1: Use of Data Link Service Primitives *[ballot closed 7.1.92]*
ISO TR 10029	Operation of an X.25 Interworking Unit *[published 15.3.89]*
ISO 10177	Intermediate System Support of the OSI CONS using ISO 8208 in Accordance with ISO 10028 *[awaiting publication]*
ISO DIS 10588	Use of X.25 PLP in Conjunction with X.21/X.21 *bis* to Provide the OSI CONS *[ballot closes 17.4.92]*
ISO DIS 10732 CCITT X.614	Use of X.25 PLP to provide the OSI CONS over the telephone network *[ballot closes 17.4.92]*

Routing

ISO 9542	End System to Intermediate System Routing Information Exchange Protocol for Use in Conjunction with the Protocol for the Provision of the Connectionless-mode Network Service *[published 15.8.88]*
ISO 9542/PDAM1	Amendment 1: Dynamic Discovery of OSI NSAP Addresses by End Systems *[ballot closed 22.12.91]*
ISO TR 9575	OSI Routing Framework *[published 1.6.90]*
ISO DIS 10028	Definition of the Relaying Functions of a Network Layer Intermediate System *[awaiting DIS ballot]*
ISO 10028/DAM1	Amendment 1: Connectionless relaying functions *[ballot closes 26.6.92]*
ISO 10030	End System to Intermediate System Routing Information Exchange Protocol for Use in Conjunction with ISO 8878 *[published 15.12.90]*
ISO 10030/PDAM1	Amendment 1: Dynamic Discovery of OSI NSAP Addresses by End Systems *[ballot closed 22.12.91]*
ISO 10030/PDAM3	Amendment 3: Intermediate System Interactions with a SNARE *[ballot closed 12.12.91]*
ISO DIS 10030-2	Part 2: PICS Proforma *[ballot closes 28.5.92]*

ISO 10589	Intermediate System to Intermediate System Routing Information Exchange Protocol for Use in Conjunction with ISO 8473 *[awaiting publication]*
ISO CD 10747	Protocol for Exchange of Inter-Domain Routing Information among Intermediate Systems to Support Forwarding of ISO 8473 PDUs *[ballot closed 9.12.91]*

Management

ISO DIS 10733	Specification of the Elements of Management Information Related to OSI Network Layer Standards *[ballot closes 28.5.92]*

Security

ISO CD 11577	Network Layer Security *[ballot closes 20.4.92]*

ISDN

ISO 9574	Provision of the OSI Connection-mode Network Service by Packet-mode Terminal Equipment Connected to an ISDN *[published 15.12.89]*
ISO 9574/DAM1	Amendment 1: Provision of CONS over an ISDN Circuit-Switched Channel Connecting Directly to the Remote Terminal *[ballot closed 4.10.91]*

Private Integrated Services Digital Networks (PISN)

ISO CD 11571	Addressing in Private Integrated Services Digital Networks *[ballot closed 21.1.92]*
ISO CD 11572	Circuit-mode Bearer Services – Inter-exchange Signalling Procedures and Protocol *[ballot closed 21.1.92]*
ISO CD 11573	Synchronization Methods and Technical Requirements for PISNs *[ballot closed 1.2.92]*
ISO CD 11574	Circuit-mode 64 kbit/sec Bearer Services – Service Definition – Functional Capabilities and Information Flows *[ballot closed 15.2.92]*
ISO CD 11579	Reference Configuration for PISN Exchanges *[ballot closed 18.5.92]*

Data Link Layer Standards

ISO DIS 8886 CCITT X.212	Data Link Service Definition *[third DIS ballot closed 16.9.88]*
ISO DIS 9234	Industrial Asynchronous Data Link for Two-way Simultaneous or Two-way Alternate Mode
ISO CD 11575	Protocol Mappings for the OSI Data Link Service *[ballot closed 1.3.92]*

High-level data link control (HDLC)

ISO 3309	High-level Data Link Control (HDLC) – Frame Structure *[fourth edition published 1.6.91]*
ISO 3309/Add.1	Addendum 1: Start/Stop Transmission *[final text 12.3.90]*
ISO 3309/Am.2	Amendment 2: Extended Transparency Options for Start/Stop Transmission *[published 15.1.92]*
ISO 3309/DAM3	Amendment 3: Seven-bit Transparency Option for Start/Stop Transmission *[awaiting DAM ballot]*
ISO 4335	HDLC – Consolidation of Elements of Procedures *[fourth edition published 15.9.91]*
ISO 4335/Add.1	Addendum 1: (no title; contains UI and SREJ extensions) *[published 1.8.87]*
ISO 4335/Add.2	Addendum 2: Enhancement of the XID Function Utility
ISO 4335/Add.3	Addendum 3: Start/Stop Transmission *[final text 12.3.90]*
ISO 4335/Am.4	Amendment 4: Multi-Selective Reject Option *[published 1.10.91]*
ISO 7478	Multi-link Procedures *[third edition published 1.7.84]*
ISO 7776	HDLC – Description of the X.25 LAPB-compatible DTE Data Link Procedures *[published 15.12.86]*
ISO 7776/DAM1	Amendment 1: PICS Proforma *[ballot closed 15.2.92]*
ISO 7809	HDLC – Consolidation of Classes of Procedures *[second edition published 15.9.91]*
ISO 7809/Add.1	Addendum 1 (no title; contains UI extensions) *[published 15.6.87]*
ISO 7809/Add.2	Addendum 2: Description of Optional Functions *[published 15.6.87]*
ISO 7809/Add.3	Addendum 3: Start/Stop Transmission *[final text 12.3.90]*
ISO 7809/DAM5	Amendment 5: Connectionless Class of Procedures *[ballot closed 18.1.92]*

ISO 7809/Am.6	Amendment 6: Extended Transparency Options for Start/Stop Transmission *[published 15.1.92]*
ISO 7809/Am.7	Amendment 7: Multi-Selective Reject Option *[published 15.9.91]*
ISO 7809/DAM9	Amendment 9: Seven-bit Transparency Option for Start/Stop Transmission *[awaiting DAM ballot]*
ISO 8471	HDLC Balanced Classes of Procedures – Data Link Layer Address Resolution/Negotiation in Switched Environments *[published 1.4.87]*
ISO 8885	HDLC – General Purpose XID Frame Information Field Content and Format *[second edition published 1.6.91]*
ISO 8885/Add.1	Addendum 1: Additional Operational Parameters for the Parameter Negotiation Data Link Layer Subfield and Definition of a Multilink Parameter Negotiation Data Link Layer Subfield *[published 1.10.89]*
ISO 8885/Add.2	Addendum 2: Start/Stop Transmission *[final text 12.3.90]*
ISO 8885/DAM3	Amendment 3: Definition of a Private Parameter Negotiation Data Link Layer Subfield *[second DAM ballot closed 11.4.91]*
ISO 8885/Am.4	Amendment 4: Extended Transparency Options for Start/Stop Transmission *[published 15.1.92]*
ISO 8885/Am.5	Amendment 5: Multi-Selective Reject Option *[published 1.7.91]*
ISO 8885/PDAM6	Amendment 6: Seven-bit Transparency Option for Start/Stop Transmission *[ballot closed 10.3.91]*
ISO 8885/PDAM7	Amendment 7: Frame Check Sequence Negotiation Using the Parameter Negotiation Subfield *[ballot closed 21.8.90]*
ISO TR 10171	List of Standard Data Link Layer Protocols that Utilise High-Level Data Link Control (HDLC) Classes of Procedures *[awaiting publication]*
ISO 10171/PDAM1	Amendment 1: Registration of XID Format Identifiers and Private Parameter Set Identifiers *[ballot closed 10.3.91]*

Basic mode

| ISO 1155 | Use of Longitudinal Parity to Detect Errors in Information Messages *[second edition published 15.11.78]* |
| ISO 1177 | Character Structure for Start/Stop and Synchronous Character Oriented Transmission *[second edition published 15.8.85]* |

ISO 1745	Basic Mode Control Procedures for Data Communication Systems *[published 1.2.75]*
ISO 2111	Basic Mode Control Procedures – Code-Independent Information Transfer *[second edition published 1.2.85]*
ISO 2628	Basic Mode Control Procedures – Complements *[published 1.6.73]*
ISO 2629	Basic Mode Control Procedures – Conversational Information Message Transfer *[published 15.2.73]*

Local area networks (LANs)

ISO 8802-1	Local Area Networks, Part 1: Introduction
ISO DIS 8802-1E	Local Area Networks, Part 1: Introduction, Section E: System Load Protocol *[ballot closed 7.3.91]*
ISO 8802-2	Part 2: Logical Link Control *[published 16.7.90]*
ISO 8802-2/DAM1	Amendment 1: Flow Control Techniques for Bridged Local Area Networks *[ballot closed 19.11.88]*
ISO 8802-2/DAM2	Amendment 2: Acknowledged connectionless-mode service, Type 3 operation *[ballot closes 28.5.92]*
ISO 8802-2/ PDAM3	Amendment 3: PICS Proforma *[second PDAM ballot closed 27.2.92]*
ISO 8802-2/DAM4	Amendment 4: Editorial Changes and Technical Corrections *[ballot closed 24.11.90]*
ISO 8802-2/ PDAM5	Amendment 5: Bridged LAN Source Routing Operation by End Systems *[was PDTR 10734; ballot closed 31.12.91]*
ISO 8802-3	Part 3: Carrier Sense Multiple Access with Collision Detection – Access Method and Physical Layer Specifications *[second edition published 21.9.90]*
ISO 8802-3/DAM1	Amendment 1: Medium Attachment Unit and Baseband Medium Specifications for Type 10BASE2
ISO 8802-3/DAM2	Amendment 2: Repeater Set and Repeater Unit Specification for use with 10BASE5 and 10BASE2 Networks
ISO 8802-3/DAM3	Amendment 3: Broadband Medium Attachment Unit and Broadband Medium Specifications, Type 10BROAD36 *[ballot closed 28.12.90]*
ISO 8802-3/DAM4	Amendment 4: Physical Medium, Medium Attachment, and Baseband Medium Specifications, Type 10BASE5 (StarLAN) *[ballot closed 28.2.91]*
ISO 8802-3/DAM5	Amendment 5: Medium Attachment Unit and Baseband Medium Attachment Specification for a Vendor Independent Fiber Optic Inter-repeater Link

ISO 8802-3/DAM6	Amendment 6: Summary of IEEE 802.3 First Maintenance Ballot *[ballot closed 22.2.92]*
ISO 8802-3/DAM7	Amendment 7: LAN Layer Management *[ballot closes 24.4.92]*
ISO 8802-3/DAM9	Amendment 9: Physical Medium, Medium Attachment, and Baseband Medium Specifications, Type 10baseT *[ballot closes 12.6.92]*
ISO 8802-4	Part 4: Token-passing Bus Access Method and Physical Layer Specification *[published 17.8.90]*
ISO DIS 8802-5	Part 5: Token Ring Access Method and Physical Layer Specification *[second DIS ballot on consolidated document containing part 5 and its first three addenda closed 1.9.90]*
ISO 8802-5/ PDAM1	Amendment 1: 4 and 16 Mbit/s Specification *[ballot closed 13.1.89]*
ISO 8802-5/ PDAM2	Amendment 2: MAC Sublayer Enhancement *[ballot closed 10.11.89]*
ISO 8802-5/ PDAM3	Amendment 3: Management Entity Specification *[ballot closed 10.11.89]*
ISO 8802-5/DAM4	Amendment 4: Source Routing MAC Bridge *[ballot closed 3.7.91]*
ISO 8802-5/DAM5	Amendment 5: PICS Proforma *[ballot closed 1.5.91]*
ISO CD 8802-51	Part 51: MAC Sublayer Conformance Test Purposes *[ballot closes 25.4.92]*
ISO CD 8802-6	Part 6: Distributed Queue Dual Bus Access Method and Physical Layer Specification *[ballot closed 27.12.91]*
ISO 8802-7	Part 7: Slotted Ring Access Method and Physical Layer Specification *[final text distributed 13.7.89]*
ISO DIS 10038	MAC Bridging *[ballot closes 15.7.92]*
ISO 10038/PDAM1	Amendment 1: Specification of Management Information for CMIP *[awaiting PDAM ballot]*
ISO 10038/DAM2	Amendment 2: Source Routing Supplement *[awaiting DAM ballot]*
ISO 10039	MAC Service Definition *[published 1.6.91]*
ISO TR 10178	The Structure and Coding of Logical Link Control Addresses in Local Area Networks *[awaiting publication]*
ISO PDTR 10734	Guidelines for Bridged LAN Source Routing Operation by End Systems *[cancelled; superseded by 8802-2/PDAM5]*
ISO DTR 10735	Standard Group MAC Addresses *[ballot closed 12.2.92]*

Fiber distributed data interface (FDDI)

ISO 9314-2	Fiber Distributed Data Interface, Part 2: Medium Access Control *[published 1.5.89]*
ISO DIS 9314-5	Part 5: Hybrid Ring Control (FDDI-II) *[ballot closed 8.12.91]*
ISO CD 9314-6	Part 6: Station Management (SMT) *[working draft]*

Conformance testing

ISO DIS 8882-2	X.25 DTE Conformance Testing, Part 2: Data Link Layer Test Suite *[ballot closed 3.7.91]*
ISO DTR 10174	Logical Link Control (Type 2 Operation) Test Purposes *[awaiting DTR ballot]*

Management

ISO CD 10742	Elements of Management Information Related to OSI Data Link Layer Standards *[ballot closes 15.4.92]*

Physical Layer Standards

ISO 10022 CCITT X.211	Physical Service Definition *[published 1.8.90]*
ISO TR 7477	Arrangements for DTE to DTE Physical Connection Using V.24 and X.24 Interchange Circuits *[published 15.9.85]*
ISO 7480	Start–Stop Transmission Signal Quality at DTE–DCE Interfaces *[published 15.12.91]*
ISO 8480	DTE–DCE Interface Backup Control Operation Using the 25 Pin Connector *[published 15.11.87]*
ISO 8481	DTE to DTE Physical Connection Using X.24 Interchange Circuits with DTE-provided Timing *[published 15.9.86]*
ISO 8482	Twisted Pair Multipoint Interconnections *[published 15.11.87]*
ISO 9067	Automatic Fault Isolation Procedures Using Test Loops *[published 1.9.87]*
ISO 9543	Synchronous Transmission Signal Quality at DTE–DCE Interfaces *[published 1.4.89]*
ISO 9549	Galvanic Isolation of Balanced Interchange Circuits *[published 15.11.90]*

Fiber distributed data interface (FDDI)

ISO 9314-1	Fiber Distributed Data Interface, Part 1: Physical Layer Protocol *[published 15.4.89]*
ISO 9314-3	Part 3: Physical Layer Medium Dependent (PMD) *[published 1.8.90]*
ISO CD 9314-4	Part 4: Single-Mode Fiber/Physical Layer Medium Dependent

Physical connectors

ISO 2110	25 Pole DTE–DCE Interface Connector and Contact Number Assignments *[third edition published 1.10.89]*
ISO 2110/Am.1	Amendment 1: Interface Connector and Contact Number Assignments for a DTE/DCE Interface for Data Signalling Rates Above 20K Bits per Second *[published 15.9.91]*
ISO 2593	34 Pole DTE–DCE Interface Connector and Contact Number Assignments *[third edition awaiting publication]*
ISO 4902	37 Pole DTE–DCE Interface Connector and Contact Number Assignments *[second edition published 1.12.89]*
ISO 4903	15 Pole DTE–DCE Interface Connector and Contact Number Assignments *[second edition published 1.10.89]*
ISO 8877	Interface Connector and Contact Assignments for ISDN Basic Access Interface at Reference Points S & T *[published 15.8.87]*
ISO 8877/Am.1	Amendment 1: ISDN Basic Access TE Cord *[published 15.5.91]*
ISO TR 9578	Communication Interface Connectors Used in Local Area Networks *[published 15.11.90]*
ISO 10173	ISDN Primary Access Connector at Reference Points S and T *[published 15.9.91]*
ISO DTR 10738	Use of Unshielded Twisted Pair Cable (UTP) for Token Ring Data Transmission at 4 Mbit/s *[ballot closes 17.4.92]*
ISO CD 11569	26-Pole Interface Connector Mateability Dimensions and Contact Number Assignments *[ballot closed 27.12.91]*

C

Character sets

This appendix contains the code tables of the T.50 (IA5) and T.61 (teletex) character sets, taken from the appropriate CCITT recommendations.

Table C.1 The IA5 character set (basic version for national or application-specific character sets).

b4	b3	b2	b1	b7→	0	0	0	0	1	1	1	1
				b6→	0	0	1	1	0	0	1	1
				b5→	0	1	0	1	0	1	0	1
					0	1	2	3	4	5	6	7
0	0	0	0	0	NUL	DLE	SP	0	(3)	P	(3)	p
0	0	0	1	1	SOH	DC1	!	1	A	Q	a	q
0	0	1	0	2	STX	DC2	"	2	B	R	b	r
0	0	1	1	3	ETX	DC3	$\#/\pounds^{(2)}$	3	C	S	c	s
0	1	0	0	4	EOT	DC4	$\square/\$^{(2)}$	4	D	T	d	t
0	1	0	1	5	ENQ	NAK	%	5	E	U	e	u
0	1	1	0	6	ACK	SYN	&	6	F	V	f	v
0	1	1	1	7	BEL	ETB	'	7	G	W	g	w
1	0	0	0	8	BS	CAN	(	8	H	X	h	x
1	0	0	1	9	HT	EM	)	9	I	Y	i	y
1	0	1	0	10	LF$^{(1)}$	SUB	*	:	J	Z	j	z
1	0	1	1	11	VT$^{(1)}$	ESC	+	;	K	(3)	k	(3)
1	1	0	0	12	FF$^{(1)}$	IS4	,	<	L	(3)	l	(3)
1	1	0	1	13	CR$^{(1)}$	IS3	-	=	M	(3)	m	(3)
1	1	1	0	14	SO	IS2	.	>	N	(3)	n	(3)
1	1	1	1	15	SI	IS1	/	?	O	_	o	DEL

(1) The recommended meaning of these control characters is horizontal (CR) or vertical (LF, VT, FF) positioning.

(2) In a specific formulation of the character set these positions may have one of the two permitted graphical representations.

(3) The graphical representations of these positions may be freely chosen for national or application-specific character sets.

Table C.2 The IA5 character set (international reference version).

b4	b3	b2	b1	b7=0 b6=0 b5=0 → 0	0 1 → 1	0 1 0 → 2	0 1 1 → 3	1 0 0 → 4	1 0 1 → 5	1 1 0 → 6	1 1 1 → 7
0	0	0	0	0	NUL	DLE	SP	0	@	P	`	p
0	0	0	1	1	SOH	DC1	!	1	A	Q	a	q
0	0	1	0	2	STX	DC2	"	2	B	R	b	r
0	0	1	1	3	ETX	DC3	#	3	C	S	c	s
0	1	0	0	4	EOT	DC4	¤	4	D	T	d	t
0	1	0	1	5	ENQ	NAK	%	5	E	U	e	u
0	1	1	0	6	ACK	SYN	&	6	F	V	f	v
0	1	1	1	7	BEL	ETB	'	7	G	W	g	w
1	0	0	0	8	BS	CAN	(	8	H	X	h	x
1	0	0	1	9	HT	EM	)	9	I	Y	i	y
1	0	1	0	10	LF	SUB	*	:	J	Z	j	z
1	0	1	1	11	VT	ESC	+	;	K	[	k	{
1	1	0	0	12	FF	IS4	,	<	L	\	l	|
1	1	0	1	13	CR	IS3	-	=	M	]	m	}
1	1	1	0	14	SI	IS2	.	>	N	^	n	~
1	1	1	1	15	SO	IS1	/	?	O	_	o	DEL

Table C.3   The teletex character set (T.61, primary character set, columns 0 to 7).

b4	b3	b2	b1		b8=0 b7=0 b6=0 b5=0 → 0	b8=0 b7=0 b6=0 b5=1 → 1	b8=0 b7=0 b6=1 b5=0 → 2	b8=0 b7=0 b6=1 b5=1 → 3	b8=0 b7=1 b6=0 b5=0 → 4	b8=0 b7=1 b6=0 b5=1 → 5	b8=0 b7=1 b6=1 b5=0 → 6	b8=0 b7=1 b6=1 b5=1 → 7
0	0	0	0	0			SP	0	@	P		p
0	0	0	1	1			!	1	A	Q	a	q
0	0	1	0	2			"	2	B	R	b	r
0	0	1	1-	3			⓸	3	C	S	c	s
0	1	0	0	4			⓸	4	D	T	d	t
0	1	0	1	5			%	5	E	U	e	u
0	1	1	0	6			&	6	F	V	f	v
0	1	1	1	7			'	7	G	W	g	w
1	0	0	0	8	BS		(	8	H	X	h	x
1	0	0	1	9		SS2 (1)	)	9	I	Y	i	y
1	0	1	0	10	LF	SUB	*	:	J	Z	j	z
1	0	1	1	11		ESC (1)	+	;	K	[	k	
1	1	0	0	12	FF		,	<	L		l	|
1	1	0	1	13	CR	SS3 (1)	−	=	M	]	m	
1	1	1	0	14	LS1 (1)		.	>	N		n	
1	1	1	1	15	LSO (1)		/	?	O	_ (1)	o	

(1)   In the videotex context, underscore is used as a data delimiter.

(4)   Instead of these characters, the characters 10/6 (#) and 10/8 (◻) should be used. On receipt, 2/3 should be represented as # and 2/4 as ◻.

Table C.4 The teletex character set (T.61, supplementary character set, columns 8 to 15).

b8		1	1	1	1	1	1	1	1
b7		0	0	0	0	1	1	1	1
b6		0	0	1	1	0	0	1	1
b5		0	1	0	1	0	1	0	1
b4 b3 b2 b1		8	9	10	11	12	13	14	15
0 0 0 0	0				°	(5)		Ω	K
0 0 0 1	1				¡	±	`	Æ	æ
0 0 1 0	2			¢	²	´		Đ	đ
0 0 1 1	3			£	³	^		a̲	ð
0 1 0 0	4			$	×	˜		Ħ	ħ
0 1 0 1	5			¥	µ	‾			ı
0 1 1 0	6			#	¶	˘		IJ	ij
0 1 1 1	7			§	·	˙		Ŀ	ŀ
1 0 0 0	8			¤	÷	¨		Ł	ł
1 0 0 1	9					(2)		Ø	ø
1 0 1 0	10					˚		Œ	œ
1 0 1 1	11	PLD	CSI	«	»	˛		º	ß
1 1 0 0	12	PLU			¼	(3)		Þ	þ
1 1 0 1	13				½	˝		Ŧ	ŧ
1 1 1 0	14				¾	¸		Ŋ	ŋ
1 1 1 1	15				¿	ˇ			'n

(2) In the 1980 edition position 12/9 was the umlaut character. Position 12/8 is now used for this.

(3) This character may be used in combination with other characters for underlining.

(5) These control characters should not be used in the basic teletex service.

List of X.400 products

D

This appendix gives an overview of X.400 products from various manufacturers which are available today or which will be available in the near future. The list is up to date (March 1990) and is based on manufacturers' product specifications, verbal information received from company representatives (mostly technically-oriented or sales-support staff) and our own experience. We have attempted to ensure that the entries are as correct and complete as possible, but neither the completeness nor the correctness can be guaranteed.

In presenting this product overview our aims are the following:

- We wish to underline the breadth of the range of available products.

- We would like to provide the reader with the opportunity to look specifically for the desired information by manufacturers.

Using the information available, it was impossible to answer all the questions for all products. Empty fields mean that the information was not available.

The model form (described below) used to evaluate X.400 products was formulated according to the guidelines given in Part II. The characterization used is not the only one possible. However, in our opinion, it includes the most important criteria relevant to the selection of X.400 products.

Manufacturer: *Manufacturer of the X.400 product*

Product: *Name of the X.400 product*

Description:	*Short description of the system (functions, MTA, UA, configurations).*
Hardware:	*Hardware needed or supported.*
Operating system:	*Operating system(s) on which the product runs.*
Application software:	*Additional application software needed, for example, office automation system.*
Network:	*(OSI) Protocol stack used in the lower layers (LAN/X.25).*
Communication products:	*Additional (OSI) products needed in layers 1–6 or 7.*
User interface:	*Characterization of the user interface (line-oriented, full-screen menu-oriented, window/mouse). Is it an X.400 UA user interface or is it that of the manufacturer's conventional e-mail system?*
Programmer interface:	*Does the user have access to a programmer interface? To which functions (MTS, IPMS)?*
Gateway functions:	*Are gateways to other technologies supported (mainly to the manufacturer-specific e-mail system)?*
Conformance:	*Which of the CEPT (ENV 41202), CEN/CENELEC (ENV 41201) or NBS (NBS implementation agreement) profiles are supported?*
Management:	*Which management functions are present (routing, user-management, operational data acquisition)?*
Additional functions:	*Possible additional functions (directory service, message archiving). Local directories (aliases) and simple archiving systems are usual and are not be mentioned specifically.*
Remarks:	*Any other comments.*

Manufacturer: Alcatel

Product: DPX400

Description:	Message transfer and interpersonal messaging for public and private management domains.
Hardware:	ALCATEL 8300, modular multiprocessor system.
Operating system:	ATHOS 2/ATHOS 3.
Application software:	DPX400.
Network:	PSPDN (X.25), dedicated lines.
Communication products:	
User interface:	Line-oriented; user-guidance provided; there are various PC products that emulate the DPX400 user interface (for example, TELINO, MESTRA).
Programmer interface:	
Gateway functions:	Fax G3; teletex; telex.
Conformance:	ENV 41202; Swiss PTT OSI-LAB.
Management:	Network manager (NMX400) on VAX.
Additional functions:	Accounting (by dedicated NMX400) and management functions.
Remarks:	This system is used by the Swiss PTT for message transfer in arCom[400]; its functionality takes account of the needs of public service providers (for example, charging and accounting).

Manufacturer: ascom Zellweger Telecommunications

Product: Mailstream400

Description:	Complete X.400 solution with dedicated communication computers and software.
Hardware:	DEC VAX as part of the overall system, VAXServer 3100 a minimal solution.
Operating system:	DEC VMS.
Application software:	
Network:	X.25, IEEE 802.3, DECnet, LAT, ISDN.
Communication products:	IEEE(2) or PSI(1–3), VOTS(4), OSAK(5).
User interface:	Line-oriented, full-screen mask control for VT terminals, window- and mouse-oriented user interface for PC terminals.
Programmer interface:	
Gateway functions:	Fax, telex, radiopager; voice-alert, VMSmail, UNIX-Mail, IBM DISOSS, IBM PROFS.
Conformance:	CEPT: A/311; CEN/CENELEC: A/3211.
Management:	User management, statistics, operational data acquisition and security functions.
Additional functions:	Archiving/retrieval (full-text search, search for fields in the IPMS heading), directory service, intelligent database interface, form generation, public key management.
Remarks:	EDI/EDIFACT converter service in development.

Manufacturer: Bull SA, France

Product: DOAS 6 V250 Distributed Office Automation System

Description:	MTA on central server, UA on office clusters, user interface on workstation.
Hardware:	Recommended: DPS 6 Plus with DOAS 6 on Ethernet or X.25, Cluster Q 460 with UA on Ethernet or X.25, Workstation Q 400 with STARPOST, PC with Micropost.
Operating system:	DPS 6: GCOS 6 Rel. 3.1 ET 4, DPS 6 Plus: HVS 6; Cluster Q 460: Starsys 9.07 VM; Workstation Q 400: Starsys 9.07; PC: MS-DOS 3.3.
Application software:	STARISO for cluster Q 400, STARPOST for Workstation Q 400, Micropost, Micropass, Microname for PC.
Network:	X.25 via V.24 or V.35, IEEE 802.3 (Ethernet).
Communication products:	ISO communication software for DPS 6, Cluster (session ISO 8327; transport ISO 8073, classes 2 and 4), X.400 software supports P3.
User interface:	Workstation Q 400: controlled by function keys, integrated in STARSYS; PC: Micropost under MS-Windows 2.03.
Programmer interface:	DPS 6: MTS access for Pascal and Cobol; Cluster: UAL access for Pascal and Cobol.
Gateway functions:	None.
Conformance:	From June 89: tests with test systems in France and Germany; interoperability tests with ATLAS 400 (France) and arCom[400] (Switzerland).
Management:	Integrated into Bull-ISO/DSA network; centralized nameserver mapped onto regional directories; operational data acquisition available as extension.
Additional functions:	Directory service (queries based on 'surName' and 'organizational unit names'), distribution lists.
Remarks:	Bull HN USA: OneMail X.400 gateway; QX400: X.400 MTA and UA on Bull DPX under UNIX.

Manufacturer: Control Data Corporation

Product: CDC Mail/VE (Version 2.0)

Description:	Complete package for messaging service and message distribution.
Hardware:	Cyber 800/900 series.
Operating system:	NOS/VE.
Application software:	
Network:	All networks supported by CDCNET (for example Ethernet, X.25, X.29).
Communication products:	
User interface:	Mail/VE2 optionally line-oriented or full-screen interface with function keys.
Programmer interface:	Easy for users themselves to realize by SCL call from applications.
Gateway functions:	SMTP, RFC 987.
Conformance:	COS validation (NBS, GOSIP) in progress; 1987 X.400 (84) implementation agreement.
Management:	
Additional functions:	Simple message archiving and retrieval.
Remarks:	Successful tests have been carried out with Bull, Data General, Unisys and others; an X.400 mail system specific to France with 20 different suppliers was demonstrated at CeBIT.

Manufacturer: Danet GmbH, Germany

Product: OSITEL/400

Description:	Portable X.400 and directory services software (initially for UNIX systems).
Hardware:	CADMUS (PCS) with System V.2, VAX 11/7xx with ULTRIX, HP 9000/300 with HP-UX, Motorola S8000 with System V.3.
Operating system:	Demonstrated on UNIX System V, 4.2/4.3 BSD.
Application software:	Integrated RDBMS.
Network:	Depends on the specific implementation.
Communication products:	Depends on the specific implementation.
User interface:	English or German, line-oriented or full-screen, profiling by the user.
Programmer interface:	The system has a layer architecture so that various programmer interfaces are possible.
Gateway functions:	
Conformance:	CEN/CENELEC, CEPT (NBS, X.400 (88) planned).
Management:	Operational monitoring, operational data acquisition, user administration.
Additional functions:	Encryption, directories, development tools (for OEM).
Remarks:	Developed from an X.400 test system used in COMTEX-LAB (now OSI-LAB).

Manufacturer: Data General

Product: DG/X.400

Description:	Communications extension of the CEO office automation system.
Hardware:	ECLIPSE MV1000 to MV/40000.
Operating system:	AOS/VS, AOS/VS II.
Application software:	CEO office automation environment.
Network:	X.25.
Communication products:	AOS/VS XTS or XTS II.
User interface:	CEO: menu-driven, available in six languages.
Programmer interface:	Not planned.
Gateway functions:	CEO gateways to X.400, IBM PROFS, DISOSS, telex, teletex, MCI-Mail, etc.
Conformance:	CEN/CENELEC ENV 41201, CEPT A/311, NBS/COS.
Management:	Special UA for management of connections, users and accounting.
Additional functions:	User-management and user-directory from CEO, distribution lists and alias mechanism.
Remarks:	A node may be a gateway to X.400 for a whole CEO mail network; successfully connected to arCom[400].

Manufacturer: Digital Equipment Corporation

Product: DEC MRX400 (Message Router X.400 Gateway)

Description:	Gateway to MAILbus (DEC-specific mail system); functionality of an MTA, no UA.
Hardware:	Micro-VAX II to VAX clusters.
Operating system:	VMS.
Application software:	UA via MAILbus supported (for example, VMSmail).
Network:	IEEE for LAN; X.25.
Communication products:	IEEE(2) or PSI(1–3); VOTS(4); OSAK(5).
User interface:	None.
Programmer interface:	Programmer interface to MAILbus.
Gateway functions:	MAILbus; VMSmail; IBM.
Conformance:	CEPT: A/311; CEN/CENELEC: A/3211; NBS: X.400.
Management:	Connection management, user management via directory service.
Additional functions:	Directory service (not conforming to X.500).
Remarks:	X.400 UA in development.

Manufacturer: Hewlett Packard

Product: HP X.400/9000

Description:	Gateway to X.400 for office communications environments on UNIX-(HP9000) and MPE-(HP3000) based systems.
Hardware:	HP-9000 series 300 or 800.
Operating system:	HP-UX, Version 7.0 or later.
Application software:	HP OpenMail, ELM/Mailx (HP NewWave Mail in preparation).
Network:	X.25, ISO 8802.3.
Communication products:	X.25/9000: X.25 hardware and software, (CCITT 1984); LAN/9000: ISO 8802.3 hardware and software; OTS/9000: OSI transport service (TP 0, 2 for X.25, TP 4 for ISO 8802.3, session BAS).
User interface:	ELM/Mailx for UNIX-Mail; HP OpenMail menu control for PC, MacIntosh, UNIX-workstations.
Programmer interface:	Via HP DeskManager.
Gateway functions:	To UNIX-Mail via 'sendmail'; to HP DeskManager; to PROFS and DISOSS via HP DeskManager.
Conformance:	CEN/CENELEC, CEPT.
Management:	Menu-based management functions for operation, maintenance, configuration and fault location; event logging for MTA, RTS.
Additional functions:	Directory service when HP OpenMail or HP DeskManager used.
Remarks:	

Manufacturer: IBM

Product: IBM X.400 Message Transfer Facility

Description:	MTA functions for VM, MVS and VSE systems.
Hardware:	IBM/370, 30xx, 43xx, 9370.
Operating system:	IBM VM, MVS, VSE.
Application software:	MVS: DISOSS, CICS; VM: PROFS, CMS.
Network:	X.25; SNA.
Communication products:	MVS: DISOSS X.400 adaptation; VM: PROFS X.400 adaptation, VSAM; for all operating systems: VTAM with NCP/NPSI, OTSS, OSNS; alternatives: connections via 9370 or 4361 by communication adapter.
User interface:	The manufacturer-specific products DISOSS and PROFS are used. Under VSE the user interface must be realized as an application program.
Programmer interface:	X.400 MTF has a programmer interface to the MTS.
Gateway functions:	To DISOSS and PROFS.
Conformance:	CEN/CENELEC (A3211, ENV 41201), CEPT (A311, ENV 41202).
Management:	MTA and user administration, access authorizations.
Additional functions:	Directory services.
Remarks:	Extension of Screenmail to X.400 UA functionality announced.

Manufacturer: ICL

Product: ICLMAIL

Description:	UNIX-based implementation of X.400, compatible with the ICL office system Office Power.
Hardware:	ICL UNIX servers from the full DRS line.
Operating system:	UNIX V.5, Release 3.2/3.4.
Application software:	Office system 'Office Power'.
Network:	WAN X.25; LAN 802.3 (OSLAN).
Communication products:	Office Power on X.25 or 802.3; DRS NX X.25; DRS NX OSLAN.
User interface:	Office Power, menu-oriented, complete office system.
Programmer interface:	UA interface which permits sending of ASCII text.
Gateway functions:	Connection to ICL mainframes.
Conformance:	CEN/CENELEC (ENV 41201), CEPT (ENV 41202), UK GOSIP 3.0.
Management:	Local mail administration functions: establishment/ release of mail connections, search functions.
Additional functions:	Global directory service.
Remarks:	

Manufacturer: NCR (Switzerland)

Product: NCR X.400 (Tower)

Description:	NCR X.400 consists of UA, MTA and RTS.
Hardware:	NCR Tower 32/200, 32/4X0, 32/6X0, 32/8X0, 32/300, 32/500, 32/700.
Operating system:	from UNIX V Release 3.
Application software:	NCR ALIS V 2.0 or NCRmail.
Network:	X.25.
Communication products:	NCR OSI Application, NCR OSI Network, X.25 software, HDLC driver.
User interface:	Window/mouse.
Programmer interface:	API (application programming interface) to IPMS and MTS.
Gateway functions:	
Conformance:	CEPT, CEN/CENELEC, NIST (1988), UK GOSIP V.3, UK GOSIP level 1.0.
Management:	Tools for configuration and administration, online help.
Additional functions:	Directory service: private, local and central (X.500).
Remarks:	

Manufacturer: NCR (Switzerland)

Product: NCR/ITX X.400 (10000)

Description:	NCR-400 consists of the UA, MTA and RTS.
Hardware:	NCR system 10000, NCR I-9500, NCR I-9400IP.
Operating system:	From ITX Rel. 7.0.
Application software:	NCRMail.
Network:	X.25.
Communication products:	NCR OSI Application, NCR OSI Network, X.25 software, HDLC driver.
User interface:	Window/mouse for intelligent workstations, menu on line-oriented screen.
Programmer interface:	API (mail server API) to IPMS and MTS; API (on PC side): accessed from MS-Windows, application on NCRMail.
Gateway functions:	
Conformance:	CEPT, CEN/CENELEC, NIST (1988), UK GOSIP V.3, UK GOSIP level 1.0.
Management:	Tools for configuration and administration, online help.
Additional functions:	Directory service: private, local and central (X.500).
Remarks:	NCRMail may be used locally and permits the exchange of arbitrary files and formats.

Manufacturer: Nixdorf Computer

Product: Targon Mail 2.0

Description:	UA and MTA.
Hardware:	Targon /31 and /35.
Operating system:	From TOS 3.3 (Targon Operating System) and UNIX V.2.
Application software:	Targon Office (office automation) with Targon Mail.
Network:	X.25, X.21, tty, Ethernet.
Communication products:	Communication Management System CMS, LNC (Ethernet), ICC (X.25).
User interface:	Surface of Targon Office.
Programmer interface:	Present, programming language C.
Gateway functions:	Telex, teletex.
Conformance:	
Management:	Connection management, user administration.
Additional functions:	
Remarks:	

Manufacturer: Olivetti Computer

Product: X_MAIL

Description:	Integrated office information system with standardized interfaces and a uniform user interface.
Hardware:	Servers: UNIX computers of the LSX-3000 series or PC; workstations: PC, UNIX terminal or Olivetti system.
Operating system:	Servers: UNIX system V 3.2 or X/OS, Olivetti UNIX systems conforming to AT&T SVID and X/OPEN with BSD and Olivetti extensions; workstations: MS-DOS, OS/2 or PB.
Application software:	IBIS (Integrated Business and Information System) with X_MAIL (component of IBIS).
Network:	LAN Manager on StarLAN, Token Ring or Ethernet, Olinet via StarLAN or Ethernet; TCP/IP via Ethernet between IBIS servers.
Communication products:	RTS via RS-232, TCP/IP on Ethernet, IBM SNA/SDLC or via X.25 between MTA.
User interface:	Optionally line-oriented window system (for terminals), MS-Windows or OS/2 Presentation Manager on PC.
Programmer interface:	Macros for end users, UNIX shell procedures for all IBIS services, C programmer interface via special program libraries.
Gateway functions:	Fax, telex, teletex (all via X_GATE/TLC), UNIX-Mail, Q-Office Mail.
Conformance:	X.400, ENV 41201, ENV 41202, GOSIP.
Management:	X_MAIL user and communications configuration, directory service within IBIS.
Additional functions:	Automatic message archiving, directory service (X.500 from IBIS R 5.0).
Remarks:	

Manufacturer: Siemens

Product: MAIL.X

Description:	X.400 for Siemens UNIX computers (SINIX).
Hardware:	MX2, MX300, MX500, at least 4MB, 40MB disk.
Operating system:	MX2: SINIX M-C V2.1, MX500: SINIX V5.2, MX500: SINIX V5.1.
Application software:	Informix DBMS, OCIS DESK (Office Communications and Information Services).
Network:	X.25, 802.3.
Communication products:	CCP-WAN, CCP-LAN (layers 1–4), the session layer is part of MAIL.X.
User interface:	Window technique with pull-down menus.
Programmer interface:	MAIL-X-IAPL (optional).
Gateway functions:	
Conformance:	ENV 41201, ENV 41202.
Management:	MTA management, user administration, operational data recording.
Additional functions:	Connection to distributed printer service.
Remarks:	The product is universally developed according to ISO/OSI standards (no gateway solution).

Manufacturer: Siemens

Product: Siemens MAIL-2000

Description:	MAIL-2000 V1.0 contains the MTA (MAIL-2000 MT) and the UA OASE-DTA (Desk Top Application) with an AU (Access Unit); OASE-TEXT is a software prerequisite for MAIL-2000.
Hardware:	System 75xx.
Operating system:	BS2000V8.x/V9.x.
Application software:	OCIS-DESK (BS2000) V1.0, particularly OASE-TEXT V1.1.
Network:	LAN, X.25.
Communication products:	Telepac, X.25, LAN (ISO 8802), X.21/V.24, HDLC, NEATE, ISO 8073.
User interface:	Integrated in OASE-DTA and in the OASE-TEXT text processing: menu control.
Programmer interface:	For the MTA (MAIL-2000 MT) the IMTS; for MAIL-2000 V1.0 interfaces in OASE-DTA and OASE-TEXT.
Gateway functions:	Telex/teletex; ODIF(Q112) and telefax in preparation.
Conformance:	Cooperation in Comtex Lab.
Management:	Planned.
Additional functions:	Document archiving and search (separate component of OCIS-DESK); OASE-CONNECT: document exchange between HIT (SINIX) and OASE-TEXT (BS2000).
Remarks:	

Manufacturer: Siemens–Albis (Switzerland)

Product: Siemens SWISSMAIL

Description:	ISDN implementation of X.400 services based on MAIL.X; the system contains centrally run ISDN MH nodes and user interfaces for various devices (PC, terminals); the dialogue on the terminals is controlled by an ISDN MH node.
Hardware:	ISDN nodes: Siemens MX 500, ISDN connection; subscriber connections: PC or terminal.
Operating system:	MX5000: SINIX V5.1; PC: specific PC operating systems.
Application software:	
Network:	Servers: ISDN (SWISSNET in Switzerland) and X.25; subscriber connection: ISDN B channel.
Communication products:	Telepac, X.25, ISDN.
User interface:	
Programmer interface:	
Gateway functions:	Gateways planned to public 'value-added services', such as Telex, teletex, videotex.
Conformance:	CCITT X.400.
Management:	Planned for the ISDN computer.
Additional functions:	Implementation of 'value-added services' such as EDIFACT planned.
Remarks:	Trial operation on SWISSNET from beginning of 1990.

Manufacturer: Softlab

Product: Softlab OSI server

Description:	X.400 MTA with access units to telex, teletex and fax.
Hardware:	All UNIX V.3 systems, adaptable to other systems.
Operating system:	UNIX system V.3.
Application software:	
Network:	LAN and X.25.
Communication products:	Retix software.
User interface:	Menu- or MOTIF-based user interface for administrator and postmaster.
Programmer interface:	
Gateway functions:	Access units to telex, teletex, fax.
Conformance:	CEN/CENELEC, NIST 500–150, UK GOSIP MHS.
Management:	Management of user and operational data, postmaster.
Additional functions:	Connection to X.500 message archive.
Remarks:	Adaptable to any UA, office automation systems. Adaptable to other mail systems for gateway functionality.

Manufacturer: SUN Microsystems

Product: SunLink MHS

Description:	MTA and gateway to UNIX-Mail.
Hardware:	Sun 2, 3 and 4, 4MB main memory, optional MCP X.25 processor board, LAN controller board.
Operating system:	SunOS 3.2 or more recent.
Application software:	SunView (contained in the standard configuration).
Network:	X.25, IEEE 802.3, IEEE 802.4.
Communication products:	SunLink OSI 5.2 or later (OSI session, transport, network, data link for LAN and session to network for X.25), SunLink X.25 5.2 or later for X.25 connection.
User interface:	SunView, Window-oriented on full graphics screen; geared to RFC 822.
Programmer interface:	Via Berkeley UNIX system program 'sendmail'.
Gateway functions:	X.400 to SMTP, UUCP and other protocols via 'sendmail'.
Conformance:	CEN/CENELEC, CEPT, NBS.
Management:	Table- and directory-controlled conversion of addresses between X.400 and RFC 822.
Additional functions:	
Remarks:	

Manufacturer: OSIware

Product: Messenger 400

Description:	X.400 system for interconnected PC environment and VAX.
Hardware:	IBM PC and compatible systems, DEC VAX, Tandem, VLX, CLX.
Operating system:	MS-DOS, DEC VMS, UNIX, Guardian 90 XF.
Application software:	No additional application software needed.
Network:	X.25, TCP/IP, DECnet.
Communication products:	According to the operating system Novell Netware, PC-LAN, PSI, etc.
User interface:	Line-oriented.
Programmer interface:	Present for IPMS and MTS.
Gateway functions:	RFC 987 gateway between RFC 822 mail and X.400, interface to EDIFACT planned.
Conformance:	CEN/CENELEC.
Management:	Management functions for the management of an MTA and for user management.
Additional functions:	Gateway to Eurokom, message store and remote UA announced, X.500 announced, currently an intermediate solution is used.
Remarks:	Document conversion from Wang format into X.409, successfully connected to an eMTS; exhibited by Tandem at CeBIT 89.

Manufacturer: UNISYS

Product: BTOS OFIS ACCESS X.400

Description:	UA and MTA; UA: OFIS Mail, MTA: OSI MHS mail server.
Hardware:	Unisys BTOS systems (B28, B38, B39, XE530).
Operating system:	BTOS II.
Application software:	Optional OFIS Mail, OFIS access to X.400.
Network:	X.25, ISO 8802.3.
Communication products:	BTOS OSI session, OSI transport, classes 0, 2 and 4.
User interface:	Menu-oriented.
Programmer interface:	At all levels, all programming languages offered are supported.
Gateway functions:	X.400 to OFIS Mail.
Conformance:	NBS, CEN/CENELEC (ENV 41201), CEPT (ENV 41202).
Management:	Operational data acquisition.
Additional functions:	Distribution lists, local directory.
Remarks:	

Manufacturer: UNISYS

Product: MHS 1100

Description:	UA and MTA.
Hardware:	Unisys 1100/2200 systems.
Operating system:	OS1100/2200.
Application software:	Optional DPS screen interface to IPMS.
Network:	X.25, ISO 8802.3.
Communication products:	ISO session, ISO transport, classes 0 and 2.
User interface:	Line- and menu-oriented.
Programmer interface:	IPMS and MTS access for COBOL.
Gateway functions:	X.400 IPMS to OFIS Mail (OFIS Link).
Conformance:	NBS, CEN/CENELEC, CEPT.
Management:	Configuration utilities, operational data acquisition.
Additional functions:	Distribution lists, local directory.
Remarks:	

Manufacturer: UNISYS

Product: OSI MHS A series

Description:	UA and MTA.
Hardware:	A series.
Operating system:	MCP/AS.
Application software:	
Network:	X.25, ISO 8802.3.
Communication products:	OSI session, OSI transport, X.25, CP2000 LAN.
User interface:	Menu- and line-oriented.
Programmer interface:	Present for MTL and UAL.
Gateway functions:	
Conformance:	NBS, CEN/CENELEC, CEPT.
Management:	Configuration utilities, operational data acquisition.
Additional functions:	Distribution lists, local directory.
Remarks:	

Manufacturer: UNISYS

Product: OSI MHS U series

Description:	UA and MTA.
Hardware:	Unisys 5000 and 6000 series.
Operating system:	UNIX V.3.
Application software:	
Network:	X.25, ISO 8802.3.
Communication products:	OSI application services (session BCS, BAS), OSI transport, classes 0, 2 and 4.
User interface:	Menu- and line-oriented.
Programmer interface:	Present for MTL and UAL.
Gateway functions:	X.400 to UUCP mail.
Conformance:	NBS, CEN/CENELEC.
Management:	Operational data acquisition.
Additional functions:	Distribution lists, local directory.
Remarks:	

Manufacturer: Wang

Product: Wang Office X.400

Description:	Communications extension for WangOFFICE.
Hardware:	Wang VS.
Operating system:	VS.
Application software:	WangOFFICE office automation environment.
Network:	X.25, ISO 8802.3.
Communication products:	X.25 and IEEE 802.3 or WSN, under ISO 8473, connection-oriented classes 0, 2, 3 and 4, BAS, BSS and BCS.
User interface:	Menu-driven.
Programmer interface:	Present for transport and session layer.
Gateway functions:	Gateway between X.400 and WangOFFICE.
Conformance:	CEN/CENELEC, CEPT, NBS.
Management:	Menu-based management functions.
Additional functions:	Use of the WangOFFICE online directory, distribution lists.
Remarks:	An MTA in a PC network may serve all other PCs as MTA.

List of abbreviations

AC	Application Context
ACSE	Association Control Service Element
ADMD	Administration Management Domain
AE	Application Entity
ANSI	American National Standards Institute
AP	Application Process
APDU	Application Protocol Data Unit
arCom	ADMD of the Swiss PTT
ARPANET	Research network of the 'Defense Advanced Research Project Agency'
ASCII	American Standard Code for Information Interchange
ASE	Application Service Element
ASN.1	Abstract Syntax Notation One
ASP	Abstract Service Primitive
ATS	Abstract Test Suite
AU	Access Unit
Bisync	Binary Synchronous Control
BSC	Binary Synchronous Control
BSI	British Standards Institution
CA	Certificate Authority
CASE	Common Application Service Element
CC	Clearing Centre
CCITT	Comité Consultatif International Télégraphique et Téléphonique
CCRSE	Commitment, Concurrency and Recovery Service Element
CEC	Commission of the European Community
CEN/CENELEC	Comité Européen de Normalisation/Comité Européen de Normalisation Electrique
CEPT	Comité Européen des Administrations des Postes et des Télécommunications

CLNS	Connectionless Network Service
CLTS	Connectionless Transport Service
CONS	Connection Oriented Network Service
COSINE	Cooperation for Open Systems Interconnection Networking in Europe
COTS	Connection Oriented Transport Service
CPMU	COSINE Project Management Unit
CSMA/CD	Carrier Sense Multiple Access with Collision Detection
DAP	Directory Access Protocol
DARPA	(US) Defense Advanced Research Projects Agency
DDA	Domain Defined Attribute
DECnet	'Digital Equipment Corporation' network architecture
DFN	Deutsches Forschungsnetz (German research network)
DIT	Directory Information Tree
DL	Distribution List
DNA	Digital Network Architecture (DEC)
DNS	Domain Name System
DS	Directory Service
DSA	Directory System Agent
DSP	Directory System Protocol
DUA	Directory User Agent
EARN	European Academic Research Network
EBCDIC	Extended Binary-coded Decimal Interchange Code
ECE	Economic Commission for Europe
ECMA	European Computer Manufacturers Association
EDI	Electronic Document Interchange
EDIFACT	Electronic Document Interchange for Finance, Administration, Commerce and Transport
EDMD	Electronic Document Message Directory
EDSD	Electronic Document Segment Directory
EFTA	European Free Trade Association
EIA	Electronic Industries Association
EOC	End of Content
ETS	Executable Test Suite
EWICS	European Workshop on Industrial Computer Systems
EWOS	European Workshop for Open Systems

FL	First Level
FTAM	File Transfer, Access and Management
GE	Group of Experts
GOSIP	Government Open Systems Interconnection Profiles
IA5	International Alphabet No. 5
IBCN	Integrated Broadband Communication Network
IEEE	Institute of Electrical and Electronics Engineers
IFIP	International Federation for Information Processing
IM-UAPDU	Interpersonal Messaging User Agent Protocol Data Unit
IP	DARPA Internet Protocol
IPMS	Interpersonal Messaging System
ISDN	Integrated Services Digital Network
ISO	International Organisation for Standardisation
ISO IP	ISO Internetwork Protocol
ITSTC	Information Technology Steering Committee
IUT	Implementation under Test
IXI	International X.25 Interconnect
JANET	Joint Academic Network
JTM	Job Transfer and Manipulation
LAN	Local Area Network
LAP-B	Link Access Protocol, Balanced
LLC	Logical Link Control
LT	Lower Tester
MAC	Media Access Control
MAN	Metropolitan Area Network
MAP	Manufacturing Automation Protocol
MASE	Message Administration Service Element
MD	(1) Management Domain; (2) Message Development Group.
MDC	Manipulation Detecting Code
MDSE	Message Delivery Service Element
MHS	Message Handling System
MHTS	Message Handling Test System
MMDF	Multi-channel Memorandum Distribution Facility
MMS	Manufacturing Message Service
MOTIS	Message Oriented Text Interchange System
MPDU	Message Protocol Data Unit

MRSE	Message Retrieval Service Element
MS	Message Store
MSAP	Message Store Access Protocol
MSSE	Message Submission Service Element
MTA	Message Transfer Agent
MTAE	Message Transfer Agent Entity
MTL	Message Transfer Layer
MTS	Message Transfer System
MTSE	Message Transfer Service Element
NFS	Network File System (Sun Microsystems)
NIST	(US) National Institute for Standards and Technology (formerly National Bureau of Standards (NBS))
NRS	(UK) Name Registration Scheme
NSAP	Network Service Access Point
O/R	Originator/Recipient
OSI	Open Systems Interconnection
OSI-RM	ISO Reference Model for Open Systems Interconnection
P1	Message Transfer Protocol
P2	Interpersonal Messaging Protocol
P3	Submission and Delivery Protocol
P7	Message Store Access Protocol
$\mathbf{P_c}$	A class of application-specific protocols of the UAL for exchange of messages between UAEs
$\mathbf{P_t}$	Interactive Terminal to System Protocol
PATS	Parameterized Abstract Test Suite
PC	Personal Computer
PCI	Protocol Control Information
PCO	Point of Control and Observation
PCTR	Protocol Conformance Test Report
PDAU	Physical Delivery Access Unit
PDU	Protocol Data Unit
PETS	Parameterized Executable Test Suite
PICS	Protocol Implementation Conformance Statement
PIN	Personal Identification Number
PIXIT	Protocol Implementation Extra Information for Testing
PO	Post Office

PRMD	Private Management Domain
PSAP	Presentation Service Access Point
PSDN	Packet Switched Data Network
PSDU	Presentation Service Data Unit
RARE	Réseaux Associés pour la Recherche Européenne
RDN	Relative Distinguished Name
RFC	Request for Comment
RJE	Remote Job Entry
ROS	Remote Operations Service
ROSE	Remote Operations Service Element
RPC	Remote Procedure Call
RSA	Asymmetric public key coding system (Rivest, Shamir and Adleman)
RSCS	Remote Spooling and Control Subsystem (IBM)
RTS	Reliable Transfer Service
RTSE	Reliable Transfer Service Element
SAP	Service Access Point
SAS	SWITCH Access System
SASE	Specific Application Service Element
SATS	Selected Abstract Test Suite
SCS	SWITCH Central System
SCTR	System Conformance Test Report
SDE	Submission and Delivery Entity
SDU	Service Data Unit
SETS	Selected Executable Test Suite
SIG	Special Interest Group
SMTP	Simple Mail Transfer Protocol (RFC 821)
SNA	Systems Network Architecture (IBM)
SPAG	Standards Promotion and Application Group
SR-UAPDU	Status Report User Agent Protocol Data Unit
SUT	System under Test
SWITCH	Swiss college and research network
TCP	Transmission Control Protocol
TDED	Trade Data Elements Directory
TDID	Trade Data Interchange Directory
TOP	Technical and Office Protocols

TP	Transport Protocol
TSAP	Transport Service Access Point
TTCN	Tree and Tabular Combined Notation
UA	User Agent
UAE	User Agent Entity
UAL	User Agent Layer
UAPDU	User Agent Protocol Data Unit
UCL	University College, London
UMPDU	User Message Protocol Data Unit
UN	United Nations
UT	Upper Tester
UUCP	UNIX to UNIX Copy
VT	Virtual Terminal
WAN	Wide Area Network
WEP	Well Known Entry Point
WG	Working Group
WIN	Wissenschaftsnetz (scientific network in Germany)
WP	Working Party
Y-NET	X.400 network for ESPRIT and other CEC research programmes

Bibliography

Beyschlag U. and Pitteloud J. (1988). MHS Conformance Testing. In *Proc. Seminar on Digital Communications* (Plattner B. and Günzburger P., eds.), Zurich IEEE

Birolini A. (1981). *Qualität und Zuverlässigkeit technischer Systeme*. Berlin: Springer-Verlag

Birrel A. D., Levin R., Needham R. M. and Schroeder M. D. (1982). Grapevine: an exercise in distributed computing. *Comm. ACM*, 25(4), 260–74

CCITT (1985). *Red Book*. ITU. Geneva

CCITT (1986). *X.400-Series Implementor's Guide Version 5*

CCITT (1988). *CCITT Conformance Testing Specification Manual X.403/ CTSM.1 Version 2.0*

CCITT (1989). *Blue Book*. ITU. Geneva

CEN/CENELEC (1988). *Private Message Handling System User Agent and Message Transfer Agent: Private Management Domain to Private Management Domain*. (ENV 41 201). Brussels

CEPT (1988). *Protocol for Interpersonal Messaging between Message Transfer Agents Accessing the Public Message Handling Service*. TE.3 (MH) (88) 12 (ENV 41 202)

Clyne L. (1988). LAN/WAN interworking. *Computer Networks and ISDN Systems*, 16(1–2)

Courtois P. J. (1975). Decomposability, instabilities and saturation in multiprogramming systems. *Comm. ACM*, 18

Craigie J. (1988). *Migration strategies for X.400 (84) to X.400 (88)/MOTIS*. COSINE Eureka Project 8, Specification Phase, Technical Reports, Vol. 7, Report 8.2

Crocker H. (1982). Standard for the Format of ARPA Internet Text Messages, RFC 822. In *DDN Protocol Handbook*. SRI International

Danet GmbH (1987). *MHTS/400 User's Manual*. Darmstadt

Dijkstra E. W. (1968). The structure of THE multiprogramming system. *Comm. ACM* 11(5)

DIN (1988). *EDIFACT – Elektronisher Datenaustausch für Verwaltung, Wirtschaft und Transport, Einführung Entwicklung, Grundsatz und Einsatz*

EWICS (1982). *Up-to-date Report I-1-12*

Giese E., Görgen K., Hinsch E., Schulze G. and Truöl K. (1985). *Dienste und Protokolle in Kommunikationssystemen*. Berlin: Springer-Verlag

Grimm R. (1987). *A minimum profile for RFC 987: mapping between addresses in RFC 822 and X.400 standard attributes*. DFN

Grimm R. and Heagerty D. (1989). *Recommendation for a shorthand X.400 address notation.* RARE WG1 recommendation

ISO (1988). *ISO Draft International Standard 10021.* The Hague

Kille S. E. (1986). *Mapping between X.400 and RFC 822.* RFC 987. London, University College

Kingston D. P. III (1984). MMDF II – A Technical Review. In *Proc. Usenix Conference,* Salt Lake City, August 1984

Lange W. (1988). MHS Conformance Testing Experiences in Designing a Test Suite. In *Proc. Seminar on Digital Communications* (Plattner B. and Günzburger P., eds.), Zurich IEEE

Lubich H. and Plattner B. (1989). Electronic Mail Systems and Protocols. In *Proc. Conf. IFIP WG 6.5,* Costa Mesa. Amsterdam: North Holland

Maier G. E. (1984). Entwurf und Realisierung einer Methode zur Exceptionsbehandlung und Synchronisation in Echtzeitprogrammen. *Dissertation Nr. 7583,* ETH Zurich

Maier F. (1989). Zwischenbetrieblicher Informationsaustausch. *SWISSPRO Infobulletin,* (4)

Manros C. -U. (1989). *X.400 Blue Book Companion.* Technology Appraisals

McQuillan J. M. and Walden D. C. (1977). The ARPA Network Design Decisions. *Computer Networks and ISDN Systems* 1, 243–289

Mockapetris P. V. (1984). *The Domain Name System. Computer Based Message Services.* Elsevier Science Publishers B.V.

Nakao K. and Suzuki K. (1989). Proposal on a secure communications service element (SCSE) in the OSI application layer. *IEEE Journal on Selected Areas in Communications,* 7(4)

Neufeld G. (1983). EAN: a distributed message system. In *Proc. Canadian Information Processing Society National Meeting,* Ottawa

NIST (1988). *Stable Implementation Agreements for Open Systems Interconnection Protocols* Version 2 Edition 1. U.S. Department of Commerce, NIST Special Publication 500-162

Oppen D. C. and Dalal Y. K. (1983). The Clearinghouse: A decentralized agent for locating named objects in a distributed environment. *ACM Trans. Office Automation Systems,* 1(3)

Parnas D. L. (1974). On a buzzword – 'hierarchical structure'. In *Information Processing 1974.* Amsterdam: North-Holland

Parnas D. L., Handzel G. and Würges H. (1976). Design and specification of an operating system family. *IEEE Trans. Software Engineering,* 2(4)

Plattner B. (1988). The Swiss national network for research and education (SWITCH). *Computer Networks and ISDN Systems,* 16(1–2)

Postel J. B. (1982). *Simple Mail Transfer Protocol.* RFC 821

Quarterman J. S. and Hoskins J. C. (1986). Notable Computer Networks. *Comm. ACM,* 29(10)

RARE (1989). *RARE Annual Report 1989.* Amsterdam: RARE Secretariat

Rayner D. (1987). OSI Conformance Testing. In *Protocol Specification, Testing and Verification: VII Tutorial Notes* (Rudin H. ed.). IFIP TC6

Rivest R. L., Schamir A. and Adleman L. (1978). A method for obtaining digital signatures and public-key cryptosystems. *Comm. ACM* 21, 120–126

Rose M. T. (1990). *The ISO development environment – user's manual*, Version 6.0, vol. 1–5. The Wollongong Group, Palo Alto

SIGCOMM (1991). *Computer Communication Review*, 21(2)

SPAG (1987). *Guide to the Use of Standards*. Amsterdam: North-Holland

UN/ECE (1990a). *UN Trade Data Interchange Directory*. Geneva: UN

UN/ECE (1990b). *UN Trade Data Elements Directory*. Geneva: UN

UN/ECE WP4 (1990). *Trade Facilitation News*. Geneva: UN

Index